The
VEGAN
CHINESE
KITCHEN

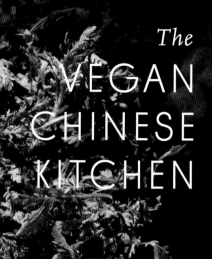

The
VEGAN
CHINESE
KITCHEN

Recipes and
Modern Stories from
a Thousand-Year-Old
Tradition

Hannah Che

Photographs by Hannah Che

Clarkson
Potter/
Publishers
New York

To Mom and Dad.
No matter where I go, your
table will always be home.

CONTENTS

INTRODUCTION

"AI-YA, I didn't think my daughter would become one of those hippie types," I overheard my mother say to a friend over the phone. I had decided to go vegan my junior year of college, and determined to learn to cook for myself, I looked up meal plans and recipes on Pinterest, followed popular bloggers, bought cookbooks, and stocked my pantry with lentils and chickpea pasta. I packed overnight oats to school and invited friends over to my tiny Houston apartment to make vegan pizza and grain bowls on weekends. I even started a recipe blog, posting photos on Instagram of the meals I made.

But it was different back at home, sitting at our scratched walnut table as my mom busied about the kitchen, preparing food for the holidays. My parents cooked mostly Chinese meals—a spread of shared dishes to go with rice—and they couldn't understand why I would forgo a special dish of expensive seafood, or a stir-fry that had ground meat or a few pork slivers. "Just pick around and eat the vegetables, at least you still get the flavor from the meat," my mom offered.

Over the winter break, I was determined to convert my family to a plant-based diet. I talked about the horrors of factory farming and the environmental footprint of meat and dairy. I pulled out my arsenal of recipes: Thai curries, walnut-meat tacos, creamy cashew pastas, and quinoa burgers. My siblings liked them well enough, but my dad gingerly bit into one patty and refused to eat the rest. "I'm cooking duck for dinner," he announced. For Lunar New Year, our family gathered to make pork dumplings, as we did every holiday. It was my favorite tradition, and I usually helped make the filling, but this time, my dad looked up as he kneaded dough and saw me watching from the side.

"Rongrong, you aren't participating?" he asked.

It hadn't occurred to me until then that my decision to go vegan wasn't just about food or even a personal choice. My parents were immigrants; food was the way they taught us about our roots; certain dishes were central not just to my family's memories, but also connected us to a lifetime of people and occasions and places and times that went before and beyond me. I wondered if my commitment to eat more sustainably meant I was turning away from my culture. Talking to my peers, I realized I wasn't alone in these fears. It's impossible to separate who we are from what we eat, and animal products are deeply ingrained in the food traditions of most cultures. How do you remove yourself from these traditions without a fundamental sense of loss?

But as I tried re-creating my favorite childhood dishes, I began to realize how much of Chinese food was inherently plant-based. And I learned that vegetarian and vegan cooking is its own cuisine in China, a rich tradition that had existed for more than 2,000 years, motivated by the Buddhist tenets of compassionate eating. On my trip to visit relatives in China one summer, I ate at temple restaurants, plant-based lunch canteens, and buffets, astonished by the flavor and ingenuity of dishes like clay pot tofu skin and delicate layered soups made with mung beans and shiitake mushrooms. This cuisine was beautiful, alluringly delicious, and rich in history—I wanted to learn more.

So, just a few months after I finished graduate school, I packed my bags and moved to China to go to culinary school. For the past few years, my journey to learn Chinese vegetarian cooking has taken me back to my parents' hometown in Harbin, to Shanghai, to Chengdu, to Suzhou, and to Guangzhou, where I trained as a chef at the only professional vegetarian cooking program in the country. It's taken me to Taiwan, where I lived for a year, cooking and eating and learning from the vibrant Buddhist community who have preserved a microcosm of regional Chinese vegetarian traditions and developed new ones of their own. I've talked to old artisans who have been making tofu and soy milk skin for their entire lives, and have called up my parents to ask about our own family's history, learning stories I was never interested in hearing before. Over the years, my dad has decided to cut most of the meat out of his diet for health reasons, and he's always asking when I'm coming home so he can eat the food I cook. And unsurprisingly, my knowledge of Chinese culture has deepened. Becoming vegan didn't alienate me from my heritage, as I'd feared, but actually motivated me to understand it even more.

In Chinese, 素 *su* translates literally to "vegan" or "vegetarian," and you'll see it on menus indicating dishes free of meat. But *su* also means simple, quiet and plainly unadorned, the elemental nature or essence of something larger. I began this book thinking I'd write about vegan recipes, but along the way I realized that this kind of cooking was actually at the heart of Chinese cuisine: the inventive transformation of frugal ingredients like vegetables, tofu, and grains into a breathtaking variety of simple and delicious dishes. China has eight major regional cuisines, each influenced by wildly different climates, agriculture, geography, and history, and each of the country's twenty-three provinces has its own local vegetarian traditions and dishes. It's impossible to cover them all, so instead I've drawn from my own experiences—this is a subjective compilation of my favorites.

I've spent most of my time in southern China and Taiwan, where the availability of fresh produce year-round has generated diverse ways to cook with vegetables, so you'll find dishes like Blanched Asparagus with Sizzling Oil (page 70), Stir-Fried Water Spinach with Fermented Tofu (page 53), and Lotus Root Soup with Dried Mushrooms and Peanuts (page 237). Many of the recipes here are a tribute to the dishes I grew up eating—my parents are from Heilongjiang, the northernmost province in China, a region not exactly known for fine cuisine or banquet culture, but for hearty, delicious, and simple home fare like Steamed Eggplant with Soy Sauce and Garlic (page 109), Stewed Beans and Potato (page 104), raw salads like Napa Cabbage and Vermicelli Salad (page 54), and wonderful ways to cook tofu. I've included recipes I cook on a weekly basis, like Eight Treasure Congee (page 287) and Fragrant Dressed Tofu with Garlic and Basil

(page 139), as well as dishes I pull out for special occasions, like Vegetarian Roast Goose (page 179), Spicy Cumin Lion's Mane Mushroom Skewers (page 229), and Four Delights (page 208).

Instead of organizing by type of dish, I've chosen to present the chapters by plant type and ingredient categories, and I hope this book can serve as a reference to homestyle Chinese methods for cooking leafy greens, peppers, potatoes, cabbage, mushrooms, and other produce, as well as a guide to using proteins like tofu, tofu skin (also known as soy skin or *yuba*), and gluten (aka seitan). Chinese cooking is very resourceful by nature: it's not about following a rigid recipe but adapting the meal to what's available in your fridge. Some basic ingredients need to be sourced at an Asian supermarket, but as long as you have them in your pantry, you can come up with an entire menu of dishes using fresh vegetables found at your local grocery store or farmers' market. I do include some veganized versions of familiar Chinese dishes made with meat, like kung pao chicken and mapo tofu, but mostly, this book is an introduction to a wholly different culinary tradition that's inventive, satisfying, and delicious in its own right.

You'll meet some characters along the way, too. The modern plant-based scene in China is made up of vegan chefs, environmental activists, restaurant owners, and millions of ordinary Chinese people and families striving to eat healthier and more sustainably, just like Western eaters. Although this journey began with my own quest to learn how to cook, it isn't just my story—I wanted to showcase the community, the cooks, and the people who have carried on this culinary tradition for generations. For people unfamiliar with Chinese cooking, I hope these recipes will offer a wealth of new plant-based techniques and flavors to explore, and change the perception that Chinese cooking is daunting, time-consuming, or dependent on animal products. For those of us who grew up on Chinese food, I hope it inspires you to make your own favorite dishes and to discover a few new ones along the way.

PRACTICE

修煉

IN the morning, I ran past stray chickens and trees heavy with mangoes. Winters in the Pearl River Delta are supposed to be mild, but the air was breathless with heat even in November, and the rising sun shimmered on the glass-and-steel office buildings of the Tianhe business district in the haze across the river. A month ago, I flew to Guangzhou to train at a vegetarian culinary school for the next half year. The school was housed in an old building, with dorms next to the historic Whampoa Military Academy, and behind the school ran a gully where rickety wooden fishing boats floated by like relics from the past, bobbing past piles of torn concrete and lush overgrowth. At the orientation meeting, we all rose to our feet and bowed as the teacher walked in, a formality I'd seen only in old dramas. He instructed us to sit and then told us sternly to expect the cooking equivalent of military school.

But after meeting my ten colleagues, I relaxed. They were down-to-earth and quickly got over the fact that I was born and raised overseas. We bonded over scrubbing bathrooms, washing oil-greased exhaust vents, waking up for mandatory group runs, tossing dry rice in woks, and practicing knife skills on hunks of dough for hours on end. In the evenings, I'd hang my uniform and aprons to dry on the windy rooftop of the dorm building and gaze west toward the river's mouth, past the gardens on the balconies, past the U-bikes zipping down the alleyways, past the shipping containers and cranes and the distant patch that was Hong Kong. In the horizon, I imagined the coast of the continent I'd left and realized I hadn't even had a chance to get homesick. In the kitchen, our individual past lives seemed to fade; all we knew was the day-to-day, from the long classes in the morning, singeing our eyebrows from the volcanic heat of the wok burners in the afternoon, to the exhausted, grateful sleep of sore muscles at night.

Almost everyone at the school was a practicing Buddhist, and they treated me as an anomaly. Many of the cooking teachers were *upasaka*, having taken the highest vows a Buddhist layperson could commit to outside of becoming a monk or nun. "You aren't vegetarian because of religious observation?" they asked me, and I admitted that no, I hadn't even known of the Buddhist history of Chinese vegetarian cuisine until a few months ago. I felt like an imposter, but as we discussed our family backgrounds and talked about various trends in vegetarian cooking, I couldn't help but feel gratified, relief at our mutual understanding welling inexplicably like a lump in my throat. These were Chinese people to whom I didn't have to explain my eating choices or defend my cultural identity. Some of the older students had been vegan for decades. Many of them had flown from Liaoning, Henan, and other provinces to dedicate their next year to training, not only to learn a vocation but also to reconnect with a religious practice.

"You wouldn't imagine," Chef Wen said, "what that does to you, the daily violence." We were talking in the dining hall at lunchtime, and he had a bowl of noodles propped on the counter. "When I stopped cooking animals, I bought myself a new cleaver," he said. "It has never touched any meat." Chef Wen was our head teacher, a short and wiry man with a gentle, weathered face and a temper in the kitchen. Every morning, he drove up to the school on his moped, instantly recognizable from the building by his Angry Bird helmet. He carried in a *you tiao*, fried dough cruller, that he bought on the street, and ate his breakfast with a steaming bowl of soy milk from our tofu room. At lunch he would rather eat a bowl of leftover stir-fried noodles than the elegantly plated dishes the private chefs had prepared for tasting. He taught in Mandarin, the official language for teaching, but occasionally he reverted to his native Cantonese.

Wen Wenhui (溫文輝) didn't start off as a chef. He had a college degree and was working as an engineer before he decided to pursue cooking professionally, leaving behind the security of a high-paying career and the respect of his peers and family. "After all the education he had supported me through, my father was furious," he recalled. "He kicked me out of the house." In China, cooking was considered a lowly profession, despite the country's long and revered culinary history. Scholars, writers, and gourmets were celebrated, but the people in the kitchen were considered low status, coarse, and uneducated. Boys from poor households went into the service industry because they would be given room and board at the restaurants where they apprenticed. Even today, there remains a deep prejudice against cooking as a respectable profession. It made no sense for someone with a good family and education to choose a life of drudgery.

Chef Wen's career began with a job as a prep cook, but two decades later he had made a name for himself as a distinguished Cantonese chef, working until the mid-2000s as head chef at one of Guangzhou's finest hotel restaurants. He spent his hours cooking endless banquet-style meals for parties of businessmen and government officials who ordered platters of expensive meat, poultry, seafood, and fine delicacies out of social expectation and mutual backslapping, but left tables with dishes only half eaten. And behind those plush private dining rooms, the kitchen was a stressful and often violent environment, governed by ego, toughness, and an inescapable machismo. Chefs would scream at their line cooks if they made a mistake. "If you guys asked the same stupid questions you ask me, they'd *zou si ni,* beat you to death," Wen once said to us, lightly.

In the kitchens he worked in, chefs smoked and drank heavily after the long hours to de-stress. To Wen, there was a clear connection between the violence in the animals they cut up and the anger that would erupt in any conflict. He eventually couldn't ignore the disconnect between the food he was cooking and his personal values, and in 2007, he made the decision to switch his career to vegetarian cuisine. Since most vegetarian kitchens were Buddhist-run, their culture was diametric to that of conventional restaurant kitchens. Chefs who chose to work in vegetarian restaurants often connected their job to self-cultivation and spiritual practice.

These restaurants have been opening in cities across China at a rapidly increasing rate, with the revival of traditional vegetarian cuisine and the influence of ethical eating in the West. In the late 1990s, Beijing had only about two vegetarian restaurants; twenty years later, that number had grown to one hundred. In Shanghai, the number grew from forty-nine in 2012 to over a hundred in 2017. Many of these were inspired by a Buddhist ethos, but others were secular in nature and promoted a green lifestyle, catering to business areas with working professionals and middle-class families. Most hired conventional chefs, who often had no idea how to create flavor without meat (and without alliums, if they were strictly Buddhist), and other restaurants relied on old styles of temple and banquet cooking with elaborate mock meats, which were beginning to look dated to modern

Chinese eaters. After eight years of working with the chefs in these restaurants, Wen realized there was a problem.

"There was a new demand for vegetarian chefs but no professional standard," he said. This was markedly different from the system in place in China for conventional chefs. In the late 1970s, the Culinary Association of China was established to codify and modernize Chinese cuisine, and schools like the Sichuan Institute of Higher Cuisine were founded to train cooks in a systematic way, with a curriculum that presented dishes and techniques in order. There were regional cookbooks and an official hierarchy with ranks and examinations. But for vegetarian cooks, nothing like this existed yet, because the commodification of vegetarian cuisine had only just begun. Wen began developing a curriculum of his own, and in 2016, he helped to found the first professional vegetarian vocational school in China, tucked away on Changzhou Island in his hometown of Guangzhou. Wen was proud of the standards he had instilled. "When my students started working in vegetarian restaurants in Guangzhou and Shenzhen, Shanghai, Beijing, even Dali in Yunnan, they could recognize each other in the kitchens by how the other person tied their aprons and how they placed their knives at rest," he said.

Chef Wen had a favorite analogy. "Cooking vegetarian food isn't just about removing all the meat," he said. "You can't cut off the wings of an airplane and call it a submarine." It required an entirely different approach to thinking about flavor. Since the flavors of vegetables are subtle and their cell walls more delicate, cooking vegetables is about preserving and building. "The flavor of meat grows over time, and a bone broth simmered for hours becomes more intense in its meaty flavor," Wen said. But after cooking a soup of vegetables past a certain point, its flavor quickly deteriorates. Cooking well also means knowing when to stop cooking.

In his definition, using meat was about subtracting and intensifying. When preparing an animal, you first trimmed off the inedible portions—the

素食的概念.
1. 不含动物性原料食品;
2. 不食用含动物性食材的饮食方式.
3. 不食用含(蛋奶外)动物性食材的饮食方式.
4. 不食用含动物性食材与五辛食材的饮食方式.

当代素食标准的划分
1. 全 素 —— 中国素、东方素
2. 蛋奶素 —— 现代素
3. 蔬 素 —— 西方素、西式素

优秀的素食厨艺师应该具备哪些素质
一. 正确的素食思维
二. 诚敬谦和的品质
三. 敬业乐业, 甘于奉献的作为
四. 具有专业扎实的厨艺功夫和健康养生知识
五. 具有一定的文化素质修养和艺术灵感.

skin and hide and blood and bone, the gristle and organs and fluids and feathers. You had to cook off the unsavory gamey tastes (腥味 *xīngwèi*) and "urine-y" tastes (臊味 *sāowèi*), using Shaoxing wine, scallions, and onions. In the markets, there was a clear hierarchy with different prices for prime cuts and lesser cuts, as well as for offal. But an entire vegetable was sold at the same price, and the stem of one plant could be just as valuable as its fruit for a different use.

The meaning of 淡 *dàn* in Chinese cooking doesn't have a good English equivalent—the closest would be "light" or "bland," although "bland" has an unwanted negative connotation. Simply put, *dan* just describes the innate flavor of a vegetable, its natural taste without any seasoning. A carrot, for example, is innately sweet, a radish spicy, mustard greens bitter, and celery salty, depending on the season and minerals in the earth. By definition, *dan* contains all the flavors—salty, sweet, sour, bitter, and spicy. "You must highlight every vegetable's original flavor (本味 *běnwèi*) and not cook it away or conceal it under heavy seasonings," Wen said.

Certain vegetables have flavors that are only brought out when paired with other ingredients—a concept called 惹味 *rěwèi*, meaning to draw or coax out flavor. "Bitter greens like gai lan and lotus root need sweetness, squashes and root vegetables have affinity with the flavor of fermented black beans," Chef Wen explained. The cook has to know the yin and yang energy temperatures of each ingredient to make a dish balanced and nourishing for the eater (寒熱均衡 *hánrè jūnhéng*). Chef Wen said the beauty of Chinese vegetable dishes is their endless variations, based on combinations. "There are many potential medleys. Eggplant and green beans. Bitter melon, eggplant, and tomato. Each one is a different flavor," he said. "Add the permutations, the seasonal vegetables"—he scribbled down a formula for a combination, with *N*s and *R*s, and I was tempted to let out a laugh at the sudden swerve into mathematics—"just for this one dish, with sixteen other vegetable possibilities, you have five hundred

and sixty combinations. You can never run out of ideas for vegetarian dishes," he said.

"Out of the cooks I've trained over the past few years, I see two types," Chef Wen said. "You have the devout, studious student who is interested in Buddhism and the philosophy of cooking. But put them in the kitchen, and they do not know how to work. They cannot handle the grease and the dirtiness and the physical labor. They cook too slowly, and their movements are clumsy and inefficient. Then you have the cooks who have minimal education, who are used to hard labor. Maybe they cannot read, but they can cook naturally. They have physical stamina and can toss a wok in a restaurant, but when true creativity and innovation is needed, they're lacking. As a vegetarian chef, cooking demands both technical skill and creativity."

Chef Wen said he hoped to train vegetarian chefs who did not just cook but innovate and push the bounds of what Chinese vegetarian cuisine can be in the future. In his mind, the four most exciting ingredients for vegetarian chefs are tofu and potatoes—versatile ingredients that can be reinvented—and mushrooms and seaweed, the foods of the future. Ultimately, it was all about flavor. If nonvegetarians weren't convinced that plants could be delicious, then he had failed. "I don't want people to come away from a meal saying, 'Wow, that vegetarian dish was just like meat,'" he said. "I want them to say, *bǐròu hái hǎochī*—it was better than meat."

The first day of class, we were taught the "three virtues and six tastes" (三德六味 *sāndé liùwèi*), a traditional set of guidelines for the head of the kitchen at a monastery, as he prepared meals for the community. I'd scribbled down a rough translation in my notebook: *If the food provided is not sanitized and clean, it loses its pure virtue; if it is not refined and has tough, sinewy, or inedible parts, it loses its tender virtue; if it is not handled appropriately and prepared with judicious cooking and timing, it loses its harmonious virtue.* When applied to the cook, pure (清淨 *qīngjìng*) means cooking with pure intentions, to make it about the food, not about your ego. Tender (柔軟 *róuruǎn*) means refinement, gentleness, and restraint of heart—a cook should not be careless with kitchen equipment, hasty, or rough, but work with intention in each step. According to order (如法 *rúfǎ*) means planning dishes in harmony with what is available in season, and judiciously using the appropriate method of cooking to bring out the beauty and flavor of the vegetable.

I used to cook haphazardly—going through the motions while my mind was elsewhere, or racing to get food on the table as quickly as possible, or focusing so much on rigidly following a recipe and worrying about the end results that I wasn't fully experiencing what I was cooking half the time. But in Chinese cooking, you can't fire the wok until every element for the dish is washed, chopped, measured out, and ready at hand: the prep work is the most important part. Cooking mindfully isn't dependent on externalities in the kitchen or on silence, but on sharpening your sensory attention and fully inhabiting your physical movements. "When you wash the rice, wash the rice, when you stir the soup, stir the soup," Chef Wen once said, quoting a Zen master.

It meant noticing the weight of a radish in your hand as you prepared it, its smooth, marble-like heaviness, and smelling its spicy, sweet aroma as you sliced into it with your knife. I learned to focus on my breath while doing repetitive tasks like stirring and folding peanuts as they slowly heated in a wok, and giving my wholehearted attention to subtle feedback, like the sound of peppercorns popping in hot oil. I learned to respond to the food as it talked back to me, and to trust my instincts.

At the end of the day, cooking was not just working on food, but working on yourself and on others. "Vegetarian cooking represents the beauty of Chinese culture, not just because of the food, but because it engages with a tradition of respect, modesty, restraint, and compassion for all living things," Chef Wen said. "As a vegetarian chef, you do not just practice cooking, but make cooking a practice."

INGREDIENTS

This is a list of ingredients called for in this book. If you'd like to fully stock your kitchen with everything here, I'll offer some notes on my preferences and things to look for as references. But you really don't need much to get started with Chinese cooking. The basics are simple. As long as you have this list of pantry ingredients, you can make a majority of the dishes in this book.

THE BASICS

cooking oil
sugar
salt
pure starch, such as potato starch or cornstarch
fresh aromatics: garlic, scallions, and ginger
soy sauce
Chinkiang black vinegar
Shaoxing wine
toasted sesame oil
chili oil
dried shiitake mushrooms
dried red chiles
star anise pods
whole Sichuan peppercorns

COOKING OIL
油 yóu

Try to use a cooking oil with a mild flavor and a high smoke point that can withstand the high heat of wok cooking. Traditionally, peanut oil is popular, and its subtle peanut scent lends a delicious, delicate aroma to dishes. But any neutral-flavored vegetable oil like rapeseed (canola) oil, grapeseed oil, avocado oil, soybean oil, sunflower oil, and rice bran oil will work great.

All that said, my parents have always used extra-virgin olive oil from Costco for stir-frying, which is neither neutral in flavor nor has a high smoke point, but what can I say—it's worked for them for two decades.

SUGAR
糖 táng

Sugar is typically added to savory dishes to round out the flavors. It's also a key component in sweet-and-sour sauces. Unless otherwise specified, in these recipes "sugar" refers to granulated sugar, which dissolves quickly in sauces. I use organic granulated sugar, as regular white sugar is bleached with bone char, meaning it's not vegan.

Rock sugar (冰糖 *bīngtáng*) is sugar crystallized into large chunks—the yellowish crystals are preferable to bleached white crystals. It does not leave a sour aftertaste like granulated sugar does, and gives braised dishes a glossy look and caramelly flavor. Note that rock sugar is different from brown slab sugar (片糖 *piàntáng*), which is made of sugar formed into alternating dark brown and light sheets. To break up rock sugar, use a mortar and pestle. For big or stubborn pieces, I place them in a clean muslin cloth or cheesecloth and crush them with a large rolling pin or hammer.

Chinese brown sugar, also called black sugar (黑糖 *hēitáng*), is used to sweeten teas, congees, and dessert soups. Unlike American brown sugar, which is often just cane sugar crystals with added molasses, Chinese brown sugar is raw and unrefined, with a dark color and smoky, almost malt-like flavor; the closest substitutes are Okinawan black sugar (*kokuto*) and coconut sugar.

POTATO STARCH
生粉 shēngfěn

Potato starch is a great all-purpose starch: it is widely available and flavorless, and a tiny amount stirred into water to make a slurry will quickly thicken sauces. It's also good for coating or to batter foods before frying, as it generates a light and crispy exterior. Cornstarch is also common in Chinese cooking, but after testing I've found it doesn't thicken as powerfully, so if you're using cornstarch, increase the amount specified in the recipe by at least 50 percent (for example, if a recipe calls for

½ teaspoon potato starch, increase to ¾ teaspoon cornstarch; if it calls for 1 tablespoon potato starch, increase to 1½ tablespoons cornstarch).

STOCK
高湯 gāotāng

I always keep some stock on hand, either homemade stock I make when I'm not too busy on weekends and freeze (see pages 309 to 311), or granulated vegetarian or mushroom bouillon powder.

CHINKIANG BLACK VINEGAR
香醋 xiāngcù

This is a dark vinegar made by fermenting glutinous rice with grains and herbs. Because it's aged for months or sometimes years, similar to balsamic vinegar, it develops a fruitier, more complex flavor than pale rice vinegar. It's famously produced in the city of Zhenjiang (Chinkiang) in Jiangsu Province, from which it gets its name. Use it in sauces, marinades, dressings for cold dishes, and dipping sauces for dumplings or steamed buns.

PALE RICE VINEGAR
米醋，白醋 mǐcù, báicù

Usually sold labeled as just "rice vinegar," this unseasoned vinegar is used for pickling, in sweet-and-sour sauces, and to add a clean, bright taste.

SHAOXING COOKING WINE
紹兴酒，料酒，黃酒 shàoxīngjiǔ, liàojiǔ, huángjiǔ

This amber-colored rice wine is also called "yellow wine" or Chinese cooking wine, and the Shaoxing variety is a specialty of the ancient city of Shaoxing in Zhejiang Province. It has a nutty grain flavor and mushroomy note, and smells faintly sweet as it evaporates and deglazes the wok. My go-to is the red-and-gold bottle from the Taiwan Tobacco and Liquor Corporation, containing just rice, water, and salt. It's not labeled "Shaoxing," but in taste and function, it's generally interchangeable.

Dry sherry is a great substitute if you can't find Shaoxing wine. Or simply leave it out.

Fresh Aromatics and Herbs

GINGER
薑 jiāng

Fresh ginger is one of the essential aromatics in Chinese cooking. At the grocery store, select firm, plump ginger segments with unwrinkled skin and a slightly glossy sheen. The typical brown-skinned kind is mature ginger, but sometimes you'll find tender young ginger in Asian supermarkets—the rhizomes are pale and almost ivory in color with pink-tinged ends, and they are wonderful used as a garnish, in salads, or pickled.

Store in the refrigerator in a small zip-top bag. I'll sometimes throw peeled ginger in the freezer, where I can keep it on hand for practically forever.

GARLIC
蒜 suàn

Garlic is not used in traditional Chinese Buddhist vegetarian cuisine, but it's an important aromatic in northern and Sichuan-style dishes. At the grocery store, look for plump, fat heads of garlic with no withered cloves or green tips.

SCALLIONS
蔥 cōng

Scallions are also called green onions or spring onions, and they come in two varieties: slender small onions with straight bulbs and long, thick-stalked green onions that resemble leeks in size. The latter is used mostly in northern China. In Chinese cooking, the green portion is often reserved for garnish, while the bottom white part is bloomed in oil at the beginning of stir-fries, since it is more pungent.

Buddhist vegetarian cooks avoid alliums (vegetables in the onion family) and often will substitute Chinese celery for scallions. Chinese celery has delicately thin, hollow stalks and a strong taste, and acts as an aromatic.

CILANTRO
香菜 xiāngcài

Also known as coriander, cilantro is one of the few fresh herbs used in Chinese cooking. It's called "fragrant vegetable" and adds a distinctive aroma to salads and a pop of color as a garnish. The best way to store cilantro is to wrap it in a paper towel and refrigerate it in an airtight container or zip-top bag.

DILL
茴香 huíxiāng

An intensely fragrant savory herb beloved in the northern and southwestern regions of China, fresh dill is often used as a dominant ingredient in dumpling and steamed bun fillings.

THAI BASIL
九層塔 jiǔcéngtǎ

Thai basil is also known as Asian basil, and it's beloved in Taiwanese cooking, where it is used most notably in "three-cup" dishes. Thai basil has dark, narrow leaves, purple stems, and a strong fragrance and peppery anise flavor that stands up well in cooked dishes. But you can certainly substitute Italian basil if you can't find it.

Dry Aromatics and Spices

DRIED SHIITAKE MUSHROOMS
香菇 xiānggū

Dried shiitake or black mushrooms have a potent earthy fragrance and deep meaty savoriness. Typically rehydrated and used in stir-fries, soups, and stews or simmered to make a flavorful stock, the mushrooms are sold in Asian supermarkets in two varieties: the small, thick ones with a cracked pattern on their caps that resemble tortoise shells are highly prized for their flavor and are called "flower mushrooms" (花菇 huāgū), while the thinner, darker, and smooth-capped mushrooms are called "winter mushrooms" (冬菇 dōnggū) and are more affordable. Look for mushrooms harvested in Japan or

PREPPING AROMATICS

If you are cooking a meal with multiple dishes, determine how much of each aromatic you will need in total and whether they need to be minced, shredded, or sliced. Prepare them all at the same time and keep them in separate piles, one for each dish.

GINGER

Scrub the root well. For thinly sliced ginger, you can leave the peel on—the area under the peel is flavorful and highly nutritious. For minced ginger, I usually peel it first. Use the edge of a small spoon to gently scrape off the thin skin and to nimbly peel around the nooks and crannies.

TO SLICE: Cut the root crosswise into ⅛-inch-thick coins or long oblong slices.

TO SHRED: Cut the ginger into thin slices the width of a quarter, then stack a couple of slices on top of each other and slice them into very thin shreds.

TO MINCE: Position the pile of thin shreds (see above) horizontally. Cut them crosswise into tiny ⅛-inch pieces.

GARLIC

The best way to peel garlic is to smash it with the blade of a Chinese cleaver: Position the clove under the flat of the knife blade, close to the handle, with the sharp edge facing away from you. Place the heel of your hand on the blade over the clove. Lift the blade and then press down firmly until the clove breaks. Remove and discard the papery skin—it should slip off easily.

Slice or mince the garlic as directed in the recipe.

SCALLIONS

Rinse under running water to remove any grit between the roots and tops. Trim off the bottom root end and tear off any yellowing or wilted leaves.

TO SHRED: Cut scallions into 2-inch segments and then halve each piece lengthwise. Cut lengthwise into thin shreds.

TO THINLY SLICE: Cut scallions crosswise into ⅛-inch-thick coins or rings. You can also angle the knife and cut them into thin slices that resemble "horse ears."

Korea, as they are usually better in quality; when you open the bag the aroma should be powerful. Store in a covered container in a dark, cool place.

Soak the dried mushrooms in cool water for at least 4 hours to plump up, or if you're in a hurry, cover them with boiling water and soak for 30 minutes. A tip I learned to speed up the process is to add a pinch of salt to the water. Don't discard the soaking water; use it as a stock.

DRIED RED CHILES
乾辣椒 gānlàjiāo

In Chinese cooking, dried chiles don't lend much heat and are used in stir-fries for their aroma and robust flavor. The type of dried chile called for in this book is the whole dried red chile: look for 1- to 2-inch-long Tianjin chiles (朝天椒 cháotiānjiāo), or 4- to 5-inch-long Sichuan chiles (二荆條 èrjīngtiáo). Avoid tiny dried bird's-eye or Thai chiles: they're far too hot for these recipes. If you can't find Chinese chiles, dried japones chiles and guajillo chiles are the closest equivalents. Look for chiles with a deep red color, rich fragrance, and soft, pliable skin, and avoid brittle, fading, and discolored chiles, which may be several years old.

SICHUAN PEPPERCORNS
花椒 huājiāo

Intensely aromatic, Sichuan peppercorns have a piney scent with a citrusy note. They don't provide any heat, causing a numbing and tingling sensation on the tongue instead. In this book, "Sichuan peppercorn" refers to the red ones; unripe green peppercorns are deliciously lemony in flavor and more numbing, but hard to find.

Purchase them online or from a Chinese supermarket, and look for a vibrant dark red, not brown, color; there also shouldn't be too many visible seeds and stems in the bag. Store the peppercorns in an airtight container in a cool, dry place away from direct sunlight. Their flavor will start to diminish after two months, so to preserve their aroma for even longer, store them in a closed bag in the freezer for up to a year.

GROUND SICHUAN PEPPERCORN
花椒面 huājiāomiàn

I recommend grinding Sichuan peppercorns yourself, since their flavor fades quickly and the store-bought ground variety always tastes dusty and dull in comparison to freshly ground. Toast the peppercorns for 3 to 4 minutes in a wok over low heat before grinding with a spice grinder or mortar and pestle. You can sift the powder through a fine strainer to discard the white inner husk, which has no flavor. In her cooking, my grandma uses ground peppercorns in place of whole to avoid the possibility of anyone accidentally biting into one.

WHITE PEPPERCORNS
白胡椒 báihújiāo

White pepper is the pepper of choice in Chinese cooking. It has a subtler aroma than black pepper, with an intriguing musty note.

When stir-frying, sprinkle a dash of ground white pepper into the wok just before serving to get the full benefit of its flavor. A light dusting on a bowl of rice congee adds a warming effect and peppery aroma.

I highly recommend grinding your own for best flavor: lightly smack them first with the flat blade of a knife to crack them. Toast them in a dry pan until fragrant and grind them in small quantities. Store both whole and ground white peppercorns in airtight containers in a dark, dry cupboard for up to a month.

FIVE-SPICE POWDER
五香粉 wǔxiāngfěn

Five-spice is a sweet-smelling aromatic blend often made up of more than five spices, usually some combination of ground Chinese cinnamon, fennel seed, clove, star anise, Sichuan peppercorn, coriander, and cumin. Although these spices are used whole in braises, the powder is very convenient for marinades, dry rubs, and spiced salts, and for sprinkling into dishes. Thirteen-spice powder, which you might also find at the Asian supermarket, is a special blend with a few more spices like ground

ginger, bay leaf, dried tangerine peel, and black cardamom and can be used interchangeably with five-spice powder. Don't buy too much at once—like any ground spice, the flavor dissipates after two or three months.

STAR ANISE
八角 bājiǎo

This rust-colored star-shaped seedpod with a pungent, licorice-like aroma is used for braising and pickling—one or two pods are usually enough to flavor a dish. Store them in a zip-top bag or airtight container in a dark, dry cupboard for up to a year.

Seasonings and Condiments

SALT
鹽 yán

I always use coarse sea salt or kosher salt (Diamond Crystal). Avoid iodized table salts, which leave an unpleasant chemical aftertaste. Unless otherwise specified, "salt" in this book refers to kosher salt, and if a volume measurement is given, use Diamond Crystal. If you are using Morton kosher salt, reduce the measurement by one-third to one-half.

MSG
味精 wèijīng

I love MSG. It's not meant to replace good cooking techniques for flavor, but a little bit goes a long way for a boost of savoriness. If you taste a dish and it doesn't need more salt or soy sauce but still lacks that certain something you can't put your finger on, add a pinch of MSG—it will round out and enhance all the flavors. Some people incorporate the seasoning by creating a blend with salt: make a 10:1 mix of kosher salt to MSG (roughly 1 tablespoon of MSG for every ⅔ cup of salt), and then use it to season dishes as you regularly would. You can find Ajinomoto brand MSG at Asian supermarkets. I prefer the fine crystals over the coarse flakes since they dissolve faster when mixed into sauces.

MSG

Monosodium glutamate (MSG) is the salt form of naturally occurring free glutamates found in foods such as cheese, soybeans and soy sauce, corn, tomatoes, radishes, mushrooms, breast milk, and seaweed. It is a source of umami, which gives a savory, craveable taste to food, and was discovered over a hundred years ago by Kikunae Ikeda, a Japanese chemist, who extracted it from a broth of kombu seaweed. In my grandparents' kitchens, you could always find salt, MSG, and chicken bouillon (精 *jījīng*) by the stove, a classic trio of seasonings in Chinese cooking. Despite being extensively used in Asian cuisines, MSG has been vilified in popular conception due to "Chinese restaurant syndrome," a claim in an American newspaper in 1968 allegedly linking harmful side effects to the consumption of MSG in Chinese restaurants. (Most people are not aware that MSG is also added to most canned soups, dressings, chips, snacks, sandwich meats, and frozen entrées, not just Chinese food.) The myth of MSG's side effects caught on in large part due to xenophobia, but it has long been debunked by rigorous scientific studies—MSG is a harmless ingredient for most people and can be used judiciously as a seasoning, just like salt.

In the vegan food world, nutritional yeast (or "nooch") is a beloved flavor enhancer, and although it's also extracted from yeast and shares the same chemical compound that makes MSG savory, nooch is enthusiastically sprinkled onto food for its boost of cheesy umami while MSG is viewed with suspicion. I hope the perception of MSG changes soon, as it is especially useful in vegan cooking. Some purists argue that true Chinese cooking shouldn't utilize MSG, since chefs traditionally relied on quality ingredients and fine stocks. That's obviously ideal, but for home cooks who don't have these on hand or simply prefer something more convenient, I don't see why you should deprive yourself of extra flavor in your cooking, especially if it gets you to eat and enjoy more vegetables.

Left to right: light soy sauce, dark soy sauce, vegetarian oyster sauce, pale rice vinegar, Chinkiang black vinegar, Shaoxing cooking wine, sesame oil

SOY SAUCE
醬油，生抽 jiàngyóu, shēngchōu

Unless otherwise specified, "soy sauce," in this book, refers to light soy sauce (生抽 shēngchōu), as opposed to dark soy sauce (老抽 lǎochōu). Light soy sauce is all-purpose: it's lighter in color, thin, and salty (whereas dark soy sauce is intense in color and used primarily for braising). My favorites are Kimlan (金蘭 Jīn Lán) and the organic soy sauce from Wan Ja Shan (萬家香 Wàn Jiā Xiāng).

Soy sauce lasts almost indefinitely, but the flavors can change after a few months. Store the tightly capped bottle on the counter away from the stove, or in a cool, dark cupboard. Some chefs refrigerate their best soy sauces to preserve their flavor and freshness.

Typical soy sauce is made with a combination of wheat and soy; for a gluten-free soy sauce, look for tamari, which is made without wheat. It has a bolder, richer flavor and can be used in place of regular light soy sauce.

VEGETARIAN OYSTER SAUCE OR VEGETARIAN STIR-FRY SAUCE
素蠔油 sù háoyóu

Used in place of traditional oyster sauce in vegetarian cooking, this thick sauce has a dark, reddish tinge, slightly gel-like consistency, and rich umami flavor that is derived from mushrooms. Sometimes it's labeled "mushroom stir-fry sauce" or "vegetarian stir-fry sauce." I particularly like the one from the Wan Ja Shan brand labeled "Vegetarian Mushroom Oyster Sauce."

FERMENTED BLACK SOYBEANS ("BLACK BEANS")
豆豉 dòuchǐ

Look for dry and plump little beans speckled with salt, sold in little plastic bags, not the marinated kind sold in jars. These are intensely savory, the main flavor in black bean sauce. They're not actually "black beans," but soybeans that have turned black as a process of dry fermentation. Before cooking, I first rinse them to wash off the surface salt and then lightly mash or

Left to right: fermented black soybeans, fermented soybean paste, Sichuan chili bean paste, fermented tofu, sesame paste, olive-preserved greens, homemade pickled mustard greens, chili oil, Sichuan pickled greens (yácài)

coarsely chop them with the blade of my knife. This will release more of their flavor in the wok.

SICHUAN CHILI BEAN PASTE
辣豆瓣醬 là dòubànjiàng

Also labeled broad bean paste, Sichuan hot bean paste, or doubanjiang, this spicy, deep red paste is made with pickled red chiles and fermented broad beans, and it's an essential ingredient in Sichuan cooking, often paired with Sichuan peppercorns. The most famous is from the Pixian County in Sichuan Province. You can find this online or in Chinese supermarkets. Brands vary widely in saltiness and sweetness, so taste the sauce and adjust the salt and sugar amounts in the recipe if needed.

FERMENTED SOYBEAN PASTE
黃豆醬 huángdòujiàng

I love the rich, savory flavor of a good basic yellow soybean paste and use it often as a base in braised dishes—it offers umami depth and saltiness without the color of soy sauce or heat of Sichuan chili bean paste. It's a thick yellowish-brown paste containing broken pieces of soybeans, and it smells and tastes like good soy sauce. There are various brands—look for one with minimal ingredients, containing just soybeans, water, salt, and sugar.

SESAME PASTE
芝麻醬 zhīmájiàng

Chinese sesame paste is ground from roasted sesame seeds, and it's darker and thicker than tahini. It resembles peanut butter and has a wonderfully nutty aroma. Sesame paste is usually used in noodle sauces or added to cold-dressed dishes and salads. Stir the jar well, as the oil will rise to the top, leaving a drier paste at the bottom. The best sesame pastes contain just roasted sesame seeds; avoid ones with added sugar or oil. To make it yourself, see page 305.

FERMENTED TOFU
豆腐乳 dòufurǔ

Sold in little glass jars, this funky condiment is made by brining and fermenting tofu in wine and spices.

The aged cubes are creamy and ripe like soft cheese and can be eaten with rice porridge (it's quite salty, so a tidbit swiped up on a chopstick goes a long way) or mashed into a smooth paste to lend luscious flavor to stir-fries. It's also used in hot pot sauces. Store opened jars in the fridge.

OLIVE PRESERVED GREENS
橄欖菜 gǎnlǎncài

A dark, umami-rich relish and Cantonese specialty of the eastern Chaozhou region of Guangdong Province, *ganlancai* or "olive vegetable" is made by simmering salted mustard leaves with crushed Chinese olives and preserving them in jars with the olives' inky green oil. I always keep a jar in my fridge, as it's fantastic on top of pan-fried tofu, spooned onto plain rice or noodles, or used to stir-fry green beans or other vegetables.

SESAME OIL
香油，麻油 xiāngyóu, máyóu

"Sesame oil" in this book refers to toasted sesame oil. The amber-colored oil is added to dishes as a finishing touch, not used as a cooking oil, since its strong nutty aroma quickly dulls once heated. Sesame oil is also used in dressings for cold dishes and dips for dumplings. Check the ingredient list to make sure it's 100 percent sesame oil and doesn't have any added filler oils. My mom's favorite is the Japanese Kadoya brand, which comes in an economical rectangular metal can, but since sesame oil doesn't improve with age, I recommend buying a small bottle to start.

CHILI OIL
紅油，辣椒油 hóngyóu, làjiāoyóu

Ruby-red chili oil is used in both hot and cold dishes, adding an arrestingly brilliant color and a deep, toasty flavor. Although you can find bottled chili oils in Asian supermarkets, they can taste stale and not particularly aromatic, so I recommend making chili oil at home—you simply infuse ground red chiles and spices in hot oil (see page 301)—a jar of the stuff will last a long time in the refrigerator.

Other Dried Goods

WOOD EAR OR CHINESE BLACK FUNGUS
木耳 mù'ěr

Usually sold dried, wood ears are a common Chinese fungus with a very mild flavor and delicate, slippery crunch. Keep the dried wood ears in a covered container in a dark, cool place and soak them in hot water for 20 to 30 minutes before using. These are better digested when blanched first.

GOJI BERRIES
枸杞 gǒuqǐ

Dried goji berries or wolfberries can be found in most Chinese supermarkets, as well as Western health food shops; my mom purchases organic goji berries in bulk online. They have a very subtle flavor and are used mostly as a garnish sprinkled on soups or savory dishes, cooked into sweet congees, or simmered in teas, where they tint the liquid a beautiful amber color. Store them in an airtight container or sealed bag in a dry cupboard for up to a month, or stash them in the freezer, where they'll stay vibrant for a long time.

JUJUBE DATES
紅棗 hóngzǎo

Jujubes or Chinese red dates are the fruit of a deciduous tree native to northern China. The mottled yellow-green or reddish surface of the fresh fruit dries into a wrinkly, glossy red skin. Dried jujubes are studded in steamed buns to add color and sweetness, mashed and used in pastries as a filling, or cooked until plump in soups, congees, and teas. Keep them in a covered container in a dark, cool place, or refrigerate them in a sealed bag.

DRIED DAYLILY FLOWERS
金針花，黃花菜 jīnzhēnhuā, huánghuācài

The long, unopened brownish-yellow buds of the daylily flower have a delicate, earthy flavor and slightly floral fragrance. They can be found in any Asian supermarket—look for lighter-colored, flexible buds and avoid brittle-looking ones. Refrigerate them in a sealed bag. To rehydrate, simply soak them in cold water for 30 minutes. Trim off the bottom ¼ inch of each bud and cut any longer ones in half before cooking.

LILY BULBS
百合 bǎihé

These edible, ivory-colored petals are peeled from the skinless bulbs of the daylily flower (*Lilium brownii*), and you can find them fresh in Asian markets in the spring through late summer. They are added to stir-fries and soups for their refreshingly crunchy, sweet taste and subtly floral smell. Separate the petal-like bulbs and add them at the very end of cooking, as they take very little time to cook. Unopened bulbs will keep in the refrigerator for up to two weeks.

NORI SHEETS
海苔 hǎitái

Dried seaweed, sold in unseasoned sheets, is used in traditional vegetarian cooking to wrap ingredients and shape mock eel and mock fish, since it provides a dark skin-like look and savory, briny flavor. Get the flexible untoasted sheets used for sushi, not the toasted or salted ones, which crumble easily.

BEAN THREAD NOODLES, SWEET POTATO VERMICELLI
粉絲，粉條 fěnsī, fěntiáo

Somewhat confusingly, very different noodles are referred to as "glass noodles." Bean thread or mung bean vermicelli are thin, transparent noodles that come in small bundles, sold several in a pack—they are hard and white when dried, and must be soaked in cool water for 20 minutes to soften before cooking.

Sweet potato vermicelli or potato starch noodles tend to be thicker and much chewier in texture, and are the kind used for *japchae* in Korean cooking. These often require boiling until soft before using.

BASIC EQUIPMENT

The foundational tools for cooking Chinese food are a wok with a lid, a sharp knife, and a steamer, but here are a few more that make certain things possible and others easier.

WOK
鍋 guō

While it's certainly possible to cook Chinese food using a flat frying pan or skillet, I still believe a wok is essential, even for the beginner cook. It's inexpensive and durable, and its functionality lies in its shape. For stir-frying, the wok's roomy belly and high sloping sides make it ideal for turning and tossing bulky vegetables, and its rounded base also requires less oil for stir-frying than a flat-bottomed pan does. It can also be used to boil noodles, blanch vegetables, and steam (simply stack bamboo steamer baskets on top). Deep-frying is a lot less of a hassle in a wok, since the bowl shape requires less oil to cover a greater area than a straight-sided stockpot.

For most American stoves, I recommend a **flat-bottomed 14-inch carbon-steel wok.** Carbon steel heats quickly and evenly, and it's both light and inexpensive. A flat-bottomed wok will be stable on both the grate of a gas burner or the flat surface of an electric stove. Don't use a round-bottomed wok without a wok ring, as it can easily tip over.

I love a good cast-iron wok, but cast iron is much heavier than carbon steel. And since it retains heat for longer, unlike quick-cooling carbon steel, you have to remove the food immediately to prevent it from overcooking. Stainless-steel and aluminum woks don't need seasoning, but they also don't prevent food from sticking at high temperatures, so you'll have to compensate with a larger amount of oil.

I do not recommend a nonstick wok. The type of high heat required for stir-frying will damage the nonstick coating and release potentially harmful chemicals. If you properly season and heat a carbon-steel wok, it will develop a patina and become nonstick over time.

WOK SPATULA AND LADLE
鍋鏟, 湯勺 guōchǎn, tāngsháo

A wok spatula is shaped like a shovel and fits the curvature of the wok. It's good for stirring, folding, and scooping ingredients, and for transferring sauces to the wok.

A Chinese ladle is used to scoop food, sauces, and stock. The shape is different from a Western ladle—the bowl is more flush with the handle, and its curved bottom fits the bottom of the wok well.

You can use any cooking spoon or wooden spatula with a wok, but these are more efficient since they're designed for the wok. You can find these in any Asian supermarket or Chinese cookware shop.

WOK LID
鍋蓋 guōgài

Find a flat-topped or domed wok lid that fits snugly into the wok, resting ½ inch or so below the rim.

CLAY POT
砂鍋 shāguō

I never understood the necessity of a clay pot until my mom gifted me one and I started using it regularly to make rice, stews, and braised dishes. Dishes cooked in a clay pot just taste better to me. The clay transmits heat gently, allowing food to cook gradually and evenly over a longer period of time. A clay pot makes for great presentation, too. Smaller, shallower ones are used for braising, whereas large, deeper ones hold soups or porridges.

Don't brown aromatics or fry ingredients in a clay pot—do this separately in a metal pot or wok. The clay pot is designed for use on the stovetop, but it should be heated starting at a low setting and gradually increased to no more than medium heat.

SKIMMER OR SPIDER
笊籬 zhàoli

Used for draining food after boiling or frying, these are basically strainers you use to scoop food from the wok.

WOK BRUSH
鍋刷 guōshuā

This bristly bamboo brush is perfect for scrubbing out a hot wok under water between dishes, as the square split bamboo bristles won't melt like plastic ones. You can substitute a long-handled brush with natural bristles.

SEASONING A WOK

Cooking with a carbon-steel wok, it takes some maintenance to develop and preserve the pan's dark metallic patina, which acts as a nonstick coating. Many cooks find the process of building and maintaining this patina satisfying.

FIRST SEASONING

Scrub the new wok with a steel-wire ball. Wash it well with hot, soapy water to remove any machine oils left over from the manufacturing process. Dry with a paper towel, then place the wok on the stove over low heat, and wipe off any remaining moisture. Open the windows, increase the heat to high, and allow the wok to sit for 10 minutes to allow the grease residue to burn off. It will start to darken during this time. Then continue on the stovetop or in the oven.

STOVETOP: Cut 1½ cups of fresh ginger slices (about ¼ inch thick). In the wok, heat ¼ cup vegetable oil (cold-pressed flax oil is best) over medium-high heat, then add the ginger (and a handful of Chinese chives, if you have them), sliding it around in the wok with your spatula to coat the entire inside surface well. Stir-fry for 15 minutes, or until the ginger looks blackened and cooked to a crisp, then remove from the heat, discard the ginger, and wipe out the inside of the wok with a paper towel. Repeat this process for even better seasoning.

OVEN (RECOMMENDED): Preheat the oven to 450°F (230°C). Unscrew the wooden handle of the wok and set it aside. (If it isn't removable, wrap it in a few layers of damp paper towels, then cover with a layer of aluminum foil.) Rub the entire inside of the wok with a very thin coating of vegetable oil or cold-pressed flax oil. Set it upside down in the oven for 45 to 60 minutes, until the inside has developed a caramel-colored patina. Repeat this process for even better seasoning. Be sure to keep your kitchen well-ventilated; you can also do this in an outdoor grill.

MAINTAINING THE PATINA

Using the wok frequently is key to maintaining and developing the patina. It might look mottled or discolored at first, but after years of use, the patina will become more even and develop a beautiful black shine.

Wash the wok immediately after each use, while the surface is still hot. Try to avoid using detergent or soap, which can damage the patina. Scrub lightly with a bamboo brush under running water, then dry it well with a towel. You may also heat it to make sure all the moisture steams off, then lightly rub it all over with a little oil.

If you have used a wok for steaming, you'll have to quickly re-season the wok to get its finish back. Dry the wok well with a paper towel and then rub the inside surface with a thin layer of oil. Heat the wok again over medium-high heat for 5 minutes, or until the oil starts to smoke. Remove the wok from the heat and wipe out the oil with another paper towel.

STEAMER BASKETS
蒸籠 zhēnglóng

A wok with bamboo steamer baskets is the most versatile steaming setup. The bamboo absorbs any condensation, so it doesn't drip onto the food, and it also infuses everything with its lovely fragrance. Steaming will boil off the seasoned shine in the wok, so use a separate wok dedicated to steaming and boiling, or just re-season the wok to develop the patina again after use. A 12-inch-diameter steamer will fit a 14-inch wok. They are usually sold in a set of two baskets with a cover. Don't use more than two, since a third level will not receive enough steam to cook properly.

When steaming in a wok, place two pennies in the water. This is a trick I learned from author Carolyn Phillips that allows you to monitor the boiling water without lifting off the baskets—as long as you hear the pennies rattling cheerily at the bottom of the wok, you have enough water, but once they start slowing down (or you don't hear them at all), that's an indication to refill the water, as the bottom will start burning soon.

You can also use a dedicated stainless-steel steamer pot with stainless-steel steamer racks. The advantage is that it holds a lot more water than a wok, so you won't have to refill the water for longer steaming times, but it tends to create more condensation.

CHINESE CLEAVER
菜刀 càidāo

This all-purpose Chinese knife looks like a cleaver but is light, dextrous, and utilitarian, with a very thin yet wide rectangular blade. This is literally the only knife I use. You can use it to cut slices, slice fine threads, julienne strips, dice cubes, make rolling cuts, and mince aromatics. Because the blade is wide, you can use the flat side to scoop up ingredients, smack garlic, and even smash cucumbers.

Cleaver handles come in two styles: a metal handle molded with the blade, and a round wooden handle fastened to the blade. I find the latter easier to grip. A standard large blade is 8 or 9 × 4 inches, but they also come in a 7 × 3-inch size, which is more comfortable if you have smaller hands. Some people like stainless-steel blades, but I find them slippery and prefer dark carbon-steel knives because they're easier to sharpen. Carbon steel does need to be wiped completely dry after every use so it doesn't rust. Asian supermarkets sometimes carry Chinese cleavers, but the quality will vary; I recommend the Wok Shop for a good online source.

ROLLING PIN
擀麵杖 gǎnmiànzhàng

Look for a thin wooden Chinese rolling pin at any Asian supermarket or Chinese cookware shop. These are about 1 inch in diameter and 1 foot long, sometimes with tapered ends, and are used to roll out baozi and dumpling wrappers. You can use a standard Western rolling pin to flatten the doughs in this book, but the smaller Chinese rolling pin is designed to be used with one hand while the other turns the dough, which makes for a much more efficient process if you are making dozens of dumplings.

MUSLIN CLOTH OR CHEESECLOTH

A big square of lightweight unbleached muslin is useful for shaping and pressing tofu, and forming and steaming imitation meats like vegetarian chicken.

ELECTRIC PRESSURE COOKER

An electric multicooker or pressure cooker like an Instant Pot is invaluable for speeding up the cooking process for congees, porridges, and soups. You can also use it to cook rice.

HOW TO USE THIS BOOK & HOW TO PLAN A MEAL

The serving sizes of the recipes in this book are based on the guiding principle of a Chinese meal, in which you serve enough rice for everyone to eat their fill, along with a spread of accompanying dishes. As a rule, aim to have one dish per person, plus one extra. So, if you're cooking for two people, two or three dishes is perfect; for four people, five dishes will be plenty. (There's actually a Chinese saying that a good meal should have 四菜一湯 *sìcài yītāng*, "four dishes and one soup"). If a recipe says "Serves 4," I'm assuming that the dish will be part of a meal with multiple dishes and rice, not served alone. This doesn't necessarily apply to noodle recipes or other one-dish meals (or appetizers and desserts).

When planning a menu, aim for a variety of textures, tastes, and colors. If there will be a richer and strong-flavored dish like Fish-Fragrant Eggplant (page 88), Braised Tofu Skins in Chili Bean Sauce (page 189), or Mapo Tofu (page 159), pair it with a refreshing cold dish like Napa Cabbage and Vermicelli Salad (page 54), or something more vegetal like Simple Stir-Fried Greens (page 48). If there's a drier, intensely fragrant dish, like Spicy Dry-Fried Potato (page 116) or Kung Pao Mushrooms (page 226), serve it with something soupier, like Gluten Puffs with Napa Cabbage (page 207), Frozen Tofu and Sour Napa Cabbage Stew (page 153), or a soup of broth seasoned with salt with some leaves simmered in. Try to include dishes with different cooking methods: a cold appetizer or salad you can make in advance and keep in the fridge, a braised dish or soup with a more involved marinade or sauce, plus a simple wok-cooked dish to stir-fry at the last minute.

A Note on Terms and Romanization

Since I grew up speaking Mandarin, I've romanized the Chinese characters in this book in Hanyu Pinyin, with diacritics (four marks describing tone) to help with pronunciation. Instead of Simplified Chinese, I chose to use Traditional Chinese characters (except in a small number of cases), which are used in Taiwan, Hong Kong, and Macau, so that Taiwanese and Cantonese readers will be able to understand the characters as well. When the Cantonese name of an ingredient is more well-known, like choy sum or gai lan, I will include it along with the Mandarin.

Many Chinese vegetables have multiple names just in Mandarin (green cabbage, for instance, is called 大頭菜 *dàtóucài*, 包菜 *bāocài*, 圓白菜 *yuánbáicài*, and 高麗菜 *gāolìcài* in different regions), and especially for store-bought condiments like bean paste and tofu products, there are even more English translations of varying accuracy. This can be confusing, but while shopping, go by the ingredient list and look there rather than at the name on the package. The English words for many Chinese ingredients are often their Japanese names, like tofu, shiitake, goji berry, and daikon radish, but rather than use lesser-known Chinese translations, I've stuck with the most popular name for recognizability (and an easier time at the supermarket).

Dietary Terms

The Chinese concept of 素 *su* and the English definition of "vegan" or "vegetarian" overlap, for the most part, but don't exactly coincide with each other, which can create confusion for Western eaters in China and vice versa. See the list that follows for the distinctions. All the recipes in this book are vegan in the Western sense—they do not contain eggs, dairy, meat, honey, or animal products—but will include alliums (the onion family), which traditionally are not used in Buddhist vegetarian or vegan cooking.

This is a nonexhaustive list of terms that describe the categories you'll come across in Chinese-speaking parts of the world, including China, Taiwan, Hong Kong, and Singapore. This glossary should be useful if you're traveling, but the variations also reveal the complexity and flexibility in Chinese vegetarianism that have created the need for specific definitions.

OVO-LACTO VEGETARIAN
蛋奶素 dànnǎisù

Traditionally, Buddhist vegetarian dishes may include eggs or dairy. Buddhists do not eat meat to avoid taking life, but since eggs and milk produced by industrial farming are lifeless, they have less objection to eating them. However, with increasing awareness of the cruelty of the modern egg and dairy industries, many Buddhists who are ovo-lacto vegetarians are switching to "complete" vegetarianism (see below).

PURE OR COMPLETE VEGETARIAN
純素，全素 chúnsù, quánsù

Pure vegetarian is the strictest and most traditional form of Chinese vegetarianism, the diet eaten in monasteries and by devout lay Buddhists. A dish labeled *chun su* will not contain meat, alliums, dairy, or eggs.

"FIVE ALLIUM" VEGETARIAN
五辛素 wǔxīnsù

Equivalent to the Western definition of vegetarian, this is also called "health-based vegetarian" (健康素 *jiànkāng sù*) or "plant-based vegetarian" (植物素 *zhíwù sù*) to distinguish it from religion-motivated vegetarianism. These dishes may contain dairy, eggs, and alliums.

PLANT-BASED
蔬食 shūshí

This is a general term that means plant-based, and just like in English, it's flexible in meaning and neutral in connotation.

"WEI GEN," VEGAN
維根 wéigēn

This is a relatively new term and translates to vegan in an ethical sense—that is, applying not just to diet but encompassing all lifestyle choices, like avoiding fur, leather, animal-tested products, and so on. This term is used mostly in Taiwan and isn't very widespread in China yet.

"SIDE OF THE POT" VEGETARIAN, FLEXIBLE VEGETARIAN
鍋邊素，方便素 guōbiānsù, fāngbiànsù

Many Chinese vegetarians who live in a household with a nonvegetarian partner or family members eat "side of the pot" vegetarian. This means they can still eat dishes cooked with meat, but they avoid the visible pieces of meat and eat only the vegetables. "Flexible" or "convenient" vegetarian means eating vegetarian whenever it's practical. When offered something with meat in it, the flexible vegetarian will often eat it so as not to offend the giver. Some Buddhists choose to cook vegetarian meals at home and during religious observations but are flexible in other settings.

THE HISTORY OF VEGETARIAN EATING IN CHINA

THE earliest Chinese vegetarians can be traced back to the Xia dynasty (2070–1600 BCE). They were seekers of immortality who attempted to use a diet free of animal foods along with meditation and physical exercises to extend their lifespans. Later these ancient traditions merged into the tenets of Taoism. Taoists sought to minimize harm to all life forms, and seekers of *dao*, "the way," believed that diet, and especially the amount of qi (life force) in foods, was intrinsically tied to their physical, mental, and spiritual health and that eating certain foods would interfere with their bodily harmony. "Quit meat and meditate thoughtfully—do not eat living things that contain blood, to support your vitality," Laozi instructs in the 化胡經 *Huàhújīng*, a foundational text from the mid-third century BCE.

During the Shang dynasty (1600–1046 BCE), Chinese people began to associate eating meat with indulgence and immoral excess. The last king of the Shang dynasty, Di Xin, was infamous for throwing extravagant feasts, inspiring the idiom 酒池肉林 *jiǔchíròulín*, "lakes of wine and forests of meat." His corrupt reign precipitated his kingdom's downfall, and during the ensuing Zhou dynasty, rulers were warned of a similar fate and instructed to fast from meat and alcohol on the first and fifteenth days of the lunar month (初一十五 *chūyī shíwǔ*). In Chinese folk religions, offerings of meat and animal sacrifices were an important part of ancestor veneration, but even these rituals were preceded by specified periods of vegetarianism, where no meat or alcohol could be consumed. During that time, Confucius advocated a simple, frugal lifestyle for noblemen and promoted vegetarianism as a mark of sophistication and refinement for intellectuals. Later, his successor Mencius encouraged benevolent kindness toward animals, saying, "A superior man is affected toward animals, that, having seen them alive, he cannot bear to see them die; having heard their dying cries, he cannot bear to eat their flesh."

All these traditions paved the way for Buddhism. Monks from India introduced the religion to China around 220 CE. The emphasis on vegetarianism was largely a Chinese interpretation of Buddhist teachings. Killing animals intentionally made one complicit in the killing of life (殺生 *shāshēng*), one of the five precepts forbidden in Buddhist morality. Originally, monks would beg for alms and eat whatever they received, even if it was meat, since the life had already been taken. But with the rise of monasteries in China, monks no longer begged for alms but grew and cultivated their own food with support from wealthy donors and benefactors. During the Liang dynasty (464–549 CE), Emperor Wu, a devout Buddhist, established lifelong vegetarianism for monks and nuns and encouraged laypeople to eat vegetarian on sacred days or festivals (齋期 *zhāiqī*). These practices

explain why most Chinese people don't consider being vegetarian an ideology or lifelong commitment, but a beneficial practice that you engage in periodically, like fasting and meditation.

Over the next thousand years, Buddhism became the dominant religion in China. Ritual vegetarianism was integrated into the belief systems of ordinary Chinese people. Along with Buddhism, monks spread an emphasis on vegetarianism and the use of ingredients like soy milk, tofu, tofu skin (*yuba*), and gluten (seitan) to Japan, Korea, and Vietnam. Even the use of chopsticks stemmed from vegetarian tenets: Confucius decried the act of carrying swords and knives at the meal table as barbarous, believing that sharp points evoked images of the slaughterhouse and the violence of warmongers and thus should have no place in a hospitable environment. Buddhist monks later instituted the *fan wan jing*, a code to the Vinaya that banned knives for eating and encouraged using chopsticks for a more comfortable and nonaggressive feeling around a table. The widespread use of chopsticks shaped the development of Chinese cuisine—the reason there's so much preparatory chopping involved in making a Chinese meal is because dishes had to consist of bite-size pieces that could easily be grasped with chopsticks, since nothing was sliced at the table.

Buddhist temples were also the country's first public restaurants. Monasteries doubled as inns for travelers and pilgrims, and although monks ate simply, they prepared food for visitors, benefactors, and worshippers at the temple. These dishes were centered on mock meat (仿葷素 *fǎnghūnsù*), dishes that captured the flavors and textures of meat made with ingredients including mushrooms, gluten, and soybeans. Especially in the Ming dynasty (1368–1644), a sophisticated cuisine evolved in these temple kitchens, where imitative dishes were not a just a substitute for meat dishes but a new culinary arena infused with inventiveness and playfulness. Temple vegetarian food, 寺廟素食 *sīmiào sùshí*, catered to the tastes of nonvegetarians and

lay Buddhists, who went to the temple periodically to make offerings and donations and to enjoy a vegetarian meal for spiritual fulfillment. In the Song dynasty (960–1279), when commercial restaurants began to open, they used temple kitchens and their hospitality as a reference, and these first Chinese restaurants often had vegetarian dishes (齋菜 *zhāicài*), cooked in the style of Buddhists, on the menu.

Chinese Buddhist vegetarians do not eat alliums, and this is based on a concept of food divided into two categories: 素 *sù* and 葷 *hūn*. *Su* refers to vegetables or plants; *hun* includes all animal products—meat, dairy, eggs, and seafood—and also alcohol and the "five fetid or pungent vegetables" (五葷 *wǔhūn* or 五辛 *wǔxīn*): (1) onions and scallions, (2) garlic, (3) chives, (4) leeks, and (5) asafetida. Alliums are considered 小葷 *xiǎohūn*, "lesser meat," and are said to increase cravings and stir up anger. They also give off pungent, stinky odors, which was undesirable for monks living in close quarters. My Buddhist roommate explains that eating garlic and onions hinders meditation for her, which is why she avoids them. Even in modern vegetarian restaurants in China, dishes do not contain garlic, scallions, or onions, and if they do, they are clearly marked on the menu as 五辛素 *wǔxīn sù*, "five-allium vegetarian." This reveals the fundamental difference between Chinese and Western

vegetarianism: alliums and alcohol are in the same category as meat when it comes to Buddhist religious observation, but alliums are just considered plants for Western vegetarians, who are generally motivated by secular concerns like animal rights, environmentalism, and health.

Sometimes I wonder where the lines between diet and religious observation fall in China, and if it is possible or even necessary to separate the two. Buddhism has remained the greatest pro-vegetarian force in China for the past thousand years, and the centrality of religious vegetarianism in the community is undeniable. Even as my vegan friends in China promote eating less meat as a secular and health-oriented lifestyle, most of them are motivated by their Buddhist practice or family background. The current "second-wave vegetarianism" happening in China today is distancing itself from Buddhism, and integrates the Western discussions of secular ethics, environmentalism, and animal liberation; concerns about the global food supply; and a health-oriented discourse to appeal to non-Buddhists and relate it to other Chinese values, like frugality, compassion, and simplicity. Either way, at the heart of the Chinese vegetarian movement is a history spanning three millennia that they can call their own, and the return to this tradition is extremely compelling for many Chinese people.

LEAFY GREENS

Walk into the produce section of any Chinese grocery store and the first thing you'll notice is the overwhelming variety of leafy greens. They are an essential part of the Chinese diet and usually cooked simply to showcase their freshness. Part of the preparation process is plucking and discarding any tough or chewy stalks, so every dish contains only the soft, tender leaves and juicy stems. At Chinese restaurants, my parents would ask for the "seasonal green" on the menu, because no table was complete without a hot, fragrant dish of simply stir-fried greens.

In China's temperate climates, spinach, amaranth leaves, "hollow-heart" water spinach, pea shoots, and chrysanthemum greens, and local specialties like curly "dragon-whisker" chayote leaves and satiny Malabar spinach are enjoyed year-round. Most of these are radiantly delicious with just a simple toss in a hot wok with garlic and salt, while others can be served in a soup (Pea Shoots in Silky Soup, page 57) or paired with umami ingredients like fried shallots and fermented tofu.

Some of my favorite vegetables include juicy, thick-stemmed gai lan and choy sum, both beloved brassicas in Cantonese cuisine, and head cabbage or Taiwanese cabbage, which is wonderful stir-fried (Hand-Torn Cabbage, page 50). The vast bok choy family ranges from the mild Shanghai bok choy, with its jade-colored, spoon-shaped stalks, to white-stemmed varieties like the hardy napa cabbage, a staple vegetable in the colder northern provinces. My family likes to eat it raw in a refreshing, crisp salad or stir-fried with an aromatic sauce (Stir-Fried Napa Cabbage with Vinegar Sauce, page 58).

You'll find an increasing selection of Chinese greens in Western supermarkets, but feel free to think of these recipes as templates and use with whatever you have available. Delicate leafy greens like pea shoots need to be used within a few days of purchase, but hardier greens like cabbages will keep for a week or even longer in the refrigerator.

BLANCHED SPINACH WITH SESAME SAUCE

Májiàng bōcài

麻醬菠菜

SERVES 4

Blanching transforms a mountain of spinach in seconds, reducing teeth-chalking raw leaves into juicily sweet, tender morsels. My mom would tuck the wet spinach into a ball, wring out the liquid between her palms, and chop the emerald-green pile into bite-size pieces. Soothed with a creamy sauce of nutty sesame paste, perked up with minced garlic, and brightened with rice vinegar, spinach becomes irresistible—my siblings and I literally chopstick-fought over who got to eat the last pieces. At restaurants, this dish is often served as an appetizer, and chefs will either mold the spinach into a column or pile it neatly leaf to stem and dress it just before serving. You can replace half the sesame paste with peanut butter for a creamier sauce.

Look for sturdy stemmed spinach that can stand up in your hand like a bunch of flowers, not the bagged baby variety, which tends to melt away when blanched.

Thoroughly wash the spinach, soaking the stems and leaves in water and using your fingers to loosen any dirt and grit. Rinse and repeat until the water is free of dirt. Drain in a colander. Bring a wok or large pot of water to a boil.

When the water reaches a rolling boil, add 1½ teaspoons of the vegetable oil and half the spinach and blanch until vibrant green and tender, 30 to 40 seconds. Remove the spinach from the water with a skimmer or slotted spoon and spread it out in a colander to drain. Bring the water back to a boil, add the remaining 1½ teaspoons vegetable oil, and repeat with the remaining spinach.

In a small bowl, combine the sesame paste, vinegar, soy sauce, garlic, sugar, salt, and sesame oil. Add just enough water (you can use the hot cooking water from the pot) to thin the sauce to a pourable consistency.

When the spinach is cool enough to handle, gently press out the excess water until it's not sopping wet. Lay out the pieces on a cutting board and cut them into 3-inch lengths. Pile the spinach in a serving dish, use a spoon to drape the sesame sauce on top, garnish with crushed peanuts and sliced red chile (if using), and serve.

1 pound (450 grams) bunched spinach

3 teaspoons vegetable oil, divided

2 tablespoons Chinese sesame paste, homemade (page 305) or store-bought

1 teaspoon pale rice vinegar

1 teaspoon soy sauce

2 garlic cloves, minced

1 teaspoon sugar

½ teaspoon kosher salt

½ teaspoon toasted sesame oil

2 tablespoons crushed peanuts, toasted pine nuts, or sesame seeds

Fresh red chile, thinly sliced, for garnish (optional)

BLANCHED LETTUCE WITH GINGER SOY SAUCE

Jiāngróng shēngcài

薑蓉生菜

SERVES 4

When I first encountered cooked lettuce on restaurant menus, I was skeptical, but I quickly changed my mind after eating dishes like this one. Chinese cooks treat lettuces just like any other leafy green, and varieties like sturdy-hearted romaine lettuce and the long papery fronds of stem lettuce are often stir-fried, blanched, steamed, or wilted in soups, with delicious results. Here a quick blanch intensifies romaine lettuce's sweetness and flavor, and the delicate soy sauce dressing bathes the crisp, juicy stems and dimpled leaves with sesame oil and clinging bits of ginger.

This method is also tasty with other vegetables that have some crunch to them—young asparagus, green beans, snow peas, and broccoli are all good candidates; just adjust the blanching time as needed. You can make this dish using minced garlic in place of the ginger, or a combination of the two.

Bring a large pot of water to a boil. Prepare a bowl of ice and water. Blanch the lettuce in the boiling water for about 30 seconds, until its leaves are vibrant green but still crisp. Remove the lettuce and dunk it in the ice water to halt the cooking, then drain and shake it as dry as possible (or give it a whirl in a salad spinner). Place the lettuce in a large bowl.

In a small saucepan, heat the vegetable oil over medium heat. Cook the ginger briefly until fragrant and golden, about 1 minute. Add the soy sauce, Shaoxing wine, and sugar. Bring to a boil, stirring with a spatula until the sugar has dissolved, about 15 seconds. Remove from the heat and stir in the sesame oil.

Scrape the sauce out over the drained lettuce and gently fold to coat the leaves. Arrange the lettuce in a pile on a plate and pour on the sauce that has collected at the bottom of the bowl. Serve immediately.

1 medium head (12 ounces / 340 grams) romaine or other ribbed lettuce, leaves separated

1 tablespoon vegetable oil

2 tablespoons minced fresh ginger

2 tablespoons soy sauce

1 tablespoon Shaoxing wine

1 teaspoon sugar

½ teaspoon toasted sesame oil

BLANCHED SWEET POTATO GREENS *WITH* CRISPY SHALLOTS

Tàng qīngcài

燙青菜

SERVES 4

Blanched greens are a fast-food dish at street carts and casual eateries, offered for just a tiny sum. At my favorite cart in Taipei, the vendor dunks a packed metal basket of sweet potato greens under boiling water for a minute, then drains and stirs the hot, glistening, wilted leaves with a spoonful of thick soy sauce (醬油膏 *jiàngyóu gāo*) and crispy fried shallots.

Sweet potato leaves are available in many Asian supermarkets—look for bunches of thick stems with a profusion of shiny triangular leaves. In southern China and Taiwan, they grow so thickly and luxuriously that they're gathered and sold cheap in giant bunches, but they've recently gained more attention as a superfood green with abundant vitamin C and riboflavin (vitamin B$_2$). They're mild-flavored and slippery, without the sharp-tasting, teeth-chalking oxalic acid of the comparably nutritious spinach and chard.

Use this blanch-and-season method for spinach, amaranth greens, bok choy, gai lan, pea shoots, flat-head cabbage, and even broccoli florets. Prepare the fried shallots ahead of time and keep them in the fridge to get a hot dish of greens on the dinner table in mere minutes.

Prep the greens by pinching off each leaf and tender connecting stem from its stalk. Keep any other tender parts at the tips but discard the main stalks—unless you are using pea shoots, spinach, or other tender greens, they are too tough to eat. Wash the greens thoroughly and drain in a colander.

Bring a large pot of water to a rolling boil. Drizzle in the vegetable oil, then drop in the greens and blanch them until bright green and softened, about 45 seconds. Drain and shake in a colander, then transfer the hot leaves to a serving bowl. Add the oyster sauce, crispy fried shallots, and a bit of the shallot oil to give the greens a glisten. Mix well to coat and enjoy.

10 ounces (280 grams) sweet potato greens, spinach, pea shoots, or other greens

1 tablespoon vegetable oil

2 tablespoons vegetarian oyster sauce or thick soy sauce

2 tablespoons Crispy Fried Shallots (page 302)

1 teaspoon Shallot Oil (page 302)

SIMPLICITY

簡易

WHEN I was in middle school, my family moved from Ohio to Shenzhen, a Chinese megacity across the border from Hong Kong. Every Friday, I walked a few blocks to a neighborhood music school for my piano lesson, my stomach rumbling from the smells wafting from the food carts I passed. Shenzhen had grown in twenty years from a rural fishing village to an international hub of commerce, and the population of 11 million people was mostly migrants. At dinnertime, the street outside our building smelled of every regional cuisine from a hundred different kitchens. But from January to mid-February, the city was deserted; the streets empty and silent as a ghost town, everyone traveling back to their home province for Lunar New Year. No one seemed to be *from* Shenzhen. The city was a meeting point of liminal lives, of migrant workers and expat foreigners, all drawn by the possibility of a better future, connected by their ambition and their loneliness. In this displacement, everyone cooked the food they knew.

My mom tried to make our apartment on the thirty-second floor feel like home. She filled the kitchen with gadgets, buying a new wok, a seven-tiered metal steamer, a mahogany fish tank, and a mill that polished brown rice down to white rice. But the wok is the only item my siblings remember. It was monstrously heavy and overpriced: a 20-inch, thick-rimmed black belly with a brushed-steel cover and double handles that my mom had spotted in a Carrefour supermarket. She was so charmed by the properties of *zhutie*, or cast iron—*much* better than nonstick, the salesperson said, that she bought it on the spot. When my dad's job transferred us back to the United States, she couldn't bear to leave the giant wok behind and brought it across the ocean. She would eventually carry it to eight cities over the next thirteen years. We moved a lot.

I was just about to start high school when we first arrived back in America, and after three years in China, my Mandarin had improved but my native English was now rusty. I felt displaced again. In those days, I remember my mom cooking for us every night, in that wok, and despite the ever-changing physical location, those two sights were the constants that represented home. Only recently did my mom reveal to me that she hated spending so much time in the kitchen; it was just that making every meal at home was the cheapest way to keep five kids fed, and from-scratch Chinese food was the only kind of cooking she knew. "*Jiali you shenme cai?* What vegetables are in the fridge?" she'd ask on the phone while driving back home after picking up a sibling from a violin lesson or ballet class. I'd peer in the fridge and tell her—a head of cabbage, a few tomatoes, and two peppers that had gone soft—and in the pause that followed, I could hear her mind whirring in calculation, that familiar Chinese resourcefulness. "I don't have time to go to the grocery store," she'd say. "Start the rice in the rice cooker."

Back at home, she'd slice the entire cabbage and the peppers into thin shreds, heat oil in the wok with garlic and ginger, and toss everything into an aromatic, wilted stir-fry. Then she used the same wok with its leftover oil to stir-fry the chopped tomatoes and make a tomato egg-drop soup scattered with scallions. When the rice cooker beeped, I'd pop open the lid and loosen the steaming rice with the grippy white spatula, scooping it into bowls—big shovels for my dad and brothers, small mounds for my little sisters. She'd find a leftover broccoli stem and use that, too, dicing it small and adding soy sauce and sesame oil to make a salty relish. "Time to eat, *chifanle*," she'd yell, and there would be a stampede down the stairs.

On days she went to the Chinese grocery store downtown, she brought back special varieties of greens—lacy chrysanthemum, purple-veined amaranth, and long, tapered lettuces, southern Chinese varieties we'd eaten in Shenzhen. She gave them the same treatment in her wok: a simple toss over searing heat with oil and salt was all it took to transform raw greens into something even my younger siblings found irresistible. For harder vegetables, she just added liquid, covered the wok, and walked away. We ate eggplant and peppers, string beans and potatoes, stir-fried slivered carrot, and my mom's favorite, zucchini, which she bought in bushels from the farmers' markets in the summer and stewed with garlic until it was meltingly silky in its own juices. Vegetables were never an afterthought or a duty to eat, but the main part of the meal, dishes cooked with simple methods yet so tasty we never tired of them.

Now I can only recall the particulars of her food with effort, raking through memories from high school years shrouded by teenage indifference, or maybe through a subconscious erasure in those years when I was trying to fit back into American culture. I took it all for granted. How she went shopping every week for fresh produce and never bought processed foods, how we ate seasonally with very little meat and ate fish only on special occasions, and how even that wok, that ridiculous wok, was simply a symbol of something bigger, a tradition of home cooking that I'd never stopped to understand, like so many other things about my culture.

The first time I cooked a Chinese dish for myself was in my first apartment in college. It was a simple cabbage stir-fry, but everything went wrong: the oil wasn't hot enough and my small skillet couldn't handle the amount of food, the soggy cabbage more steamed than stir-fried. I drowned everything in soy sauce and ate it all anyway, and then I called my mom for advice. "Maybe I need a bigger wok," I said. "*Baobao*, you need less cabbage," she said. "You're cooking for one person, not seven."

It feels like my Chinese American friends and I have started waking up to the heritage that is our parents' home cooking. Across the country, we're all calling our parents, looking up recipes, thinking about dishes we remember eating and wondering how to re-create them. Maybe all this shared nostalgia is expected, from too many years living away from home. Maybe it's an act of survival—we literally need to learn to cook for ourselves, for our future families—or some reclaiming of identity. In China, my friends don't share that same fondness born of being one or two generations removed, of living in another country. They're obsessed with global cuisine and Western-style food, looking outside of home, while we're still trying to figure out where home is.

My mom's big wok is gone now—abandoned, finally, at one of the last places my parents moved. And my impression of my mom's cooking has shifted after my training in China; the previous magic of that wok has turned into an understanding of what she really only ever made: a simple stir-fry and *duncai*, "big stew." But those are still the dishes I crave the most, and I still have her. On the phone now, she listens patiently as I talk about velveting and oil-poaching, dry-frying and red-braising, and at the end she sighs. "Too much hassle—*tai mafanle*," she says. "I'm a simple cook. Just throw everything in the wok. *Kai fan!*"

HANNAH CHE

PREP FOR GREENS

With all leafy greens, wash them thoroughly—grit tucks itself into every crevice of the stalks and leaves, and you don't want to crunch down on something unpleasant while eating. Rinsing the leaves under running water unfortunately won't do the job; instead, soak the separated leaves or stalks in a large bowl or a full sink. Swish the vegetables around in the water to dislodge any dirt or grit. Let sit for a couple minutes to give the fallen grit time to settle. Lift the greens out and drain the water, rinsing away the grit at the bottom of the bowl or sink. Repeat these steps as necessary until you don't see any more dirt. Shake the greens dry or spin them in a salad spinner.

AMARANTH GREENS
莧菜 xiàncài

Look for leaves with magenta hearts, as they are more tender than the solid green ones. Remove any thick stalks, cut slender stems into roughly 2-inch-long pieces, and tear and separate leaves into smaller bunches.

SPINACH
菠菜 bōcài

Pick bunches with sturdy leaves and cut both stems and leaves into 3-inch lengths.

CHRYSANTHEMUM GREENS
茼蒿 tónghāo

Trim a couple inches off the end of any tough stalks and cut the serrated leaves into 2-inch pieces. Keep the leaves separate from the stems and add stems to the wok first. The herbaceous, grassy flavor of chrysanthemum is so distinctive, you don't really need garlic or ginger. These greens overcook easily, however, so remove them from the heat before the leaves look completely softened or they will become slimy.

STEM LETTUCE / CELTUCE GREENS
油麥菜 yóumàicài

Trim off the stem ends and cut the greens into 2-inch lengths.

ROMAINE LETTUCE HEARTS
生菜 shēngcài

Trim off the ends and cut the hearts crosswise into 1½-inch-thick segments. Stir-fry very briefly so they stay crisp.

PEA SHOOTS
豌豆苗 wāndòumiáo

Pick pea shoots later in the season—summer shoots with thick, hollow, and squarish stems are more tender than the skinny spring ones. Keep the leaves and crisp stems, plucking off any hard tendrils or stems tough enough to bend without breaking.

WATER SPINACH
空心菜 kōngxīncài

These hollow-stemmed greens come in two varieties: the ones with full, arrow-shaped leaves and thick, light green stalks are more tender than those with thin, darker-green stalks and narrow leaves. To prepare them, snap the leaves off the stems and keep them separate. Hold the hollow stem and bend it; it will break where it is tough. Discard the tough ends and cut the rest into 2-inch pieces. Add the stem parts to the wok first.

SIMPLE STIR–FRIED GREENS

Qīngchǎo shícài

清炒時菜

SERVES 4

The simplest and tastiest Chinese method to cook a really fresh leafy vegetable is to stir-fry it in oil with garlic and ginger and season it with a touch of salt. The blast of high heat and constant motion in the wok wilts the greens and softens the stems while preserving their juiciness and color, and the hot, fragrant oil enlivens them with flavor. Prepping the greens inevitably takes longer than the actual cooking, which doesn't take more than 2 or 3 minutes. Since this method relies on the freshness of the ingredient, be sure to pick the most tender, vibrant greens in season, and avoid anything that looks past its prime or tough to chew.

One of my favorite leafy greens is amaranth greens—the heart-shaped magenta leaves release their vivid hue when cooked. My siblings and I would eat the stir-fried greens and gleefully stir their juices into our rice to stain it an eye-popping pink.

Prep the greens by pinching off any tough stems, then wash them well and shake dry in a colander or spin them in a salad spinner. (See page 47 for how to prep specific greens.) You should end up with roughly 8 to 10 ounces (225 to 280 grams) of prepped greens.

Heat a wok or large skillet over high heat until a bead of water evaporates on contact. Add the oil and swirl to coat the sides of the wok. Add the garlic and ginger (if using) and stir-fry until they are fragrant and just starting to color, about 30 seconds. Add the greens and fold briskly, stirring and tossing continuously to coat them evenly in the fragrant oil.

Continue stir-frying until the leaves have softened and wilted and the stems are tender, just a minute or two. During this process, if the wok seems dry, add a splash of water—you want to aim for about a tablespoon of liquid remaining in the bottom of the wok.

Sprinkle the salt evenly on top so it doesn't clump into one part of the greens, then give everything a good stir and transfer to a dish to serve immediately.

10 ounces (280 grams) amaranth greens or other tender leafy vegetable

3 tablespoons vegetable oil

1 tablespoon minced garlic

2 teaspoons minced fresh ginger (optional)

½ teaspoon kosher salt

STIR-FRIED DICED CHOY SUM & TOFU

Yóucài dòugān dīng

油菜豆干丁

SERVES 4 TO 6

Whenever you don't know how to cook a hard vegetable or thick-stemmed green, dice it up and stir-fry it—the smaller the cut, the tastier it'll be, as the flavors can be absorbed faster. Juicy greens like choy sum (also known as *yu choy*), gai lan, and mustard greens are all wonderful cooked this way, and any subtle bitterness is deliciously tempered by the sizzling ginger, garlic, and chiles. I love chewy bits of pressed tofu interspersed with the greens, but feel free to leave it out.

Wash the greens thoroughly and shake them dry. Trim the bottom of the stalks and cut any thick stalks in half lengthwise. Cut the stems into ¼-inch dice and the leaves into ¼-inch-wide shreds.

Heat a wok over medium-high heat until a bead of water evaporates within 1 to 2 seconds of contact. Add the vegetable oil and swirl to coat the sides of the wok. Add the ginger and dried chiles and stir-fry until aromatic, about 30 seconds. Turn the heat to high, add the tofu, and stir-fry until its edges are lightly browned, about 1 minute.

Add the garlic and fresh chiles and stir-fry until they are fragrant, about 15 seconds. Add all the choy sum and Shaoxing wine and stir-fry quickly until the stems are brilliant green, the leaves are wilted and softened, and the wine has cooked off, about 2 minutes. Stir in the sugar and salt, adding more salt to taste if desired. Remove from the heat, stir in the sesame oil, and serve.

1 pound (450 grams) choy sum or other thick-stemmed greens

2 tablespoons vegetable oil or Scallion Oil (page 301)

1 tablespoon minced fresh ginger

5 dried red chiles, snipped into ½-inch segments and seeds shaken out

4 ounces (112 grams) pressed tofu, cut into ¼-inch dice

1 tablespoon minced garlic

2 fresh red chiles, minced

1 tablespoon Shaoxing wine

¾ teaspoon sugar

¾ teaspoon kosher salt, plus more to taste

½ teaspoon toasted sesame oil

HAND-TORN CABBAGE

Shǒusī bāocài

手撕包菜

SERVES 4

The chefs at my culinary school in Guangzhou would often whip up this homestyle dish for our family lunches. Tossed on the stinging-hot sides of a wok, cabbage leaves wilt quickly and caramelize on the edges; this recipe makes them aromatic with dried red chiles and Sichuan peppercorns, and laces them in a savory, vinegar-tinged sauce.

Use your wok or skillet over the highest flame, and you should still get a nice seared-in juiciness and aroma without an industrial burner. If you're doubling the recipe, stir-fry it in two batches to avoid overcrowding the wok, which would steam rather than sear the cabbage. When prepping the cabbage, tear the leaves with your hands instead of using a knife for maximum raggedy edges—Chinese cooks swear it tastes better this way. The best cabbage for stir-frying is the flat-headed, looser Taiwanese cabbage, which has sweeter and more tender leaves.

MAKE THE SAUCE: In a small bowl, stir together the sauce ingredients to combine well.

PREPARE THE STIR-FRY: Tear the cabbage leaves into roughly 3-inch squares.

Heat a wok over high heat until a bead of water evaporates within 1 to 2 seconds of contact. Add the vegetable oil and swirl to coat the sides of the wok. Reduce the heat to medium, then add the ginger and Sichuan peppercorns and stir-fry until aromatic, just a few seconds. Add the dried chiles and stir-fry until they begin to darken, about 20 seconds. Add the garlic and stir-fry for 10 seconds, until fragrant but not yet browned.

Increase the heat to the highest setting and add the cabbage. Stir briskly until the leaves are coated in the fragrant oil and starting to reduce in volume, about 30 seconds. Pour the prepared sauce down the hot sides of the wok to release its flavor and stir-fry for about 30 seconds longer, until the cabbage leaves are softened and slightly caramelized on the edges but still crisp. Take the wok off the heat, transfer the cabbage to a dish, and serve.

THE SAUCE

1 tablespoon soy sauce

1 teaspoon Chinkiang black vinegar

2 teaspoons Shaoxing wine

½ teaspoon sugar

¼ teaspoon MSG (optional)

½ teaspoon kosher salt

THE STIR-FRY

12 ounces (330 grams) green cabbage leaves, preferably flat-head cabbage

2 tablespoons vegetable oil

1 tablespoon finely chopped fresh ginger

1 teaspoon Sichuan peppercorns

5 dried red chiles, cut into 1-inch pieces and seeds shaken out

3 garlic cloves, minced

Variation
HOT PEPPER & CABBAGE

Instead of tearing the cabbage leaves into pieces, cut them into thin ¼-inch shreds and add 2 thinly sliced seeded jalapeño peppers when stir-frying the aromatics. This is my mom's favorite method, and it's very tasty.

STIR-FRIED WATER SPINACH WITH FERMENTED TOFU

Fǔrǔ kōngxīncài

腐乳空心菜

Fermented tofu is the vegan chef's secret ingredient: one or two cubes of the salty, ripened tofu, mashed into a creamy paste, bolsters the savoriness of stir-fried greens and lends a slightly silky mouthfeel. Water spinach is a southern aquatic vegetable with crisp, juicy stems, and it's wonderful prepared this way, as its hollow stems and glossy leaves readily soak up the sauce. If you can't find it, regular bunched spinach is also delicious. Try to use very fresh ginger here, as it will have more juice.

SERVES 4

Wash and drain the water spinach thoroughly (see Prep for Greens, page 47). You should end up with about 10 ounces (280 grams) of prepped greens. (If using spinach, simply trim off the bottom of the stems, wash, dry, and use whole.)

On a cutting board, smack the ginger with the flat side of the blade of a knife to loosen its fibers. Grate or finely mince the ginger. Gather it up in the palm of your hand and squeeze the juice into a small bowl; you should have about 1 tablespoon. Discard the ginger pulp.

Place the fermented tofu and the liquid from its jar in the bowl with the ginger juice and mash it using a fork to combine. Add the Shaoxing wine and sugar, stirring to form a thin sauce.

Bring a pot of water to a vigorous boil and dunk the water spinach stems in until they turn bright green, about 20 seconds. Add the leaves and blanch until softened, another 10 seconds. (If using regular spinach, add it all together and blanch for 10 seconds, until just wilted.) Lift out immediately and drain in a colander. Shake dry.

Heat a wok or skillet over high heat until a bead of water evaporates within 1 to 2 seconds of contact. Add the oil and swirl to coat the sides of the wok. Add the garlic and chile (if using) and stir-fry until fragrant, about 10 seconds. Add the sauce and wait until it bubbles, then add all the blanched spinach and stir-fry quickly until the sauce is incorporated, about 1 minute.

Remove the wok from the heat and taste the greens; season with a pinch of salt, if needed (usually the fermented tofu is salty enough). Transfer to a dish and serve.

1 large bunch (1 pound / 450 grams) water spinach, or 10 ounces (280 grams) spinach

1 (4-inch) piece (30 grams) fresh ginger, peeled

2 cubes white fermented tofu (about 1½ tablespoons), plus 2 teaspoons liquid from the jar

1 tablespoon Shaoxing wine

½ teaspoon sugar

2 tablespoons vegetable oil

3 garlic cloves, thinly sliced

1 fresh red chile, thinly sliced (optional)

Kosher salt

NAPA CABBAGE & VERMICELLI SALAD

Báicài bàn fěnsī

白菜拌粉絲

SERVES 6

My mom says my grandpa's napa cabbage salad was so famous that people would specifically request it whenever he was invited to a get-together or had friends over for dinner. It couldn't be simpler: you salt napa cabbage, squeeze out the water, and toss the juicy shreds with slippery vermicelli noodles and a sesame oil vinaigrette zingy with garlic and cilantro. It's sort of like a Chinese slaw—fresh with a snap of acidity, cleansing for the palate, and fantastic cold. Start the recipe in advance to allow the flavors to be absorbed and develop as it sits. I often prepare one big batch to have at lunch during the week—with its sweet, sharp juices, it's great paired with a steamed or roasted sweet potato.

Separate the cabbage into leaves. Lay out one leaf and slice it horizontally through the white stem portion to make it thinner. Repeat with the remaining leaves, then stack and cut them crosswise into ⅛-inch shreds. Place in a colander with the cucumber and toss with the salt.

Meanwhile, bring a large pot of water to a boil. Add the vermicelli and cook according to the package instructions. Rinse under cold water and drain. Snip with kitchen scissors into shorter, more manageable lengths.

Squeeze out the excess liquid from the cabbage and cucumber by pressing them between your hands. Drop each squeezed handful into a large bowl without rinsing it. Add the vermicelli noodles, carrot, scallion, garlic, soy sauce, vinegar, sugar, MSG, and sesame oil and stir well. Taste and adjust the salt and other seasonings as needed. You can enjoy this immediately or chill it in the refrigerator, covered, for a few hours to let flavors meld. Stir in the cilantro just before serving for the freshest flavor.

½ medium head (1 pound / 450 grams) napa cabbage

1 small Persian cucumber, thinly julienned

1 teaspoon kosher salt, plus more to taste

2 ounces (56 grams) mung bean vermicelli noodles, soaked in warm water for 10 minutes

½ medium carrot, finely julienned

1 scallion, both white and green parts, cut into 3-inch segments and thinly julienned

4 garlic cloves, finely chopped

3 tablespoons soy sauce

3 tablespoons pale rice vinegar

2 tablespoons sugar

½ teaspoon MSG

2 tablespoons toasted sesame oil

½ cup coarsely chopped fresh cilantro

PEA SHOOTS IN SILKY SOUP

Shàngtāng dòumiáo

上湯豆苗

SERVES 5

At the Yi Xin vegetarian restaurant in Guangzhou, my favorite dish is a soup featuring pea shoots, the tender, delicate leaves and tendrils of green peas. The first time I had that soup, it was so fragrant with a silky richness that I could've sworn it was a meat-based broth. Later I learned that the vegetarian chefs add flavor and body to the soup by simply toasting flour and stirring it with sesame oil to form a base similar to a roux. To enjoy, eat the tender cooked greens with chopsticks and then sip the velvety, quietly sustaining broth. Feel free to use spinach or tender napa cabbage hearts instead of pea shoots for a different but equally delicious result.

Keep the leaves and crisp stems of the pea shoots and pluck off any hard tendrils and stems tough enough to bend without breaking. Wash well and drain. In a small bowl, soak the goji berries (if using) in cool water to plump.

Bring a pot of water to a boil and blanch the pea shoots until just wilted, about 20 seconds. Drain in a colander and shake dry. This step will prevent them from later turning the soup an unpleasant brownish color.

Heat a dry wok over low heat. Add the flour and toast, stirring continuously, until pale yellow and faintly fragrant, about 1 minute. Stir in the sesame oil to form a smooth paste and cook, stirring continuously, for 2 to 3 minutes, until the mixture is golden in color.

Add the stock and raise the heat to medium. The soup will look curdled and separate at first, but continue stirring from the bottom and it will come together. Bring the mixture to a gentle boil and, using a ladle, skim off any foam that rises to the top. The soup should look creamy in color and very smooth in consistency. Season with the salt.

Add the mushrooms, reduce the heat to low, and simmer for 3 minutes to cook through. Add the blanched pea shoots and cook for about 2 minutes to heat them up. Taste and add more salt if necessary.

Transfer to a large soup tureen or ladle into bowls. Garnish with a few goji berries, if desired, and serve immediately.

8 ounces (224 grams) pea shoots or bunched spinach

1 tablespoon goji berries (for color; optional)

¼ cup all-purpose flour

2 tablespoons toasted sesame oil

5 cups (1,200 mL) Light Vegetable Stock (page 310) or water

½ teaspoon kosher salt, plus more if needed

2 ounces (56 grams) fresh shiitake mushrooms, stemmed and thinly sliced

STIR-FRIED NAPA CABBAGE WITH VINEGAR SAUCE

Cùliū báicài

醋溜白菜

SERVES 4

Napa cabbage, native to the Yangtze region in China, is a common, humble vegetable considered the workhorse of the Chinese kitchen. In fact, it's the representative Chinese leafy vegetable, its form carved into jade and glass trinkets and displayed for good luck—菜 *cài*, "leafy vegetable," is a pun on 財 *cái*, "prosperity." With its waxy white barrel stalks and crinkly pale-green leaves, its versatility rivals that of any other leafy green: it can be enjoyed juicy and crunchy in raw salads, simmered until meltingly tender and silky, or stir-fried until softened but aromatic with a crisp bite. Since napa has a high water content, I salt it beforehand, which does double duty to draw out liquid and build flavor.

Here the mild-flavored cabbage is emboldened with acidity— briefly stir-fried in a lip-smacking combination of soy sauce and mellow rice vinegar. It's one of my dad's all-time favorite dishes.

MAKE THE SAUCE: In a small bowl, stir together all the sauce ingredients until blended and smooth. Set aside.

PREPARE THE STIR-FRY: Separate the cabbage leaves. Lay one leaf down and trim off the frilly, leafy parts so you are left with a "plank" of stem. Angle the knife so it's flat against the stem, almost parallel to the cutting board, and carefully slice the stem against the grain into thin 1-inch-wide pieces.

Cut the leafy parts into 1-inch strips, keeping them separate from the stems. Place the stem chips into a bowl and sprinkle the salt on them. Set aside for 20 minutes, then rinse off the salt thoroughly and squeeze gently to remove excess water.

Heat a wok over high heat until a bead of water evaporates within 1 to 2 seconds of contact. Add the oil and swirl to coat the sides. Add the garlic, scallion, and chiles and stir-fry until fragrant, about 30 seconds.

Add the cabbage stems and stir-fry until piping hot, about 1 minute. Add the cabbage leaves and stir-fry until softened, about 30 seconds more. Add the sauce and cook, stirring and folding continuously, until the stems are slightly translucent and crisp-tender and the leaves are coated in the thickened sauce. Taste and add more salt if necessary. Remove from the heat, transfer the cabbage to a dish, and serve.

THE SAUCE

¼ teaspoon kosher salt

½ teaspoon sugar

2 teaspoons vegetarian oyster sauce

2 tablespoons soy sauce

1½ tablespoons pale rice vinegar

½ teaspoon potato starch

THE STIR-FRY

½ medium head (1 pound / 450 grams) napa cabbage

1 teaspoon kosher salt, plus more if needed

2 tablespoons vegetable oil

3 garlic cloves, minced

1 scallion, both white and green parts, minced

4 or 5 dried red chiles, cut into 1-inch pieces and seeds shaken out

STIR-FRIED GAI LAN WITH VEGETARIAN OYSTER SAUCE

Háoyóu jièlán

蠔油芥蘭

SERVES 4 TO 6

Gai lan is also called Chinese broccoli or Chinese kale, and it looks like a cross between the two. Texture-wise, however, it's the most compelling sibling of the brassica family, with extremely juicy, fleshy, succulent stems and soft, glossy blue-green leaves that soak up liquid seasonings and fragrant oil.

Choose gai lan stalks with fresh-looking cut ends and small, tight buds; avoid older bunches with visible flowers, as they are more fibrous. Add a pinch of extra sugar when cooking gai lan—it helps balance the vegetable's slightly bitter nature. This method can be used to cook either choy sum, which is similar to gai lan but milder in flavor and with oval-shaped leaves, or Broccolini, their Italian cousin.

MAKE THE SAUCE: In a small bowl, combine all the sauce ingredients.

PREPARE THE STIR-FRY: In a small bowl, mix together the potato starch (if using) and 1 tablespoon water. In another bowl, soak the dried mushrooms in hot water to cover for 30 minutes to rehydrate.

Trim the bottom of the gai lan stems. Cut any stalks that are thicker than your thumb on a sharp diagonal into ½-inch-thick slices; cut slender stalks into 2-inch pieces. Once you get to the leaves, cut them crosswise into 2-inch-wide strips. Keep the stalks and leaves separate.

Snip off the mushroom stems and cut the caps at a diagonal into ½-inch-thick slices.

Heat a wok or skillet over high heat until a bead of water evaporates within 1 to 2 seconds of contact. Add the vegetable oil and swirl to coat the sides of the wok. Add the ginger slices and fry until fragrant, about 30 seconds. Add the mushrooms and cook until they begin to sear, about 1 minute.

Add the garlic, followed immediately by the gai lan stems, and stir-fry until bright green and piping hot, 2 to 3 minutes.

Give the sauce a stir and pour it in, then add the leaves and briskly fold to coat the leaves. Cover tightly and steam the vegetables for 1 minute.

Uncover, taste, and sprinkle with the salt, adding more if needed, and stir-fry until the stems are crisp-tender, about 30 seconds more. If you're using the starch slurry, give it a stir, pour it into the wok, and briskly fold it in until the sauce thickens and coats the leaves. Transfer to a dish and serve.

THE SAUCE

2 tablespoons Shaoxing wine

1 teaspoon soy sauce

1 tablespoon vegetarian oyster sauce

¼ teaspoon MSG

1 teaspoon sugar

THE STIR-FRY

1 teaspoon potato starch (optional)

3 large dried shiitake mushrooms

1 pound (450 grams) gai lan

2 tablespoons vegetable oil

1 (1-inch) piece (7 grams) ginger, thinly sliced

2 garlic cloves, thinly sliced

½ teaspoon kosher salt, plus more if needed

STUFFED CABBAGE ROLLS

Bāocài juǎn

包菜卷

SERVES 4 TO 6

In a traditional temple dish, blanched cabbage leaves are stuffed, wrapped individually, steamed, and served in a clear sauce. I love the filling but usually roll the leaves into a sushi-style log instead, for a more finger-friendly version that preserves the cabbage's bright, jewel-like colors. Each bite begins with crisp-tender, sweet cabbage, followed by chewy, savory mushrooms and tofu skin, threads of caramelized sweetness from the carrot, and a gentle crunch from peanuts and cilantro. Enjoy the sliced rolls on their own or with soy sauce and a dab of wasabi (*jie mo*).

Bring a large pot of generously salted water to a boil. Add the cabbage leaves and blanch until they are softened and vibrant green, about 1 minute. Refresh in cold water and drain in a colander.

Heat a wok over medium heat. Add the vegetable oil and swirl to coat the sides of the wok. Add the garlic and cook until aromatic, about 15 seconds. Add the mushrooms, carrot, and soy sauce. Stir-fry until the mushrooms have softened and released their liquid, about 3 minutes. Add the tofu skin, cumin, sugar, white pepper, and ½ teaspoon salt and stir until the tofu skin is heated through, scraping down any parts that stick to the wok. Remove from the heat and stir in the cilantro and crushed peanuts. Taste and add more salt, if needed. Transfer the filling to a bowl.

Lay one cabbage leaf on a cutting board and shave off its thick stem, trimming it as thin as possible without cutting into the leaf. The pared-down spine will make the leaf flatter and easier to bend. Repeat with the remaining leaves. Toss them in a large bowl with the sesame oil to lightly coat, giving the leaves a shine and aroma.

Lay out a bamboo sushi mat (or cover a tea towel with plastic wrap). Place a third of the leaves across the mat and flatten them. Place a third of the filling on the cabbage leaves, spreading it evenly and leaving an inch of the leaves exposed at the top and bottom. Hook your thumbs under the mat and lift the edge closest to you up and over the filling in the center. Press gently with curved hands along the length of the "log," then pull the edge of the mat toward you and continue to roll the cabbage up and away from you. When you reach the far edge of the cabbage leaves, press the roll tightly once more, then remove the mat. Repeat with the remaining cabbage leaves and filling to make 2 more rolls. With a sharp serrated knife, slice the rolls into 2-inch-wide segments.

Enjoy immediately or chill before serving.

Kosher salt

1 pound (450 grams) green cabbage, preferably flat-head cabbage, leaves separated (about 20 leaves)

2 tablespoons vegetable oil or Scallion Oil (page 301)

1 tablespoon minced garlic

1 medium king oyster mushroom (6½ ounces / 180 grams), both caps and stems thinly julienned

1 small carrot, thinly julienned

2 teaspoons soy sauce

4 ounces (112 grams) fresh or frozen and thawed tofu skin, cut into thin shreds

½ teaspoon ground cumin

½ teaspoon sugar

¼ teaspoon ground white pepper, or to taste

½ cup coarsely chopped fresh cilantro

⅓ cup crushed Fried Peanuts (page 304)

1 teaspoon toasted sesame oil

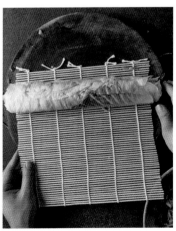

STEMS, SHOOTS & FLOWERS

As the days of darkness end and winter warms to early spring, Chinese cooks eagerly await the arrival of tender shoots and frost-hardy blossoms in the markets. There's asparagus, with bright, svelte stems and violet-tinged tips compact like an artist's paintbrush—an ingredient not native to China but enthusiastically adopted. I love the Cantonese method of blanching them whole and anointing them in a fragrant soy sauce dressing (Blanched Asparagus with Sizzling Oil, page 70). Celtuce, a lettuce grown for its thick stems, has a mild romaine-like sweetness and almost smoky aftertaste, and it can be stir-fried or thinly slivered as an appetizer. Celery is rarely eaten raw but is cooked to bring out its pleasant savory, nutty flavor and crisp sweetness. Caulini, a floppy cauliflower with crunchy pale-green stems, and broccoli are both imports that take well to Chinese cooking methods—a searing-hot wok and smoky chiles make both of these brassicas irresistible.

I once made the mistake of wandering around a market in early spring looking for lotus roots. A vendor informed me that I'd have to come back in two months—it isn't until June or July that lotus roots begin to appear, heavy, fat linked segments encrusted with mud, hauled from the thick mud of lily ponds. They're not actually roots, but the rhizomes or stems of the lotus plant that shoot out horizontally, buried underwater. These crunchy vegetables are beloved in Chinese cooking, typically cut into slices to display their delicate white color and lacy snowflake pattern of holes. And the most aromatic of all stems and shoots is the chive family—in Asian grocery stores you'll come across thick, juicy garlic scapes, big bunches of flat, blue-green garlic chives, and yellow chives, which are grown in darkness to develop their fragile, pale color and sweeter flavor. These are often chopped to make stuffings (Chive-Stuffed Boxes, page 272) or stir-fried for a simple but irresistible dish (Stir-Fried Garlic Chives with Pressed Tofu, page 82).

SLIVERED CELTUCE WITH SESAME OIL

Liángbàn wōsǔnsī

涼拌萵筍絲

If you can get your hands on fresh celtuce in an Asian supermarket, this is one of the best (and simplest) ways to showcase its distinctive, mild flavor. I fell in love with it in a restaurant in China: the raw peeled stem was cut into a pretty pile of crunchy, jade-colored slivers and dressed simply with rice vinegar and sesame oil. Even with minimal seasoning, celtuce has such an appealing freshness and buttery flavor that you just can't get enough of it.

SERVES 4 TO 6 AS AN APPETIZER

Cut off a ¼-inch slice from the fibrous base of the celtuce stem. Use a paring knife or vegetable peeler to trim off the tough outer layer until you can see its pale-green, slightly translucent interior.

Cut the stem into 3-inch segments, then cut them lengthwise into ⅛-inch slices (or use a mandoline). Stack the slices, cut them into ⅛-inch slivers, and place them in a bowl. Sprinkle the slivers with the salt and let sit for 15 minutes.

Gently squeeze any moisture from the softened slivers, then add them to a medium bowl with the sesame oil, vinegar, and more salt to taste. Toss until all the slivers are coated evenly, then pile them loosely in a dish. Serve at room temperature or chilled.

2 large (about 1½ pounds / 675 grams total) celtuce stems

1 teaspoon kosher salt, plus more to taste

1 teaspoon toasted sesame oil

2 teaspoons pale rice vinegar

BROCCOLI STALKS

Don't discard the broccoli stalks—peel off the light-green fibrous skin and cut the jade-colored inner flesh into thin slices or small dice. In a bowl, stir them with a bit of kosher salt, soy sauce, pale rice vinegar, and toasted sesame oil to taste and let sit in the refrigerator for 2 hours to marinate before serving. It makes a zingy little side dish.

STIR-FRIED BROCCOLI *WITH* SICHUAN PEPPER

Qiàngchǎo xīlánhuā

熗炒西蘭花

SERVES 4

Chef Wen has a cooking choreography that's instinctive; there's no wasted movement. His left hand grasps the heavy wok with a towel; his right hand holds the ladle. Into the heated wok goes a swirl of oil, then the dried chiles and Sichuan peppercorns, stirred until just darkened. Broccoli goes in with no hesitation. He turns up the fire, and screaming flames warp the air. Toss once. Toss twice. He swings around and flicks seasonings from the tray behind him into his ladle—a bit of soy sauce, salt, sugar, and MSG—and the ladle passes back over the wok. The sauce sizzles as it hits the searing iron. He holds the ladle under the running tap to catch about 2 tablespoons of water and swirls it into the wok. Steam hisses in a puff, the water evaporating almost instantly, and he tosses the broccoli a final time, the breath of the wok mingling and perfuming the florets. Swinging the wok up off the burner, he scoops the stir-fry onto a waiting plate, and steps back, done. The server takes it out.

To make this at home on an ordinary burner, Chef Wen recommends blanching the broccoli first. "The broccoli should be 七成熟 qīchéngshú [70 percent cooked] before you stir-fry, so you can keep the time in the wok fast," he explains. There's nothing like eating the broccoli piping hot and juicy, still infused with fragrance and dampening a bowl of rice with the absorbed sauces.

Cut the broccoli into 2-inch florets and halve each one lengthwise. Bring a pot of salted water to a boil and drizzle in 1 tablespoon of the vegetable oil. Blanch the broccoli florets for about 2 minutes, until cooked but still crisp and vivid green. Drain in a colander and shake dry.

Heat a wok over high heat until a bead of water evaporates within 1 to 2 seconds of contact. Add the remaining 2 tablespoons vegetable oil and swirl to coat the sides. Stir-fry the dried chiles for 20 seconds, then add the ground peppercorns and bloom in the oil for 10 more seconds. Add the garlic and all the broccoli florets and stir-fry briskly, tossing them over the highest heat until piping hot, about 2 minutes. Move the wok off the burner and season with ½ teaspoon salt, the soy sauce, MSG, sugar, and white pepper, then return the wok to the heat and toss a few more times to incorporate everything. Remove from the heat, stir in the sesame oil (if using), and serve immediately.

14 ounces (390 grams) broccoli

½ teaspoon kosher salt, plus more for blanching

3 tablespoons vegetable oil, divided

4 to 6 dried chiles, snipped into ½-inch segments and seeds shaken out

½ teaspoon ground Sichuan peppercorns, or 1 teaspoon whole Sichuan peppercorns

2 garlic cloves, finely chopped

½ teaspoon soy sauce

¼ teaspoon MSG

¼ teaspoon sugar

¼ teaspoon ground white pepper

½ teaspoon toasted sesame oil (optional)

BLANCHED ASPARAGUS WITH SIZZLING OIL

Báizhuó lúsǔn

白灼蘆筍

SERVES 4

In this Cantonese preparation, tender asparagus is blanched until vibrant green, bathed in a soy sauce dressing, and then anointed with a sizzling dash of hot oil to awaken the fragrance of the scallion and ginger threads. The method is typically used for choy sum, a classic in dim sum restaurants, but I think the dainty asparagus spears are easier to eat than unwieldy choy sum stems, and arguably more delicious. One bite of the crisp-tender vegetable will have you reaching for more.

Don't omit the salt and oil in the boiling water—the salt heightens the flavor and color, and the oil is important for mouthfeel. In my family, we make this almost daily whenever there is an abundance of new asparagus in the spring—the flavor of the young, pencil-thin stalks shines in this simple cooking method.

Add the ginger, soy sauce, sugar, MSG, and 2 tablespoons water to a small saucepan and bring to a boil over medium-low heat, stirring to incorporate. Remove from the heat.

Prepare a bowl of ice water.

Bring a large pot of water to a boil, then add a generous amount of salt and drizzle in ½ tablespoon of the oil. Blanch the asparagus just until it turns a vivid green color and is crisp-tender, 30 to 40 seconds for very thin stalks and 1 minute for thicker stalks. Transfer to the bowl of ice water to stop the cooking process. Drain in a colander and shake dry.

Place the asparagus in a neat stack on a serving dish. Pour the hot soy sauce mixture on and around the asparagus. Rearrange the ginger threads along with the chile and scallion in a pile on top.

In a small pan, heat the remaining 2 tablespoons oil over high heat until nearly smoking. Pour the hot oil on top of the asparagus, bathing the aromatics and releasing a vigorous sizzle. Serve immediately.

1 (2-inch) piece (15 grams) fresh ginger, peeled and finely julienned

2 tablespoons soy sauce

½ teaspoon sugar

¼ teaspoon MSG, or ½ teaspoon mushroom bouillon powder

1 pound (450 grams) young asparagus, woody ends snapped off

Kosher salt

2½ tablespoons vegetable oil, divided

Fresh red chile, seeded and finely julienned

1 scallion, white part only, cut lengthwise into thin threads

DRY-POT CAULIFLOWER

Gānguō huācài

乾鍋花菜

SERVES 4

In China, the most common cauliflower isn't the white, densely packed head available in the United States, but a variety with elongated pale-green stems and floppy, looser florets; it is also called caulilini, fioretto, and sprouting or flowering cauliflower. You can find this variety sold in farmers' markets and Asian grocery stores, but regular white cauliflower also works well; if you prefer a softer texture, blanch the florets longer before stir-frying.

MAKE THE SAUCE: In a small bowl, combine all the sauce ingredients until smooth and blended. Set aside.

MAKE THE STIR-FRY: Trim the cauliflower stalks, reserving 2 inches of stem, and cut lengthwise into thin bite-size florets.

Bring a pot of salted water to a boil. Blanch the cauliflower florets for about 2 minutes, until cooked but still crisp. Drain in a colander and shake dry.

Heat a wok over high heat until a bead of water evaporates within 1 to 2 seconds of contact. Add 1 tablespoon of the oil and swirl to coat the sides. Add the onion and stir-fry until still crisp but starting to soften on the edges, about 2 minutes. Transfer to a bowl.

Heat the remaining 2 tablespoons oil in the wok and add the ginger, dried chiles, and white parts of scallions. Reduce the heat to medium-low and fry the aromatics until fragrant, about 1 minute. Add the garlic, chili bean paste, and fermented black beans and stir-fry until the red oil from the chili bean paste is released, about 30 seconds.

Turn the heat back to high and add the blanched cauliflower and the fresh chiles. Add the sauce mixture. Stir-fry to incorporate, then cover and steam the cauliflower for 30 seconds. Uncover and stir-fry until the sauce starts to caramelize on the bottom of the wok and the cauliflower is softened and crisp-tender, about 2 minutes.

Add the onions and the scallion greens and stir to incorporate. Taste and add salt, if needed. Remove from the heat and serve immediately.

THE SAUCE

1 teaspoon soy sauce

1 tablespoon vegetarian oyster sauce

1 teaspoon sugar

2 tablespoons Shaoxing wine

THE STIR-FRY

1 pound (450 grams) caulilini or cauliflower

Kosher salt

1 medium yellow onion, cut crosswise into 1-inch-thick slices

3 tablespoons vegetable oil, divided

1 (2-inch) piece (15 grams) fresh ginger, sliced

6 or 7 dried red chiles, snipped into 1-inch sections and seeds shaken out

3 scallions, cut into 2-inch pieces, white and green parts kept separate

3 garlic cloves, thinly sliced

1 tablespoon Sichuan chili bean paste

1 tablespoon coarsely chopped fermented black beans

½ cup (50 grams) 1-inch pieces fresh red chiles or red bell pepper

STIR-FRIED LOTUS ROOT WITH CELERY & WOOD EAR

Hétáng xiǎochǎo

荷塘小炒

SERVES 4

Lotus root is adored for its crunchy texture, and this lovely Cantonese "lotus pond stir-fry" is a showcase of the five qualities desired in a vegetable stir-fry: *qīng* (light and fresh), *xiān* 鲜 (savory), *shuǎng* (juicy and refreshing), *huá* (slippery smooth), and *cuì* (snappy crisp). Because lotus root contains its own starch, you don't need a slurry—the delicate slices will naturally thicken the sauce as they cook. There are many variations on this medley: add peeled and thinly sliced water chestnuts, snow peas, a handful of crunchy fresh lily bulb petals, gingko nuts, or even roasted cashews (add directly when stir-frying, as they don't need to be blanched).

Lotus root tends to turn purplish gray in contact with iron or unseasoned steel, so for pretty white slices, I recommend cooking in a stainless-steel pan if your wok doesn't have a good patina. Soaking the lotus root in vinegar beforehand will also help prevent browning.

If fresh lotus root is not available in your Asian grocery store, look for shrink-packaged pre-blanched, pre-sliced lotus root in the refrigerated section. Cut each slice in half horizontally so that it's ⅛ inch thick and skip the blanching.

MAKE THE SAUCE: In a small bowl, whisk all the sauce ingredients with ¼ cup (60 mL) water until combined. Set aside.

PREPARE THE STIR-FRY: Soak the wood ears in hot water for at least 30 minutes, until reconstituted. Cut the lotus root in half lengthwise, then use a mandoline or a sharp knife to cut it into ⅛-inch-thick half-moon-shaped slices. You should have around 8 ounces (230 grams) of slices. Soak them in a bowl of cold water with a splash of vinegar to prevent browning.

Cut each celery stalk in half lengthwise, then cut each strip on a diagonal into 1½-inch, diamond-shaped slices. Cut the carrot crosswise on the diagonal into angled 1-inch slices, then cut them vertically into thin diamond slices that match the celery.

Bring a medium pot of salted water to a boil. Blanch the wood ears, lotus root, celery, and carrot for 2 minutes, until the celery is vibrant green but still crisp. Remove all the vegetables with a spider or skimmer and drain in a colander.

(recipe continues)

THE SAUCE

¾ teaspoon kosher salt

½ teaspoon sugar

¼ teaspoon MSG

1 tablespoon Shaoxing wine

THE STIR-FRY

¼ ounce (7 grams) dried wood ear mushrooms

1 medium segment (10 ounces / 280 grams) lotus root, washed and peeled

White vinegar, for soaking

2 celery stalks (150 grams)

½ small carrot

Kosher salt

2 tablespoons Scallion Oil (page 301) or vegetable oil

3 garlic cloves, thinly sliced

½ teaspoon toasted sesame oil

Heat a well-seasoned wok or stainless-steel pan over high heat until a bead of water evaporates within 1 to 2 seconds upon contact. Add the scallion oil and swirl to coat the sides. Add the garlic and stir-fry until fragrant. Push the garlic up the sides and add the sauce mixture to the bottom. As soon as it bubbles, tip in the blanched wood ears, lotus root, celery, and carrot, tossing to coat them in the sauce until they are piping hot, about 1 minute.

Taste and add salt, if necessary. Continue cooking to reduce the liquid until it thickens to a glossy sauce that clings to the vegetables. Turn off the heat, stir in the sesame oil, and serve.

Variation
STIR-FRIED LOTUS ROOT WITH RED FERMENTED TOFU

Nánrǔ cháo ǒupiàn

南乳炒藕片

1 (4-inch) piece (30 grams) fresh ginger, unpeeled

2 cubes (about 1½ tablespoons) red fermented tofu, plus 1 tablespoon brine from the jar

1 tablespoon Shaoxing wine

2 teaspoons sugar

This is a variation I learned in Guangzhou. Unlike the clear sauce in the original dish, the creamy, salty fermented tofu and spicy ginger juice coat the sticky-crisp lotus root slices in a flavorful, boozy, and slightly sweet sauce with a luscious red tint.

To make the sauce, mince or grate the ginger, then use your hands or cheesecloth to squeeze the ginger over a small bowl to extract 1 tablespoon of its juice; discard the fibrous pulp. Mash the fermented tofu with its brine and the ginger juice, Shaoxing wine, and sugar to form a thin sauce. Proceed with the recipe above, using this sauce instead.

BEAN SPROUTS

Homemade bean sprouts are incredibly nutritious, easy to grow, and also tastier, fresher, and nuttier in flavor than the bagged sprouts you buy in the store. They're safe to eat raw, although we typically blanch them briefly or stir-fry them. A cup of dried mung beans will yield around 3 pounds bean sprouts.

Soak 1 cup (8 ounces / 220 grams) dried mung beans in cold water for 24 hours.

Line a 10- to 13-inch container with holes (like a stainless-steel steamer rack, colander, or plastic planter) with a single layer of cheesecloth, draping the edges of the cloth over the sides. Drain the mung beans and spread them out evenly at the bottom on the cheesecloth. Place a small bowl upside down in a large basin that can catch water, and stack the lined container on top. This allows the water to drain into the basin without the bottom of the sprouts touching the water.

Water the beans generously with a cup or two of water (or run the tap over them). Flip back the edges of the cheesecloth to cover the beans and place them in a dark cupboard or cover them with a dark cloth. Water the beans as often as you can, preferably every 3 to 4 hours for best results, or at least 3 times a day—they are quite thirsty and you want to keep them damp to ensure they grow long and plump sprouts. Empty out the water in the basin periodically. The beans will start sprouting on the second day, and on the sixth day they will be long enough to harvest. Pull them up gently from the roots and store in the refrigerator, wrapped in a paper towel in a plastic bag, for up to a week.

STIR-FRIED BEAN SPROUTS WITH CHINESE CHIVES

Qīngchǎo dòuyá

清炒豆芽

SERVES 4

Bean sprouts are mild in flavor, and their juicy, bland crunch is best paired with a stronger ingredient like chives. Other common pairings for them are thinly julienned carrot or bell pepper, scallions in place of the chives, or smoked pressed tofu cut into thin slivers. For the sprouts, I recommend sprouting at home (see box) or using the ones sold in loose bulk at Asian grocery stores, but if you're buying bagged sprouts, try to use them in a day or two, as they will deteriorate quickly in the fridge. Composed mostly of water, bean sprouts easily overcook, so to avoid soggy sprouts, use high heat and keep the cooking time just brief enough to infuse the sprouts with aroma but retain their crisp bite.

Rinse the sprouts under water, then drain them in a colander and shake as dry as possible. If using home-grown sprouts, you don't have to rinse them.

Heat a wok or skillet over medium-high heat until a bead of water evaporates within 1 to 2 seconds on contact. Add the oil and swirl to coat the sides. Add the ginger and stir-fry until fragrant, about 30 seconds. Add the dried chiles and stir-fry until they begin to darken, about 30 seconds. Add the chives and stir-fry for 10 seconds, until wilted. Turn the heat to high, add the bean sprouts, and stir-fry for about 1 minute, until piping hot and reduced in volume but not yet releasing liquid. Season with salt and MSG to taste. Transfer to a dish and serve.

4 heaping cups (8 ounces / 220 grams) mung bean sprouts

2 tablespoons Scallion Oil (page 301) or vegetable oil

1 tablespoon minced ginger

5 dried red chiles, snipped into ½-inch segments and seeds shaken out

4 ounces (110 grams) Chinese garlic chives or scallions, cut into 2-inch segments

½ teaspoon kosher salt, plus more to taste

¼ teaspoon MSG, or to taste

STIR-FRIED GARLIC CHIVES WITH PRESSED TOFU

Xiānggān jiǔcài

香幹韭菜

SERVES 4

Garlic chives are a staple of Chinese home cooking—the long, spear-like blades have a pungent garlicky aroma and are delicious either chopped for dumpling or bun fillings or stir-fried with firm, chewy slivers of caramel-brown pressed tofu. Instead of the flat chives, you can also use their flowering stems, which are sold in bunches with tiny edible flower buds. Look for stiff stems with some elasticity and store them wrapped in a damp paper towel in a closed bag in the refrigerator. Another alternative is garlic scapes (蒜苔 *suàntái*), the tender, round green stems that shoot out from garlic bulbs, which are juicy with just a hint of garlic's pungent aroma and a lovely vegetal sweetness. They're often available in farmers' markets—look for completely green stems that are tender when pinched with a fingernail.

If you're using garlic chives or flowering garlic chives, cut them into 1-inch pieces. If you're using garlic scapes, snip off the spiky, hard flowering buds and dark-green tips from the stems. Use your knife to probe the stem, cutting off and discarding the end where the stem starts to feel tough. Cut the remaining tender stems into 1-inch lengths.

Cut the tofu first into ¼-inch-thick slices and then lengthwise into ¼-inch julienne.

Heat the oil in a wok or skillet over high heat until shimmering. Add the tofu slivers, distributing them evenly on the wok's surface. Do not stir for 30 seconds to sear the bottoms, then flip the tofu and sear until browned on both sides, about 30 more seconds. Remove from the wok and set aside.

Heat the wok again and add the garlic and chile slivers. Stir-fry until aromatic, about 15 seconds. Add the garlic chives or stems and stir-fry until the leaves soften or the stems look lightly wrinkled, about 2 minutes. Add the Shaoxing wine and stir-fry until evaporated, then return the fried tofu to the wok and add salt to taste. Stir-fry until the tofu is piping hot and any juices have evaporated. Serve immediately.

10 ounces (280 grams) garlic chives, flowering garlic chives, or garlic scapes

5 ounces (140 grams) smoked or five-spice pressed tofu

2 tablespoons vegetable oil

3 garlic cloves, thinly sliced

2 fresh red chiles, cut into thin slivers, or a small handful of red bell pepper strips

1 tablespoon Shaoxing wine

¾ teaspoon kosher salt, plus more to taste

TWO COMMON KNIFE CUTS

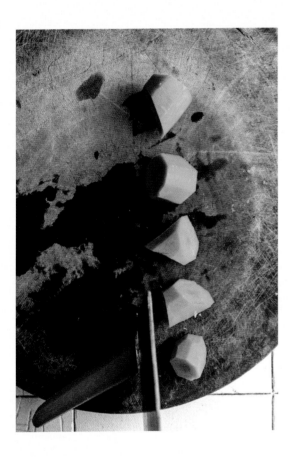

ROLL CUT
滚刀块 gǔndāokuài

Hold the trimmed vegetable (carrot, cucumber, or eggplant) at a 45-degree angle to the knife. Cut a 1-inch piece crosswise, then roll the vegetable a quarter or third, turn down, and cut another 1-inch piece. Make sure your knife stays perpendicular to the cutting board the entire time. Repeat until the entire vegetable is cut. The beauty of the roll cut is the irregular-shaped but consistent-size chunks.

DIAMOND CUT
菱形片 língxíngpiàn

For a thick-fleshed bell pepper, cut lengthwise into 1-inch-wide strips. Seed and scrape off any membrane. Lay the strip out horizontally and hold the knife at a 45-degree angle. Cut into diamond shapes.

For carrots, cucumber, or other cylindrical vegetables, cut crosswise into 1-inch pieces at a diagonal. Set the piece on its cut side like the Leaning Tower of Pisa, then slice crosswise into thin diamond slices.

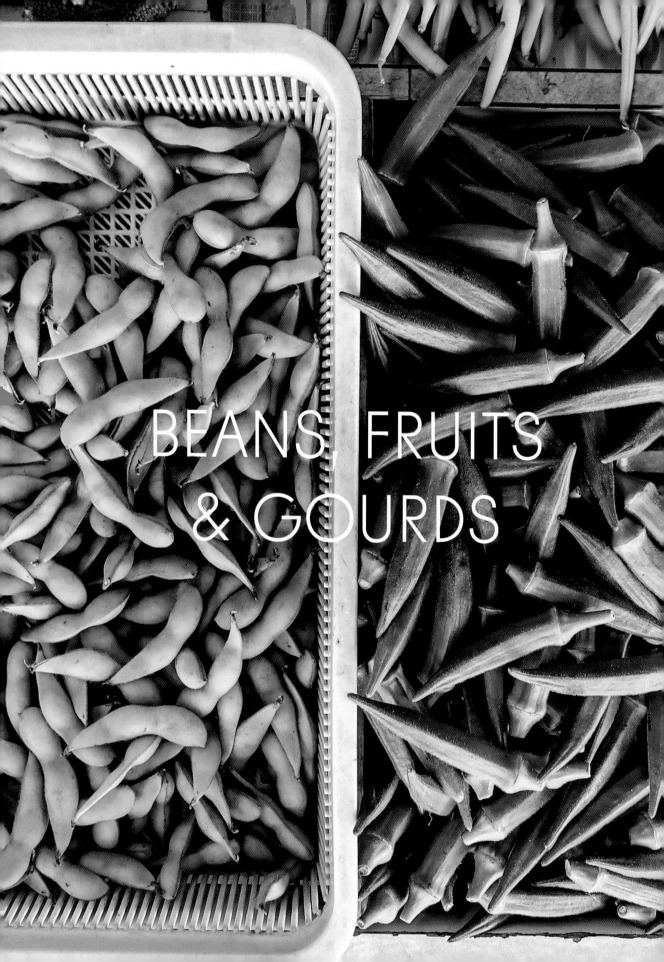

BEANS, FRUITS
& GOURDS

These are some of my favorite Chinese dishes of all time, featuring summery, vibrant fruits of the earth: gourds, peppers, squashes, eggplant, and beans. When the weather is hot, Chinese people eat cooling vegetables like bitter melon and cucumbers to "expel the heat" (解熱 *jiěrè*), either stir-fried or simply dressed as a refreshing starter. In the markets, there are hot and sweet peppers and fresh beans in abundance: the tender green bean, flat "knife" bean, and yard-long bean, enjoyed both fresh and pickled, or podded beans like green peas, green soybeans, and fava beans or broad beans. In vegetarian cooking, beans are often stir-fried and paired with preserved and fermented vegetables, which enhances their flavor in the absence of meat—just a small amount of pickled mustard greens or Cantonese olive-preserved vegetable acts like a salty, fragrant condiment to deepen the flavors of the dish, as in Blistered Dry-Fried String Beans (page 103), one of the most irresistible green bean dishes and an enduring favorite from Sichuan Province.

Eggplants are particularly beloved vegetables in Chinese cooking—the first mention of the fruit's existence is in the *Qímín Yàoshù*, an ancient agricultural study from 500 CE. They can be richly braised (Fish-Fragrant Eggplant, page 88) or steamed lightly to bring out their sweet, mild flavors and silky flesh. And when summer comes to a close and we start to crave heartier, more substantial vegetable dishes, there's nothing more satisfying than tender braised winter melon or the solace of kabocha squash stewed with fermented black beans into starchy, buttery morsels.

SMASHED CUCUMBER SALAD

Pāi huángguā

拍黄瓜

SERVES 4 AS AN APPETIZER OR SIDE

Perfumed with sesame oil and garlic, this crunchy and refreshing cucumber salad is one of the most ubiquitous Chinese starter dishes, and everyone makes it differently, so feel free to adjust until it's exactly the way you like it—a pinch more sugar for extra sweetness; black vinegar for a mellower, fragrant aroma; pale rice vinegar for sharper, fruity acidity; extra chili oil for roasted, smoky notes; or one or two thinly sliced bird's-eye chiles for heat. At some restaurants, they'll scatter a handful of crisp Fried Peanuts (page 304) on top right before serving. Avoid thick-skinned, seedy cucumbers—the best choice is slender hothouse cucumbers, Persian cucumbers, or Japanese kyuri cucumbers, which have delicate, thin skin, smaller seeds, and crunchier flesh. And be sure to whack the cucumber with the blade of a Chinese cleaver or a large rolling pin until it splits: the craggy edges look more appealing, and the rough surfaces of the cool, juicy flesh better absorb the sweet-sharp flavors of the dressing.

Trim off both ends of the cucumber. Lay it on a cutting board and smack it a few times with the flat side of a Chinese cleaver, knife blade, or heavy rolling pin until it splits into large pieces. (To prevent the seeds from flying out over your counter, you can also place the cucumber in a zip-top bag or wrap it in a towel first.) Cut the split cucumber at a diagonal into ½-inch bite-size pieces. Place them in a medium bowl and sprinkle evenly with the salt, then cover and refrigerate for 15 minutes.

Drain off any water the cucumber has released. Add the garlic, sugar, soy sauce, vinegar, sesame oil, and chili oil and toss to coat, adjusting the seasonings to taste. Serve immediately. The cucumbers will keep in an airtight container in the fridge for up to a week.

1 long hothouse cucumber, or 3 small Persian cucumbers (12 ounces / 340 grams total)

½ teaspoon kosher salt

3 garlic cloves, minced

½ teaspoon sugar

2 teaspoons soy sauce

1 tablespoon Chinkiang black vinegar or pale rice vinegar

1 teaspoon toasted sesame oil

½ tablespoon Red Chili Oil with sediment (page 301)

FISH-FRAGRANT EGGPLANT

Yúxiāng qiézi

魚香茄子

SERVES 4

If you aren't a fan of eggplant, it's because you haven't had this dish yet. Sichuan cooks fry eggplant until it's golden and buttery, then braise it briefly in a sweet-and-sour sauce. This double cooking transforms the eggplant's rather chewy, bland, spongy flesh into buttery and tender morsels that melt in the mouth, made irresistibly heady with garlic and enlivened by hot pickled red chiles and ginger. According to legend, the dish originated along the coast of the Yangtze River in Sichuan, where fishermen often cooked the fish they caught using a pungent mixture of chiles, ginger, and garlic. Today the "fish-fragrant" flavor is a standard in the canon of Sichuan cooking, with its distinctive hot, sour, and sweet profile.

MAKE THE SAUCE: In a small bowl, whisk all the sauce ingredients until blended. Set aside.

Cut the eggplants lengthwise into 3-inch sections, then slice them into ½-inch wedges. In a large bowl, combine 3 cups (720 mL) water and 1½ tablespoons salt and whisk until the salt dissolves, then submerge the eggplant and soak for 15 minutes. Drain and pat the wedges dry. Salting helps relax the flesh, reduce any bitterness, and prevent it from soaking up excessive oil.

Heat about 1½ cups (360 mL) oil in a wok or skillet over medium-high heat. Coat the eggplant lightly in the starch. When the oil reaches 375°F (190°C), fry the eggplant in batches, flipping and turning it occasionally to cook evenly, until the edges are slightly golden and the skin is glossy purple and wrinkled, 3 to 4 minutes. Transfer the cooked eggplant to a paper towel–lined plate. Pour the oil into a heatproof container and reserve for another use, leaving about 1 tablespoon oil in the wok.

Return the wok to the stove over medium heat and add the chili bean paste. Stir-fry over low heat until its red oil is released, about 30 seconds. Add the garlic, ginger, and scallion whites and stir-fry until just aromatic, about 30 seconds more. Push the aromatics up one side of the wok and pour the sauce mixture into the center. Gently fold the fried eggplant into the sauce and simmer for about 2 minutes, until the eggplant has absorbed the flavors and the liquid is thickened from the starch. Transfer to a plate, garnish with the scallion greens, and serve immediately.

THE SAUCE

½ cup unsalted stock of any kind or water

1 tablespoon sugar

1 tablespoon soy sauce

1 tablespoon Chinkiang black vinegar

½ teaspoon potato starch

1 pound (450 grams) long Chinese or Japanese eggplants (about 3 small)

Kosher salt

Vegetable oil, for frying

½ cup potato starch or cornstarch

1½ tablespoons Sichuan chili bean paste or pickled chili paste

1 tablespoon finely chopped garlic

1 tablespoon finely chopped fresh ginger

2 scallions, thinly sliced, white and green parts kept separate

STIR-FRIED FAVA BEANS & PICKLED MUSTARD GREENS

Xuěcài chǎo cándòu

雪菜炒蠶豆

SERVES 4

Tender and slightly mealy, with a delicate nutty sweetness, pale-green young fava beans are particularly tasty coaxed in the heat of a wok with the savory, peppery acidity of fermented mustard greens. Fresh podded beans need to be used within 2 days, but they are conveniently sold frozen in Chinese supermarkets (look for bags labeled "broad beans"). I like young fava beans since they don't require peeling, but you may prefer to blanch and peel the fat mature beans, which are starchier and meatier. You can also use fresh or frozen green soybeans (edamame) or green peas for a lovely springtime dish.

If you're using fresh beans, bring a pot of well-salted water to a boil and blanch the beans for 3 to 4 minutes, until they are tender and vibrant in color. Rinse with cold water and drain well. If the beans are mature and have a tough skin surrounding each bean, peel them. If using frozen beans, they are already blanched, so simply thaw them.

Heat a wok or skillet over high heat until a bead of water evaporates within 1 to 2 seconds of contact, then add the vegetable oil and swirl to coat the sides of the wok. Add the scallion and stir-fry until fragrant and starting to color, about 30 seconds. Add the fermented mustard greens and stir it around in the fragrant oil to release its flavor and cook off some of the liquid, about 1 minute.

Add the fava beans and stir-fry until they are bright green and coated in the seasonings. Season with about ¼ teaspoon salt (adjust to taste; this will depend on the saltiness of the fermented mustard greens) and cook until the beans are piping hot and tender but still holding their shape, about 2 minutes. Remove from the heat, stir in the white pepper and sesame oil, and serve.

Kosher salt

2 heaping cups (280 grams) shelled fava beans or edamame, fresh or frozen

2 tablespoons vegetable oil

1 scallion, both white and green parts, finely chopped

½ cup packed finely chopped pickled mustard greens (page 306)

⅛ teaspoon ground white pepper

½ teaspoon toasted sesame oil

BRAISED WINTER MELON

Hóngshāo dōngguā

紅燒冬瓜

SERVES 4

A giant gourd with a cucumber-like scent and very mild flavor, winter melon is not a winter vegetable or even a melon, but it gets its name from the white bloom on its pale-green skin and its watermelon-like shape. Because the frosty white flesh inside takes on flavor dreamily and withstands even hours of braising, winter melon has been used for centuries in vegetarian cuisine to imitate the tender, buttery succulence of rich meat. This recipe was inspired by the Hangzhou dish *sù dōngpōròu*, where a large slab of winter melon is scored in a cross-hatch pattern, fried, and then braised in wine, soy sauce, and spices until it turns soft, slightly sweet, glistening, and gelatinous, like a slab of red-braised pork belly. This everyday version is much easier and equally satisfying. I still remember the largest wintermelon I ever saw in an open-air market in Guangzhou during late summer—it was a foot wide in diameter and about as tall and heavy as a child. Thankfully, in most Asian grocery stores they're sold in more manageable slices, and if not, you can ask them to cut it for you.

With a sharp knife, trim the peel from the winter melon and cut out the frosty inner core and seeds. Cut it into chunks ½ inch thick and 1 inch wide, and toss with the dark soy sauce. Let sit for 10 minutes.

Combine the starch with 1 tablespoon cold water in a small bowl.

Heat 2 tablespoons of the scallion oil in a wok over medium heat until shimmering. Immediately reduce the heat to low, add the ginger, star anise, and bay leaves, and gently stir-fry until aromatic, about 3 minutes. Turn the heat to high, add the winter melon pieces, and stir-fry until the edges take on a translucent, softened quality and are beginning to caramelize on the wok's surface, about 3 minutes.

Add the soy sauce, oyster sauce, sugar, and stock and bring to a boil. Cover, reduce the heat to maintain a simmer, and cook for 8 to 10 minutes more, until the winter melon is buttery and tender but still holds its shape. If you want, you can add a tiny amount of additional dark soy sauce (¼ to ½ teaspoon) to deepen the color. Taste and season with salt as needed.

Finally, give the starch slurry a whisk and pour it into the wok, stirring continuously so that the liquid thickens into a glossy sauce. Transfer to a serving dish and scatter the scallion greens (if using) on top.

1½ pounds (700 grams) winter melon

½ teaspoon dark soy sauce, plus more as needed

½ teaspoon potato starch

3 tablespoons Scallion Oil (page 301) or vegetable oil, divided

1 (2-inch) piece (15 grams) unpeeled fresh ginger, cut into thin slices

1 star anise pod

2 bay leaves

1 tablespoon soy sauce

1 teaspoon vegetarian oyster sauce

1 teaspoon sugar

½ cup unsalted stock of any kind or water

Kosher salt

1 scallion, green part only, thinly sliced, for garnish (optional)

STIR-FRIED CUCUMBER WITH BEECH MUSHROOMS

Huángguā chǎo xiègū

黄瓜炒蟹菇

SERVES 4

If you've never had stir-fried cucumber before, you're in for a treat. In the brief searing heat of a wok, the cucumber softens and becomes slippery, satiny, and juicy with caramelized edges. The heat also brings out cucumber's delicate flavor and intensifies its sweetness. I love adding tender white beech mushrooms for an appealingly chewy, savory addition, and goji berries for garnish, but you can easily omit them.

Peel and trim the ends of the cucumbers. Cut them in half lengthwise. Use a teaspoon to scoop out the pulp and seeds—I usually eat them as I go—and cut the halves into ¼-inch-thick slices, angling the knife to elongate the slices. You'll have a few short little ends, which you can also eat.

Heat a wok over high heat until a bead of water evaporates within 1 or 2 seconds of contact. Add the oil and swirl to coat the sides of the wok. Add the garlic and stir-fry until fragrant but not yet browned, about 30 seconds.

Add the mushrooms and stir-fry until you can smell their woodsy, savory aroma, then add the cucumber and briskly stir to coat it in the fragrant oil. Sprinkle with the salt, MSG, and sugar and continue to stir-fry until the cucumber softens and turns tender and its edges are almost translucent. Taste and add more salt if needed. Transfer to a dish, garnish with the drained goji berries (if using), and serve immediately.

2 hothouse cucumbers
(22 ounces / 600 grams)

2 tablespoons Scallion Oil
(page 301) or vegetable oil

3 garlic cloves, thinly sliced

1 (5.5-ounce / 150-gram)
package white beech mushrooms,
root ends trimmed, torn into
individual pieces

1 teaspoon kosher salt,
plus more as needed

¼ teaspoon MSG

1 teaspoon sugar

1 tablespoon goji berries, soaked
in cool water to rehydrate
(optional)

Variation

A common version of this dish in southern China uses silk gourd (絲瓜 *sīguā*). Similar to cucumber, it has a delicate flavor and pale-green flesh, but is treasured for its melting, gelatinous texture. There are two main kinds of silk gourd: a fat and oblong variety (loofah gourd) with reptilian, rough-textured skin, and a very long, tapered dark-green gourd with prominent spiny ridges; either will work for this dish. To prep it, simply peel the gourd to remove its outer skin or spiny ridges and substitute it for the cucumber in the recipe above.

BRAISED WINTER SQUASH WITH FERMENTED BLACK BEANS

Dòuchǐ mèn nánguā

豆豉燜南瓜

SERVES 4

Similar to red-braising (紅燒 *hóngshāo*), when you cover and slowly cook an ingredient in a flavorful liquid, smother-braising (燜 *mèn*) is simpler and shorter and often relies on more delicate, lighter-colored condiments instead of dark soy sauce, allowing the color of the vegetable to shine through.

In this dish, the squash's natural sweetness is complemented by the salty, savory fermented black beans, and the squash is cooked until buttery and tender, on the verge of falling apart. My favorite is kabocha squash, which has a velvety, starchy softness and flavor reminiscent of roasted chestnut, but any firm-fleshed winter squash, like red kuri, butternut, or Hubbard, will work.

Peel and core the squash and cut it into 1½-inch wedges, then cut the wedges into pieces ½ inch thick and 1½ inches wide; you should have about 3 cups.

Heat a wok over high heat and add the scallion oil, swirling to coat the sides. Add the dried chiles and stir-fry until they begin to darken in color, about 10 seconds. Add the fermented black beans and garlic and let them sizzle until fragrant, about 30 seconds. Add the squash pieces and stir them around the wok to pick up all the fragrant oil, then pour in the stock and bring to a boil. Season with the sugar and salt, then cover, reduce the heat to maintain a gentle simmer, and cook until the squash has absorbed most of the liquid and is tender enough to pierce with a chopstick, 4 to 5 minutes.

Uncover and taste for salt and sugar; adjust the seasoning if necessary. Remove from the heat, stir in the sesame oil and a dash of white pepper, scatter the sliced scallions on top, and serve.

1 pound (450 grams) winter squash (about ½ small kabocha squash)

2 tablespoons Scallion Oil (page 301) or vegetable oil

4 or 5 dried red chiles, snipped into ½-inch pieces and seeds shaken out

1 tablespoon fermented black beans, coarsely chopped

3 garlic cloves, thinly sliced

1 cup unsalted stock of any kind or water

1 teaspoon sugar

½ teaspoon kosher salt

½ teaspoon toasted sesame oil

Ground white pepper

1 scallion, green part only, thinly sliced, for garnish

CLAY POT–BRAISED EGGPLANT WITH BASIL

Kǒumó qiéliǔ

口蘑茄柳

SERVES 4

Basil, garlic, and eggplant are in total harmony with each other, and this dish makes use of a clay pot to slowly infuse their flavors and tenderize the eggplant over gentle, slow heat. Thai basil is a hallmark of Taiwanese cooking, and its spicy anise-like fragrance adds both fresh color and a distinctive warming flavor to soy sauce–braised dishes. A regular wok or skillet over low heat will also work fine.

Cut the eggplants lengthwise into 3-inch sections, then slice them into ¾-inch wedges. In a large bowl, combine 3 cups (720 mL) water and 1½ tablespoons salt and whisk until the salt dissolves, then submerge the eggplant and soak for 15 minutes. Squeeze pieces as dry as possible. Salting will relax the eggplant flesh, reduce any bitterness, and prevent it from soaking up excessive oil.

In a small bowl, mix the potato starch with 1½ tablespoons cold water until blended. Set aside.

Heat ¼ cup vegetable oil in a wok or skillet over medium-high heat until shimmering. Working in batches, place as many eggplant pieces in the pan as will fit in a single layer, cut-side down. Shallow-fry the eggplant until the bottoms are golden brown, then flip and cook the other side for 3 minutes more. Transfer to a paper towel–lined plate to drain. Fry the remaining pieces in batches, replenishing the oil as needed.

Place a clay pot on the stove or use the same wok. Over medium heat, heat 2 tablespoons oil until shimmering. Add the mushrooms and stir-fry until the edges are browned, about 3 minutes. Add the ginger and garlic and stir-fry briefly just until aromatic. Add the eggplant and soy sauce, then pour in the stock and bring to a boil, seasoning with the sugar and ¼ teaspoon salt. Add the bell pepper. Cover the pot, reduce the heat to low, and simmer for 3 to 4 minutes, until the eggplant is tender and has absorbed the flavors.

Uncover the clay pot. Taste the liquid and adjust the seasonings if needed. Add most of the basil, reserving a few leaves for garnish, and fold it in to wilt. Give the starch slurry a stir and add it to the pot, folding it in gently to combine. Cook until the liquid has thickened, about 1 minute. Remove from the heat. Gently stir in the sesame oil, garnish with the reserved basil, and serve.

2 long Chinese or Japanese eggplants (1 pound / 450 grams total)

Kosher salt

1 teaspoon potato starch

Vegetable oil, for frying

3 ounces (85 grams) button mushrooms, each cut into 2 or 3 pieces

1 (2-inch) piece (15 grams) fresh ginger, cut into thin slices

3 garlic cloves, thinly sliced

2 tablespoons soy sauce

¾ cup unsalted stock of any kind or water

1 teaspoon sugar

½ red bell pepper, sliced lengthwise into wide strips and cut at a diagonal into 1-inch diamonds

1 cup loosely packed fresh Thai basil leaves

½ teaspoon toasted sesame oil

BEANS STIR-FRIED WITH OLIVE PRESERVED GREENS

Lǎncài chǎo chángdòu

欖菜炒長豆

Olive preserved greens are a savory black-green Cantonese condiment of chopped salted mustard greens preserved in oily crushed Chinese olives. A few spoonfuls of this regional Chaozhou specialty add umami to stir-fried beans, and I like to pair them with grated carrot for lovely sweetness and color. Traditionally, Chinese cooks use long beans, which come in thin, snaky lengths with slightly wrinkly skin, but any green string bean will work in this recipe. You can even try it with shelled green peas, fava beans, edamame, cooked chickpeas, or other tender, starchy beans. My family especially enjoys eating this stir-fry with Plain Congee (page 285).

SERVES 4

Heat the oil in a wok or skillet over high heat until shimmering. Add the beans and stir-fry until the exterior is slightly blistered, about 2 minutes. Add the garlic and stir-fry until fragrant and faintly golden, about 30 seconds.

Add the carrot and olive preserved greens and toss over high heat until the beans are piping hot, about 1 minute. Add the stock and sugar, stir, then cover and steam for 3 minutes, until the beans are softened but still vibrant green. Uncover, taste, season with salt if needed, and serve.

2 tablespoons vegetable oil

12 ounces (330 grams) long beans or green beans, trimmed and cut into ½-inch pieces

1 tablespoon minced garlic

1 cup (90 grams) grated or finely chopped carrot

3 tablespoons olive preserved greens (*ganlancai*)

½ cup unsalted stock of any kind or water

½ teaspoon sugar

Kosher salt

BEANS

"Do Chinese people eat beans?" It's a legitimate question. Dried beans don't seem to have the same central role in Chinese cuisine like lentils do in the savory dishes of India, chickpeas in the Mediterranean, black beans and pinto beans in Central and South America, or dried beans and pulses in other cuisines. The soybean is the most important bean in China, fermented into soy sauce and bean pastes and other essential seasonings, but the mature yellow soybean is hard to digest when simply cooked and is typically ground into soy milk or coagulated into tofu products. Other dried beans, like mung beans, red adzuki beans, and split yellow peas, are primarily used in sweet dishes, enjoyed in porridges and sweet bean toppings, or mashed into pastes for filling buns and pastries.

BLISTERED DRY-FRIED STRING BEANS

Gānbiǎn sìjìdòu

乾煸四季豆

SERVES 4

This is one of the most recognizable Chinese dishes in the West due to its popularity in Sichuan restaurants. In the original dry-frying method, the green beans are slowly cooked in a dry pan until their skins wrinkle, but restaurants almost always deep-fry the beans, which is more efficient and generates the shriveled, oil-blistered exterior people have come to associate with the dish. *Yacai* is a finely chopped Sichuan preserved vegetable that has become more widely available in Asian supermarkets in recent years and is a key ingredient in Sichuan dishes like dandan noodles. If you can't find it, omit it or replace it with 1 tablespoon fermented black beans, coarsely chopped.

MAKE THE SAUCE: In a small bowl, stir together the sauce ingredients.

TO COOK THE BEANS USING THE DEEP-FRYING METHOD (FASTEST): Heat 2 cups (480 mL) oil in a wok over high heat to 350°F (177°C), until a wooden or bamboo chopstick forms a steady stream of bubbles when inserted. Drop half the string beans into the oil and fry until the skins are blistered and slightly shriveled, about 2 minutes. Remove them with a spider or skimmer and drain them on paper towels. Repeat with the remaining string beans. Pour the oil into a heatproof container and reserve for another use.

TO COOK THE STRING BEANS USING THE DRY-FRY METHOD: Heat a wok or skillet over high heat, add 1 tablespoon oil, and swirl to coat the surface of the wok. Immediately reduce the heat to low. Working in batches, place the beans in the wok in a single layer and let them cook, without stirring, until they are wrinkled and dry on the bottom, about 5 minutes per side. Remove them from the wok, set aside, and repeat with the remaining green beans.

MAKE THE STIR-FRY: Heat 2 tablespoons oil in a wok over high heat until the oil is shimmering. Add the dried chiles, garlic, ginger, and Sichuan peppercorns and stir-fry until fragrant, about 1 minute. Add the cooked string beans to the wok along with the pickled greens and stir-fry briskly to combine. Add the sauce mixture, pouring it down the hot side of the wok to release the flavor, and toss with the string beans a few times until the liquid has mostly evaporated and the beans are piping hot and coated in the seasonings, about 2 minutes. Taste and add salt if needed (usually the pickled greens are salty enough), then transfer to a dish and serve immediately.

THE SAUCE

1 teaspoon soy sauce

1 tablespoon Shaoxing wine

Dash of ground white pepper

Vegetable oil, as needed

14 ounces (400 grams) string beans, ends trimmed, beans longer than 3 inches cut in half

THE STIR-FRY

5 or 6 dried chiles, snipped into ½-inch pieces and seeds shaken out

3 garlic cloves, minced

1 tablespoon minced fresh ginger

1 teaspoon whole Sichuan peppercorns, or ½ teaspoon ground Sichuan peppercorns

2 tablespoons minced Sichuan pickled greens (芽菜 *yácài*)

Kosher salt

STEWED BEANS & POTATO

Dòujiǎo dùn tǔdòu

豆角燉土豆

SERVES 6

This is one of my favorite northeast dishes, and I always request it whenever I visit home. I'd unfold myself by the kitchen island, warming my bare feet on the floor grate of the heating vent and chattering on about my semester as my mom tended the pot of tender flat beans with chunks of potato simmering inside. When the stew was done, she would set the entire pot down on the table, not wanting to wash an additional serving dish. It was a homey mess of cooked-down vegetables, but the buttery, meaty beans and starchy potatoes were fragrant with spices and darkened with soy sauce, and with a bowl of rice in my hand, nothing could tear me away.

In northeastern China, they use "greasy beans" (油豆角 *yóudòujiǎo*). These are wider and flatter than green beans, with glossy wide pods tinted with reddish or purple streaks, and the meaty beans can withstand long cooking times without disintegrating. You can find them in Asian supermarkets, or look for wide Italian or romano green beans, often available in farmers' markets.

Snap off the ends of the beans, carefully pulling the tough strings to remove them on both sides. Cut the beans into 3-inch pieces.

Heat the oil in a wok over medium-high heat until shimmering. Add the string beans and stir-fry until blistered and vibrant green, about 1 minute. Remove the beans from the wok using a skimmer or spider and set aside. Add the green onion, ginger, garlic, and star anise to the wok and stir-fry for 1 to 2 minutes, until the onion is softened and the spices are fragrant.

Add the potatoes and stir to coat. Add the stock, soy sauce, MSG, and five-spice powder. Add the stir-fried beans. Bring to a boil, reduce the heat to low, partially cover the wok, and simmer gently for 15 to 20 minutes, until the potatoes are tender and beans are very soft. Taste and season with salt as needed. Transfer to a large bowl and serve.

1 pound (450 grams) broad string beans, such as romano beans

¼ cup vegetable oil

1 large green onion or 3 scallions, both white and green parts, thinly sliced

1 (2-inch) piece (15 grams) fresh ginger, thinly sliced

3 garlic cloves, thinly sliced

1 star anise pod

10 ounces (280 grams) russet potatoes, peeled and cut into ¾-inch chunks

1½ cups (360 mL) unsalted stock of any kind or water

1 tablespoon soy sauce

¼ teaspoon MSG

½ teaspoon five-spice powder

Kosher salt

STIR-FRIED CORN & PINE NUTS

Sōngrén yùmǐ

松仁玉米

SERVES 4

This might seem like an odd trio, but the glossy, sweet corn with the juicy peppers and the fragrant, buttery crunch of the pine nuts is an enchanting combination. A prized export of Jilin Province, pine nuts elevate the humble ingredients in this dish, and my parents say you can always tell how good a restaurant is by their ratio of pine nuts to corn. This dish is a dream in the summer with shelled fresh peas and corn picked at its sweetest and juiciest, but it's honestly still delicious with frozen vegetables. Other possible substitutions are diced cucumber or jalapeño in place of the peppers, or edamame for the peas.

Make a slurry by combining the potato starch with 1 tablespoon cold water in a small bowl. Stir until smooth and set aside.

Bring a pot of salted water to a boil and blanch the corn kernels for 1 minute. When the water returns to a boil, add the peas and cook with the corn for 1 minute. Finally, add the carrot and blanch for 30 seconds. Remove everything with a slotted spoon and drain well in a colander. (If using frozen vegetables, skip this step and add them to the wok frozen to prevent them from becoming soggy.)

Heat a wok or skillet over low heat and add the vegetable oil, swirling to coat the sides. Add the pine nuts and stir-fry until they are light golden in color and smell wonderful, about 3 minutes. Remove the pine nuts with a slotted spoon and set them aside to drain on paper towels, leaving behind the fragrant oil.

Increase the heat to high. Add the scallions, garlic, and bell pepper and stir-fry until fragrant, about 30 seconds. Add the blanched corn, peas, and carrots to the wok and stir-fry briskly. Season with the sugar and 1 teaspoon salt. Add ¼ cup (60 mL) water and cook for about 2 minutes, until the vegetables have absorbed the flavors and the corn is juicy and tender. Give the starch slurry a stir and gradually add it to the wok, stirring continuously until the liquid has thickened and coats the vegetables with a thin, glossy sheen. Adjust the seasoning with salt and stir in the toasted pine nuts. Remove from the heat and drizzle with the sesame oil. Serve immediately.

½ teaspoon potato starch

Kosher salt

2 cups (10 ounces / 280 grams) sweet corn kernels, frozen or cut off 2 fresh cobs

½ cup (2½ ounces / 70 grams) shelled peas

¼ cup (2 ounces / 50 grams) ¼-inch-diced carrot

3 tablespoons vegetable oil

⅔ cup (2½ ounces / 70 grams) pine nuts

1 scallion, white part only, cut into ¼-inch pieces

3 garlic cloves, minced

½ small red bell pepper (2 ounces / 50 grams), seeded and cut into ¼-inch dice

1 tablespoon sugar

½ teaspoon toasted sesame oil

STEAMED EGGPLANT WITH SOY SAUCE & GARLIC

Suànróng qiézi

蒜蓉茄子

SERVES 4

Steaming is my dad's favorite way to prepare eggplant. He always bought big bags of slender purple Asian eggplants at the Chinese market, and at home he would toss a few into the steamer until their skins softened and wrinkled and then tear their buttery pale flesh into strips. On hot summer evenings, I often opened the fridge to find a container of this dish that he'd made, chilling in its marinade before dinner. He usually seasons the eggplant with soy sauce, a tremendous amount of minced raw garlic, and sesame oil, but I like to add a splash of dark Chinkiang vinegar to mellow the garlic notes and sugar and to edge it toward a more sweet-and-sour taste. Steaming is one of the healthiest cooking methods, and it brings out eggplant's delicate flavor and tender, silky texture.

Use Asian eggplants for this recipe, as they have sweeter flesh, fewer seeds, and thinner skin than the Mediterranean or globe varieties.

MAKE THE SAUCE: In a small bowl, combine all the sauce ingredients. Set aside.

Cut the eggplants into pieces to fit in your steamer. Bring water to a boil in a wok or skillet, then place the steamer on top, cover, and steam the eggplants for 10 to 12 minutes, until the skin is wrinkled and the flesh is no longer chewy or spongy but tender enough to pierce through with a chopstick. Remove the eggplants from the steamer, drain any excess water, and set them aside until cool enough to handle, about 5 minutes.

Tear the warm eggplant into long chopstickable strips and place them in a bowl. Pour in the sauce mixture and then place the scallions and ground chiles on top. Heat the oil in a small saucepan over high heat until shimmering and nearly smoking, then pour the hot oil over the eggplant and aromatics to release their flavors. Stir well to combine. Serve immediately, or chill before enjoying.

THE SAUCE

1 fresh red chile, seeded and finely chopped

3 to 5 garlic cloves, to taste, minced

3½ tablespoons soy sauce

1 teaspoon sugar

1 tablespoon Chinkiang black vinegar

½ teaspoon toasted sesame oil

1 pound (450 grams) Chinese or Japanese eggplants (about 3 small)

2 tablespoons thinly sliced scallions, both green and white parts

1 teaspoon ground chile or chile flakes

1 tablespoon vegetable oil

ROOT VEGETABLES

Before the first frost in autumn, farmers lift the tubers in the field from beneath their yellowing leaves—dark brown taro corms; mountain yams long and prickly as a hairy leg; and jewel-toned sweet potatoes and potatoes in fall shades of orange, reddish purple, yellow, and gold. These starchy roots aren't considered staple foods in Chinese cooking but are treated as vegetables and enjoyed in a wide variety of seasoned dishes.

Potatoes are called "earth beans" in the north and "little tubers" or "horse bell tubers" in the south and are often stir-fried in slivers or braised in hearty dishes (Three Treasures of the Earth, page 122). Sweet potatoes are mostly eaten in sweet dishes or roasted whole in coal barrels on the street and eaten as a snack. Mountain yams are used widely in vegetarian Buddhist cuisine as a binder in mock meats due to their intrinsic stickiness, but they can also be stir-fried with vegetables or simmered in soups (Lotus Root Soup with Dried Mushrooms and Peanuts, page 237). Taro is native to Asia and comes as a big, waxy tuber with purplish, starchy flesh or round small corms (奶芋 *nǎiyù*) with slippery, creamy white flesh. It's delicious boiled, steamed, or deep-fried; mashed into a savory or sweet paste; or cooked in savory stews and soups (Coconut Clay Pot Taro and Edamame, page 127).

The most common radish is the white Chinese radish or daikon. It it harvested year-round but is best in the winter, when the white flesh is sweetest, crunchiest, and only mildly spicy. You can eat it raw in salads, marinate it for a crisp, refreshing pickle (Soy Sauce–Pickled Radish, page 112), or cook it in soups or stews until tender and translucent. Like potatoes, carrots are a foreign import, used mostly as an ingredient in stir-fries for added color, although they are delicious stir-fried on their own or with burdock (Stir-Fried Burdock and Carrot Threads, page 124).

SOY SAUCE—
PICKLED RADISH

Jiàng luóbo

醬蘿蔔

MAKES 1 QUART

At the vegetarian restaurant Su Mao in Guangzhou, the chefs make this tangy pickled radish in large batches and serve it as an appetizer, but it's become so popular that they also sell it in small jars for customers to take home. Chef Wen Wenhui famously refused to give this recipe to a visiting diplomat who offered a few thousand yuan for it after an event, but he generously shares his special formula here. The chopped chiles add considerable heat to balance the cooling nature of the radish, so omit them for a milder version. This pickle is ready to eat after 3 days and will continue to mature in flavor over the subsequent weeks.

Scrub the radish well but do not peel it. Trim the ends and halve the radish lengthwise, then halve each piece again lengthwise to yield quarters. Remove the inner core of the radish by slicing ½ inch from each wedge. Cut each wedge into ¼-inch-thick pieces, angling the knife slightly to elongate the slices. Place the radish slices in a large bowl and sprinkle with the salt, tossing to coat. Let sit for an hour, draining the released liquid every 20 minutes.

Meanwhile, make the pickling brine: In a clean, dry wok or saucepan, toast the white peppercorns over medium-low heat until they are fragrant and starting to audibly pop in the pan. Transfer to a small bowl. Add the chiles, vinegar, sugar, and both soy sauces to the peppercorns and stir to combine until the sugar dissolves. Set aside.

Rinse the radish slices thoroughly to wash off all the salt, then gently squeeze them dry in a clean tea towel. Transfer them to a glass jar or container with a tight-fitting lid and pour in the pickling brine so that the slices are barely submerged—they will continue to reduce in size as they pickle. Seal and set in the fridge for at least 3 days. To serve, use clean chopsticks or tongs to transfer the desired amount into a dish, then reseal the rest and return them to the fridge. They will keep for up to 1 month.

1 medium (1¼ pounds /
600 grams) daikon radish

2 teaspoons kosher salt

1 tablespoon whole white
peppercorns

4 or 5 fresh Thai red bird's-eye
chiles, thinly sliced (optional)

¼ cup plus 2 tablespoons
(90 mL) pale rice vinegar

½ cup (100 grams) sugar

¼ cup (60 mL) soy sauce

1½ teaspoons dark soy sauce

STIR-FRIED POTATO THREADS WITH FRAGRANT CHILES

Qiàngchǎo tǔdòusī

熗炒土豆絲

SERVES 4

The humble potato gets a glow-up in this dish, transformed from starchy spud to exquisitely cut stir-fry. The tricky part is not cutting the potato (you can use a mandoline!), but the stir-fry technique to cook them through but keep them slightly crunchy. At my culinary school, the chefs shared their secret: rinse as much starch as possible from the potato slivers, then parboil and salt them briefly, ensuring they cook quickly in the hot wok. Then, dash in a premixed sauce, which quickly laces the potatoes with the perfect balance of savory, salty, and vinegary tang. Combined with the mouthwatering aroma of scorched chiles and Sichuan pepper, you'll get restaurant-quality results at home, every time.

MAKE THE SAUCE: In a small bowl, combine all the sauce ingredients.

PREPARE THE STIR-FRY: Peel the potatoes and cut them into 1/16-inch-thick slices (or use a mandoline), then shingle them horizontally. (You can do this by stacking them back together, then nudging them with your hand to spread them out, shingling them in one line.) Cut the slices into matchstick-width julienne.

Rinse the potato slivers in a bowl of water several times, washing off as much of the starch as possible until the water runs clear. Place the potatoes in a colander or perforated metal bowl and put the bowl in the sink, fanning the slivers out.

Bring about 2 cups (480 mL) water to a boil in a saucepan, then immediately pour the boiling water over the potatoes. Shake them dry, then sprinkle with the salt and toss to coat. After 2 minutes, use a tea towel to pat the potatoes as dry as possible. They should be damp and softened but still crisp.

Heat a wok or skillet over high heat until a bead of water evaporates immediately on contact. Add the oil and swirl to coat the sides of the wok. Reduce the heat to low and add the Sichuan peppercorns and dried chiles. Stir-fry until darkened, about 2 minutes.

Increase the heat to the highest possible heat. Add the garlic and half the sauce, dashing it along the sides of the hot wok to release its flavor. Tip in the potato threads and chile slivers (if using) and stir-fry quickly to coat. Add the remaining sauce and stir-fry for about 30 seconds, tossing briskly until the potatoes are piping hot but still have a crunch to them. Remove from the heat, taste and add more salt if needed, and stir in the chili oil (if using). Serve immediately.

THE SAUCE

2 teaspoons soy sauce

1/4 teaspoon sugar

1/2 teaspoon kosher salt

2 teaspoons Chinkiang black vinegar

1/4 teaspoon MSG

THE STIR-FRY

2 small or 1 large (350 grams) Yukon Gold, russet, or red potato

1/2 teaspoon kosher salt, plus more as needed

2 tablespoons vegetable oil

1/2 teaspoon whole Sichuan peppercorns

5 or 6 dried red chiles, snipped into 1/2-inch segments and seeds shaken out

2 garlic cloves, minced

A few thin slivers of jalapeño or other fresh hot green chile (optional)

1/2 teaspoon Red Chili Oil (page 301; optional)

SPICY DRY-FRIED POTATO

Gānguō tǔdòu piàn

乾鍋土豆片

SERVES 4

Always a crowd-pleaser, this dish is an orchestration of potent Sichuan flavors: bites of golden, piping-hot fried potato slices tossed with salty fermented black beans and red chili bean paste, kissed with the caramelized nutty aroma of Shaoxing wine and interspersed with juicy pieces of pepper and celery. Dry-frying involves no added liquid or starch-thickened sauce, but uses the dry heat of the wok to intensify the flavor of the aromatics and condiments. The crispy potato slices end up coated in all the smoky seasonings.

Peel the potatoes and cut in half lengthwise, then cut them into ½-inch-thick half-moon slices—they will shrink when fried or roasted, so keep them thick.

DEEP-FRY METHOD: In a wok, heat 2 cups (480 mL) oil to 340°F (170°C). Working in batches, drop the potato slices into the hot oil and fry until crispy and browned, about 3 minutes. They should be tender enough to pierce with a chopstick. Remove and drain on a paper towel. Pour the oil into a heatproof container, reserving 1 tablespoon in the wok.

OVEN METHOD: Preheat the oven to 400°F (200°C). Lay the potato slices in a single layer on a baking sheet and drizzle with oil, tossing to coat both sides. Bake the potatoes, flipping once, until the edges are browned, 20 to 25 minutes.

In a small bowl, combine the sugar, ground chile, and cumin.

Heat 1 tablespoon oil in a wok over low heat. Add the Sichuan peppercorns and sizzle in the oil for 3 to 4 minutes, until the peppercorns are darkened. Remove the peppercorns with a slotted spoon and discard, reserving the fragrant oil. Add the dried chiles and stir-fry until fragrant, about 30 seconds. Increase the heat to medium-high and add the fermented black beans and chili bean paste. Stir-fry until the red oil is released, about 30 seconds. Add the scallion whites, garlic slices, fresh chiles, and celery and stir-fry until aromatic, about 30 seconds.

Increase the heat to high and add the soy sauce, then immediately tip in the potatoes and stir to coat. Add the sugar mixture and toss several times until the potatoes are piping hot and coated. Season with salt if needed. Before removing from the heat, add the Shaoxing wine to deglaze the bottom, stirring until you can smell the wine's aroma. Add the scallion greens and serve.

1 pound (450 grams) russet potatoes (about 2 medium)

Vegetable oil, as needed

½ teaspoon sugar

½ teaspoon ground Sichuan chile or chile flakes

½ teaspoon ground cumin

2 teaspoons whole Sichuan peppercorns

4 dried chiles, snipped into ½-inch pieces and seeds shaken out

1 tablespoon fermented black beans, coarsely chopped

1½ tablespoons Sichuan chili bean paste

2 scallions, thinly sliced, white and green parts separated

4 garlic cloves, thinly sliced

2 medium fresh red or green chiles, or 1 bell pepper, seeded and cut into 1-inch pieces

1 wide celery stalk, cut into ½-inch-thick slices, or 3 Chinese celery stalks, cut into 1-inch lengths

1 tablespoon soy sauce

Kosher salt

1 tablespoon Shaoxing wine

HUNGER

飢餓

MY grandparents lived in Harbin for almost their entire lives. Once, during a summer visit, my grandmother took me and my brothers to the top floor of the Dragon Tower in Harbin, where we glided around an azure panorama of the city. She pointed out remnants of the old Russian community from the 1900s: the grand baroque facades of the Orthodox churches, the railways that crisscrossed the city, and the bakeries, theaters, and fashion houses that used to line the polished cobblestone streets. Even the foods eaten by the Chinese Han and Manchu population—the sour cabbage, round *lieba* sourdough breads, and smoked red sausages—reflected the mixed heritage. The only option on the menu at the Dragon Tower was a set Russian meal. As I chatted about our trip, I ate the vegetables from the sides of the meat and fish, trying to remain discreet, but my grandma's sharp eyes missed nothing.

Her disappointment remained even after I tried to explain why I wasn't eating the meat. "You are missing out on so many delicious foods," she said. She kept urging me to try things, as if my choice was a kind of childish stubbornness, and I left feeling frustrated with her lack of understanding, but also guilty, because I knew the meal had been expensive.

But a few days later she let me take her to Ming Jing Garden, a Buddhist restaurant on the outskirts of the city. We ordered fried tofu and slippery morel mushrooms in a dark sauce, a tangy salad of hot peppers and white snow ears, a cumin-pepper "pork" dish made from soy meat, and familiar northeast dishes like stewed string beans and potatoes, millet congee with diced sweet potatoes and stems of chopped greens, and fried rice with local root vegetables. "Each dish has its own taste," my grandmother remarked. She didn't say much else but was visibly impressed, eating in that slow, thorough way of someone who is savoring every mouthful, dishing up portions to fill my brothers' plates between sips of chrysanthemum tea. Downstairs, the restaurant sold artisanal and organic products, including dried shiitake mushrooms, teas, red-yeast quinoa crackers, and multigrain snacks. Free literature on vegetarianism lined a rack in the lobby, promoting nutritional info sessions, multiday Buddhist sightseeing trips, and *fàngshēng* ceremonies to release animals in captivity. As she fingered the pamphlets, I realized it was new to her, this idea of vegetarianism not as a mark of poverty but a conscious lifestyle choice, and coming from my place of privilege, I hadn't understood her wariness about it.

Last year, I was back in Harbin on the occasion of my grandfather's passing. My grandparents' apartment hadn't changed in a decade, with the lingering smell of medicinal balm, the sunflower seeds and shiny-wrapped candies scattered in little bowls on the coffee table, and the Kawai upright piano still in the corner, its dusty keys covered under a red felt cloth and doily. But it was my first time in

Harbin during the winter, and even under the open blue sky and glorious sunshine in the afternoon, I could feel the insidious cold in each sharp breath, the constant threat of frostbite circling around my numb fingertips. That night, the cold was unbearable. My grandmother looked unfazed, even as the shrieking wind nearly knocked me down. "Where are we going for dinner?" she asked.

"Your grandma lived through a time when many people suffered severe malnutrition or died of starvation," my aunt said later. For my grandparents and their parents, keeping warm and staying fed were instincts sharpened and made acute over decades of scarcity. From 1949 to the end of the Cultural Revolution in the late 1970s, there were periods of severe shortage of food in the region, and even basic foods like grains were scarce, let alone meat. Only three of the more than ten kids in my grandmother's family lived until adulthood. Growing up, my parents had coupon books and went to the grain store to pick up rationed amounts of rice, flour, and cooking oil for their families every month. For starches they ate sorghum, millet, and cornmeal, and potatoes and sweet potatoes baked in coal-lined barrels. My grandmother made steamed buns out of cornmeal and soybean pulp with a vegetarian filling of napa cabbage, because meat and white flour were scarce. "They were messy to eat because the dough fell apart easily," my dad recalled. "But we ate them out of a bowl with a spoon."

In the 1980s, the reform era led by Deng Xiaoping allowed freedom in food production, and in the summer, produce trucks would come to the neighborhood bringing crates of tomatoes, eggplants, green beans, and cucumbers. Families lined up to buy heaps of cabbage, which they stored in their underground cellars to eat all winter. "We bought celery and stir-fried it with pork, and that was a luxury," my dad said. Stir-frying required more oil, and it was considered *xìcài*, a "refined" dish, as opposed to the usual stewed dishes (*dùncài*). A palm-size piece of pork, cut into tiny slivers, would last a family for weeks. Chicken appeared

only at special occasions, like weddings and holiday dinners, often stewed with wild mushrooms and chewy glass noodles to make the flavors go further. My dad remembered the pigs that would be slaughtered for Lunar New Year and how they used every part of the animal, making *jiàng zhūtí*, braised pork hoofs; *zhūtóu ròu*, pig's head slices served with a garlicky dipping sauce; and *làcháng*, cold cuts of smoked red sausage with pork jelly. They savored those dishes because they came only a few times a year.

The Chinese appetite for meat today is just catching up to the rest of the world, and the consumption is magnified because of the size of the population. The demand for animal products was motivated by the belief that eating meat and milk were markers of a developed society, but the consumption of meat in China has quickly become a form of overcompensation during the past twenty years, especially as meat is no longer an occasional food but eaten at almost every meal. The interest in vegetarianism is increasing in the mainstream, but the nearness of those decades of famine—and the psychological fear of any possible shortage of food—still haunts Chinese people, especially those of my grandmother's generation. And this profound personal connection around the availability

of meat is something I realize is impossible for me to understand.

That ferociously cold night, we went out to dinner at my grandma's favorite restaurant, an old-style Chinese restaurant in the Xiangfang district. My aunt took charge of ordering, and she asked for mountain yam stir-fried with red peppers and wood ear in a clear sauce, blanched potato threads curled in spools and bathed in a dressing of black vinegar and chili oil, stir-fried romaine lettuce, eggplants braised with potatoes and garlic, and soft glossy ribbons of tofu sheet stewed with green peppers. You can eat all these, my aunt assured me.

She ordered an extra dish of fried sweet potato balls, and we chewed on the sticky morsels between sips of scalding tea as my uncles ate *guōbāoròu*, a sweet-and-sour pork dish. My aunt hadn't touched the meat. "I'm eating vegetarian this week," she explained. It's a Chinese custom to eat vegetarian for significant moments, in observation, in gathering, or in mourning, and she'd joined me to honor my grandfather. My grandmother nodded. In that moment, we all understood something that went beyond the food on the table.

THREE TREASURES OF THE EARTH

Dìsānxiān

地三鲜

SERVES 4

An enduring local favorite in Harbin, this was a dish my parents always looked forward to eating on special occasions while growing up, because in contrast to boiled vegetables or salty relishes, it was so richly flavored, a trio of eggplants, potatoes, and bell peppers fried luxuriously in oil and then braised with garlic and soy sauce. These are all humble, ordinary ingredients, but the combination—silky, buttery eggplant, sweet and juicy peppers, and soft, giving chunks of golden-fried potatoes—always makes my mouth water. My dad says this is the ultimate dish to *xiàfàn,* "send down the rice," and I think it literally pains him to imagine eating this dish without rice, so you're going to have to make some for the full experience. It's the most famous dish to come out of Heilongjiang Province, and you'll find it on the menu at any *dongbei* (northeastern) restaurant.

MAKE THE SAUCE: In a small bowl, whisk all the sauce ingredients until combined.

PREPARE THE STIR-FRY: Trim the ends from the eggplant and roll-cut (see page 83) them into 1½-inch pieces. In a medium bowl, combine 2 cups (480 mL) water and 1 tablespoon salt and whisk to dissolve the salt, then soak the eggplant for 15 minutes. Drain and pat the pieces dry with a tea towel. While the eggplant is soaking, cut the potato into quarters and then roll-cut them to match the size of the eggplant pieces. Slice the bell pepper lengthwise into 1-inch-wide strips and then cut the strips on the diagonal into diamond-shaped pieces to match the size of the eggplant and potato.

Heat the oil in a wok over medium-high heat to 320°F (160°C). Fry the potatoes until golden all over and each piece is tender enough that a chopstick pokes through easily, 6 to 7 minutes. Remove the potatoes with a slotted spoon or spider and drain them on paper towels.

Increase the oil temperature to 350°F (180°C). Fry the eggplant until the cut sides are golden brown and the skin is bright purple and starting to wrinkle, about 4 minutes. Remove and drain the eggplant on paper towels. Add the bell pepper slices and fry briefly for 1 minute, until their edges are turning white under the oil, then lift them out with a skimmer or spider. Pour the remaining oil through a strainer into a heatproof container, reserving 1 tablespoon in the wok.

Return the wok to the stove over medium-high heat. Add the scallions and garlic and stir-fry until aromatic, about 30 seconds. Add the sauce and ½ cup water and bring to a boil. Tip in the fried potato

THE SAUCE

2 tablespoons soy sauce

½ teaspoon sugar

1 tablespoon Shaoxing wine

½ teaspoon potato starch

THE STIR-FRY

2 small Asian eggplants (10 ounces / 280 grams total)

Kosher salt

1 medium russet potato (7 ounces / 200 grams)

1 small sweet red or green bell pepper (5 ounces / 140 grams)

2 cups (480 mL) vegetable oil, for frying

2 scallions, both white and green parts, finely chopped

3 garlic cloves, minced

and peppers, then lower the heat to medium-low and simmer briefly, folding occasionally, until the liquid is reduced by half and starting to thicken, about 2 minutes. Add the fried eggplant, folding gently to incorporate it (so it doesn't fall apart), and simmer for about 1 minute more, until the liquid has reduced into a thick, glossy sauce. Taste and add more salt, if needed. Serve immediately.

ALTERNATIVE ROASTING METHOD: If you'd prefer to roast rather than fry the ingredients, preheat the oven to 425°F (220°C). Place the eggplant and potato pieces on a baking sheet and drizzle with 2 tablespoons oil. Toss to coat. Roast for 10 to 12 minutes, and remove the eggplants when the skin is starting to wrinkle and the potatoes when they are tender enough to poke through easily with a chopstick. Then heat a wok over medium-high heat with 1 tablespoon oil and continue to the final stir-frying step above.

STIR-FRIED BURDOCK & CARROT THREADS

Niúbàng hónglúobo sī

牛蒡紅蘿蔔絲

SERVES 4

In traditional Chinese medicine, burdock is often simmered in soups or teas, but my favorite way to cook the woody root is to sliver it finely and stir-fry it, pairing it with the sweetness of carrots and sugar. Something wonderful happens in the wok with the alchemy of the soy sauce, wine, sesame oil, and caramelized sugar; with burdock's interesting nutty, earthy flavor and appealing chewiness, this dish is so delicious, you just can't get enough of it. Pick the thinnest roots you can find—the larger the root, the more fibrous it'll be—and be sure to soak the slivers in a bowl of water to rinse away as much of the oxidized color on the burdock's surface as possible before stir-frying.

Peel the burdock and cut it crosswise into 3-inch lengths. Cut each piece lengthwise into ⅛-inch-thick slices (or as thin as you can make them), then stack and cut the slices into thin slivers. Soak the slivers in a pan of cold water as you prepare the remaining ingredients. Cut the carrot into matching-size slivers. Before stir-frying, rinse the burdock slivers several times and drain away the darkened water. Shake dry in a colander.

Heat a wok or skillet over medium-high heat until a bead of water flicked onto the surface evaporates within 1 to 2 seconds of contact. Add the vegetable oil and swirl to coat the sides of the wok. Add the dried chiles and sizzle briefly until they start to darken, about 30 seconds. Add the garlic and burdock and stir-fry briskly for 30 seconds, coating them in the oil. Add the carrot slivers, soy sauce, sugar, and mirin and stir-fry for 2 to 3 minutes more, until the burdock and carrot are softened and starting to caramelize and the wine has fully evaporated. Taste and add salt as needed, then remove the wok from the heat, stir in the sesame oil, and transfer the mixture to a serving dish. Sprinkle with the sesame seeds, if desired, and serve immediately.

1 footlong piece (170 grams) burdock root

1 medium carrot

2 tablespoons vegetable oil

3 or 4 dried red chiles, snipped into ½-inch segments and seeds shaken out

3 garlic cloves, finely chopped

1 tablespoon soy sauce

2 teaspoons sugar

1 tablespoon mirin or Shaoxing wine

Kosher salt

½ teaspoon toasted sesame oil

Toasted sesame seeds, for garnish (optional)

COCONUT CLAY POT TARO & EDAMAME

Yēxiāng yùtóu bāo

椰香芋頭煲

SERVES 4

Although taro is often associated in the West with creamy sweet drinks and desserts, its delicious appeal is most obvious in savory dishes. The purple-mottled flesh cooks down to fragrant, meaty bites with a fine-textured starchiness, a quality called 麵 *miàn*, or "floury," and a stick-to-the-roof-of-your-mouth savoriness reminiscent of a hard-boiled egg yolk. This was one of my favorite menu items at Gudian Meiren, a vegetarian restaurant in Taipei, where it was featured alongside other dishes like seitan "ribs" skewered on sugarcane with a tangy hibiscus reduction, braised tofu with bamboo shoots, and crisp roast "duck" on a bed of puffed rice. You won't find coconut milk used traditionally in most regional Chinese cuisines (with the exception of Hainanese), but the influence of South Asian cuisines on modern Chinese cooking can be seen in the growing popularity of dishes with coconut milk, like this one.

In a small bowl, cover the mushrooms with the boiling water and place another bowl or plate on top to weigh them down. Soak for 30 minutes.

Meanwhile, peel the taro and cut it into 1-inch cubes. In a skillet or wok, heat 2 tablespoons of the shallot oil over medium-high heat until shimmering and then add the taro. Sear the taro in the hot oil, flipping occasionally, until golden brown on the edges, about 4 minutes. Remove from the pan.

Drain the shiitake mushrooms, reserving the soaking liquid, snip off and discard the stems, and cut the caps on a diagonal into 3 or 4 thin slices each.

Set a clay pot on or return the wok to the stovetop over medium-low heat and heat the remaining 1 tablespoon shallot oil until it shimmers. Add the ginger and mushrooms and stir-fry until the edges of the mushrooms start to brown and stick, about 3 minutes.

Add the garlic and fermented bean paste and stir-fry until most of the moisture has sizzled out of the paste and it smells delicious, about 20 seconds. Add the cooked taro and edamame, then pour in the stock and coconut milk. Season with sugar and salt to taste—this will depend on the saltiness of your soybean paste.

Cover and cook for 15 to 18 minutes, until the taro has absorbed most of the liquid and is completely cooked through and fork-tender. Add the white pepper, top with the cilantro, and serve immediately.

4 large dried shiitake mushrooms

1 cup (240 mL) boiling water

1 medium (10 ounces / 280 grams) taro root

3 tablespoons Shallot Oil (page 302) or vegetable oil, divided

1 (2-inch) piece (15 grams) ginger, unpeeled, washed and thinly sliced

3 garlic cloves, minced

2 tablespoons fermented soybean paste

1 cup cooked shelled edamame, thawed if frozen

1 cup (240 mL) unsalted stock of any kind or water

½ cup full-fat coconut milk

1 tablespoon sugar

½ teaspoon kosher salt, plus more to taste

¼ teaspoon ground white pepper

Handful of fresh cilantro, both stems and leaves finely chopped

TOFU

In the Western world, tofu is sometimes viewed as a dubious substitute for meat, inferior in its blandness and soft texture. But tofu was never meant to resemble meat. Tofu was likely inspired by milk-curdling techniques of nomadic dairying tribes that roamed the northern steppes—the name came about when the Han Chinese took the Mongol word for "cheese" and applied it to the character for bean, *dòu*. The coagulated soy milk became *dòufǔ*, "bean curdled." Tofu is thus more akin to a dairy product, and it's plain in the same way that unseasoned ricotta or paneer is plain. Treasured for its neutral color and ability to take on sauces and flavors readily, tofu can combine with virtually any ingredient in the wok, and it's said to have *bāoróng de gèxìng*, a "generous nature."

Local experimentations in the thirty-two cuisines of China over the last 2,000 years have produced a jaw-dropping variety of regionally inflected tofu products: the soy milk curds can be set into silky, quivering pudding; pressed into blocks ranging from wobbly soft to firm; stamped into thin, leathery sheets; fried into pillowy cubes and chewy golden slabs; steeped in a spiced broth; smoked with tea leaves; frozen into chewy, spongy blocks; and ripened into a funky, cheese-like relish. Paired with Chinese cooking techniques, these varieties are further transformed into dishes ranging from fragrant and mild (Fragrant Dressed Tofu with Garlic and Basil, page 139) to richly flavorful and saucy (Homestyle Braised Tofu, page 150), from chilled and refreshing (Shredded Tofu Salad, page 142) to bubbling hot and quietly sustaining (Frozen Tofu and Sour Napa Cabbage Stew, page 153).

In China, tofu is seen as frugal and commonplace and rarely rises to the level of haute cuisine, but it's gaining new attention with its artisanal traditions, culinary versatility, and increasing relevance as an environmentally sustainable protein. Nutritionally, tofu is a complete protein containing all nine essential amino acids necessary for human sustenance.

VARIETIES OF TOFU

There are over forty (and counting!) varieties of tofu in China, but the following are some of the common types found in Asian supermarkets and regular grocery stores in the States, and I'm hopeful that more will become available in the near future.

SILKEN TOFU, SOFT TOFU
内脂豆腐，嫩豆腐 nèizhǐ dòufu, nèn dòufu

Silken tofu does not have distinct curds and whey, as it's made by coagulating rich soy milk over low heat and letting it set in the container, without any pressing. The result is a cohesive block with a buttery texture that cuts smoothly. Since silken tofu breaks easily, it shouldn't be used in dishes that require too much handling, and it's best steamed, dressed whole, or scooped into pieces to simmer in soups.

Varieties within silken tofu can be labeled as soft, medium, or firm silken, depending on the brand. Firm silken is interchangeable with soft, non-silken tofu. Some brands of soft tofu are sold in the refrigerated section (I recommend the House Foods brand), whereas others are vacuum-packed in shelf-stable cardboard packages.

MEDIUM OR MEDIUM-FIRM TOFU
中嫩豆腐 zhōngnèn dòufu

This is the tofu of choice in southern China and Taiwan, and in traditional markets, it's the variety the tofu vendors sell fresh. Medium tofu has visible curds and is quite tender. It's great pan-fried, stir-fried, and braised. When deep-fried, the tofu takes on a gloriously chewy skin while retaining a soft, custardy center. In grocery stores, if a block of tofu doesn't specify its firmness, it is most likely medium-firm. My favorite brand is Trader Joe's organic tofu.

FIRM TOFU OR EXTRA-FIRM TOFU
板豆腐 bǎn dòufu

Firm tofu is called *ban doufu* ("board tofu") and is popular in northern China. The curds are tighter, and because of its firm texture, it can be picked up easily with chopsticks. This is an all-purpose tofu that holds its shape well for frying and braising. I recommend Hodo's firm tofu.

PRESSED TOFU
香乾，豆乾 xiānggān, dòugān

Pressed tofu is a category of extra-firm tofu, sold in squares, often in packs of four or eight. Also called dried tofu, the curds are compact and the texture is chewy, sometimes rubbery. Pressed tofu is often smoked or seasoned, and can usually be eaten from the package with little to no preparation.

Five-spice pressed tofu is the most common, made by infusing pressed tofu with soy sauce and five-spice powder (Sichuan peppercorns, ground cassia bark, cloves, fennel seeds, and star anise). Often it's used finely chopped in dumpling and bun fillings. **Smoked pressed tofu** is sold in either flat squares or a log-like roll. Smoked with tea leaves, it's delicious, and the flavor is said to resemble that of ham. It's particularly delightful stir-fried with chives or diced up for fried rice.

For more dishes outside of this chapter that feature pressed tofu, see Stir-Fried Diced Choy Sum and Tofu (page 49) and Stir-Fried Garlic Chives with Pressed Tofu (page 82).

PRESSED TOFU SHEETS
乾豆腐 gāndòufu

Called "dry tofu," these are made by pressing bean curds until they are as thin as cloth and as flexible as leather. They're most often sold packaged in flat stacks of sheets, either refrigerated or frozen. Look for their lightly textured, nubbly surface, a result of pressing the tofu in muslin cloth. A specialty of northeastern China (they're often labeled "dongbei thousand sheets"), chewy *gandoufu* is typically sliced into thin noodles or ribbons for stir-fries and salads, used as a wrap to roll up green onions or slivered raw vegetables, or tied into knots and braised for soups.

SPONGY TOFU, HUNDRED/ THOUSAND LEAF TOFU
百頁豆腐，千葉豆腐 bǎiyè dòufu, qiānyè dòufu

These spongy, pale rectangular blocks are made from soy protein and soybean oil, not coagulated from curds. Commonly available in Asian markets but vastly underrated in the United States, they have an irresistible chewy denseness, very similar to that of a fish cake. I've seen some brands call it "Q-tofu," which conveys the tofu's uniquely bouncy texture. Some brands contain egg white, so be sure to check the label. Spongy tofu is most often enjoyed in soups or hot pots.

DEEP-FRIED TOFU
油豆腐，炸豆腐 yóu dòufu, zhà dòufu

Packages of pre-fried tofu are sold refrigerated in Asian supermarkets, in trays of cubes or triangular wedges. You'll also find tofu puffs (豆腐泡 *dòufu pào*), light, airy tofu cubes that are made with a special leavened curd and hollow in the center. Both varieties absorb sauces beautifully and have a shrunken, chewy golden surface that adds richness to a dish. I prefer to fry my own tofu to control the quality of oil, but these offer a convenient shortcut.

FROZEN TOFU
凍豆腐 dòng dòufu

Freezing tofu changes its cellular structure; the water in the tofu freezes into ice crystals, which pierce the cell walls and leak out when defrosted, thereby removing much of the moisture in the curds. This leaves a marvelously porous tofu that absorbs flavors and sauces greedily. Freezing soft or medium tofu produces a thawed tofu with flaky, porous crevices that is delicious in soups, while freezing firm or extra-firm tofu produces a denser sponge that can withstand stir-frying or braising. You can buy frozen tofu in Asian supermarkets, or simply prepare it yourself by freezing the tofu solid, then letting it defrost in the refrigerator.

FERMENTED TOFU
豆腐乳 dòufurǔ

Fermented tofu is very savory and creamy, with the texture of a soft feta cheese, and used as a flavoring agent or condiment. You'll find it in small glass jars in the condiment aisle of Asian markets. Red fermented tofu (南乳 *nánrǔ*) is a southern version that tastes slightly funkier and sweeter, and it's tinted a deep red color from the red yeast rice in the brine. Other varieties include sesame oil fermented tofu (麻油腐乳 *Máyóu fǔrǔ*), "smelly fermented tofu" (臭腐乳 *chòu fǔrǔ*) which is an alarming gray/bluish-green color and fantastically stinky, and *mala* fermented tofu (麻辣腐乳 *málà fǔrǔ*), flavored with chiles for heat. The flavorful cubes and brine can be mashed into sauces to cook with (Stir-Fried Water Spinach with Fermented Tofu, page 53) or eaten straight in very tiny amounts as a salty relish with congee.

PRESSED TOFU SHEETS

PRESSED TOFU

FIVE-SPICE PRESSED TOFU

SPONGY TOFU

SILKEN, MEDIUM, AND FIRM TOFU

FROZEN TOFU

DEEP-FRIED TOFU

INVENTION

發
明

Soybeans planted below the
    southern mountains
are refreshed in their pods with
    frosty wind.
Grind and let the jade milk flow,
boil and steam to release the
    clear spring.
The color is smoother than the
    earth,
the fragrance stronger than
    chalcedony quartz.
The flavor has more beauty than the
    five grains,
a delicacy you should not
    indiscriminately pass on.

──鄭允端 Zheng Yunduan (c. 1327–1356, Yuan dynasty)

劉玉國 Liu Yuguo is head of Su Mao Tofu in Guangzhou, and was formerly the tofu director of the Dashu Wujie (Vegetarian World without Limits) restaurant in Shanghai. Although he's in his late sixties, he still rises at four every day to make tofu. During my time as an intern at the Su Mao restaurant, I never saw him sitting down; dressed in kitchen whites and rubber boots, his sleeves rolled up to his elbows, he moved about with a bristling, vigorous energy. Master Liu grew up in a village in the northeast, where his grandfather ran a small tofu shop.

"I am the fifth generation tofu maker in my family," he said. When he speaks, he becomes gruffly charming, with a northeastern accent that weighs each syllable. Liu said his grandfather would take him along as he pushed a small cart with a board of tofu to eight villages, a route of over ten miles. Back then, tofu making was powered by muscle. "My grandfather rose at two or three and strapped himself to a heavy quern to grind the soaked soybeans, for several hours," he recalled. To make the tofu, his grandfather collected the bean paste in a giant cloth net and squeezed out the soy milk by hand, then boiled the milk and coagulated it into curd, a process not unlike cheese making. "I learned to make tofu when I was eleven," Liu said, "and I haven't stopped making it since then."

Traditional tofu making had always been passed down in the family. But as young people abandoned their villages and large-scale tofu manufacturers grew in the post-Mao industrialization of the 1980s, factories began using additives to increase shelf life. "People were scared to buy tofu; I knew bosses who would not eat the tofu from their own factories," Liu said. "Just ten grams of 吊白塊 diàobáikuài [a common additive] could kill you." Once a Chinese food associated with gentleness and simplicity, tofu had become a fearful concoction of additives bleached an unnatural white, its natural flavor masked by the bitter, metallic aftertastes of preservatives and emulsifiers.

In their 30-liter buckets, the dusty, pale, hard little soybeans we soaked overnight had swelled into a glossy, buttery yellow mass. I squeezed a bean between my fingers to examine the split halves. "If you see a dip in the center, it means they are not soaked long enough," Liu said. He started a steady trickle of water running into the electric grinder and fed the soybeans into its conical mouth. The machine rumbled, pulverizing the soybeans into an ivory paste, separated into solids and liquid milk. He cooked this soy milk, and at 90° Celsius (194°F), the protein began rising in a foamy mass. "My grandfather would scoop some soybean oil and mix it with a little white ash from the burning firewood," Liu said. "I still use his wood-ash oil instead of artificial defoaming agents." Liu passed a few drips of it over the milk, and as the foam fell in the pot, the entire room filled with a rich, steamy fragrance.

We poured out a pitcher of the soy milk to sample, and I sipped it slowly, cradling the warm bowl in my palms and inhaling deeply. Traditional soy milk is especially fragrant when boiled in a large wok over a woodstove, since the soy milk slightly crusts on the bottom. Liu figured out that he could replicate the subtle aroma by adding some toasted soybeans to the grinder. "This soy milk has the old taste of my hometown," he said.

Coagulating the soy milk into curds requires either a salt or an acid. In southern China, tofu makers traditionally used gypsum (石膏 shígāo) or calcium sulfate, a mineral found in rock layers and deposits from ocean brine and saline lakes. "Shigao produces a more tender tofu," Liu said. The Japanese and northern Chinese prefer bittern (nigari or 鹽滷 yǎnlǔ) or magnesium chloride, derived from boiling seawater, which produces tofu with firmer curds and a subtly sweet aftertaste. Liu dissolved a few teaspoons of gypsum powder into a beaker of water, and as he stirred the solution into the milk, gelatinous clouds started to form. We covered the bucket, and after ten minutes of resting, the milk was fully curdled. I ladled out the wobbly solids and draped them into a cloth-lined square mold, then stacked weights on top to press out the water. Soon, the square boxes were surrounded by pools of yellowish whey. The curds had melded into one ivory block, still warm, with a slight resistance against my palm. With a sharp knife I extracted a thick, quivering slice, holding it up for my colleagues to see. Liu called this "tender" curd; if pressed longer, the tofu would be firmer. He crumbled a block into a bowl, then added a sprinkle of salt and a drizzle of toasted soybean oil and passed it around. I'd never eaten tofu so fresh before—buttery smooth, it glided on my tongue, melting before I could taste it, prompting me to dip in for another bite, and then another. The flavor was sublime but also exquisitely bland, rich with the lingering sweetness and aroma of soy milk.

Although tofu has a mystical, noble provenance—legend says that Liu An, the king of Huainan (in modern-day Anhui Province), accidentally invented it while in search of an elixir of immortality—the ancient food had never shaken off its association with frugality and poverty. It's a cheap, common food in China, not as refined or exalted in tradition as it is in Japan, where tofu, brought over by monks, first entered as a temple delicacy for the samurai class. For the upwardly mobile in China, tofu is an afterthought; my roommate said that ever since her parents could afford meat and seafood regularly, they didn't buy much tofu. "I eat very little tofu myself, although I am a vegetarian, and I am a little ashamed," another colleague said. Her admission echoed exactly how I felt.

I had always viewed tofu as a processed food inferior to whole beans and legumes, being ignorant of how it was made, and I even prided myself on being a vegetarian who didn't resort to tofu to get my protein. But I had internalized the surrounding distaste of a food as indispensable to the Chinese psyche and diet as bread or cheese to the French, and one made and eaten in virtually every regional cuisine in China. Tofu is symbolic of the dogged inventiveness of the Chinese people, who'd found a way to turn hard-to-digest beans into a versatile, gentler substance, a low-cost, land-efficient food that's both tasty and good for you. Standing there, even in that fluorescent-lit room, I realized this block in my hand was the same tofu passed down from generations of tofu makers who had labored over these dried beans; the alchemy of the food had not changed in 2,000 years. My misunderstanding of tofu was being replaced by a glowing sense of pride—this was also *my* heritage, although I'd underappreciated it for so long.

Back in 2006, Liu began to write down his recipes and teach tofu making to students, and he said the growing interest in traditional tofu kept him going, even as he neared his seventies. In a new market of manufactured and often expensive plant-based alternatives, tofu's three-ingredient simplicity and longstanding role in the diet makes it increasingly appealing to modern Chinese cooks and eaters. Liu pulled out his phone to show us some photos of a tofu shop one of his students had opened in Hangzhou last year with her mother. "They can close up by noon and make a comfortable living. *Piaoliang ba,* doesn't it look beautiful?" He beamed like a proud parent. In the future, Liu foresees these small-scale tofu stores could be just as ubiquitous in neighborhoods as milk-tea and coffee shops. "The tradition must keep pace with the times," Liu said. "Honoring heritage is not sticking with the old ways of doing things, but finding new ways to continue it." He patted the squat little grinder, which we had just finished cleaning, then said, "My grandfather would be happy that so many people have eaten his tofu, beyond the eight villages where he pushed our cart."

  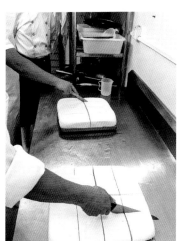

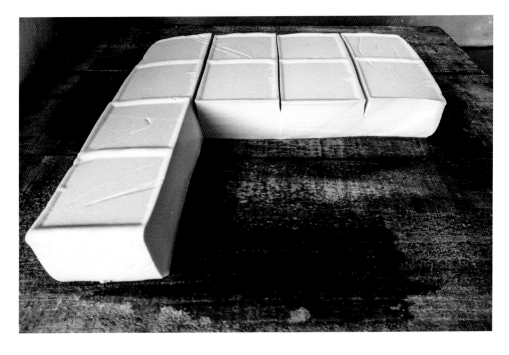

FRAGRANT DRESSED TOFU WITH GARLIC & BASIL

Liángbàn dòufu

涼拌豆腐

SERVES 4

The easiest way to cook tofu is to quickly blanch it, then season with salt and sesame oil and fold in a handful of finely chopped scallions or fresh herbs. This preparation, called *liangban*, is minimal and yet divinely tasty. My favorite version of this dish is with toon (*xiangchun*), a savory, onion-garlicky leaf common in southern China, and after some tinkering, I found that the combination of basil and garlic has a similar aroma that's just as intoxicatingly fragrant, flecking the creamy tofu cubes like a pesto. I probably make this three or four times a week, it's that good.

Cut the tofu into ½-inch cubes.

Bring a saucepan of very generously salted water to a rolling boil. Place a bowl of cold water near the stove. Carefully lower the cubes of tofu into the boiling water with a slotted spoon and let them simmer away for 3 to 4 minutes, until completely heated through. Lift the tofu cubes out and plunge them immediately into the bowl of cold water. Their outside surface will firm up as they cool. Although tofu is already cooked and edible straight from the package, blanching it will infuse it with flavor, firm up its texture, and expel any stale water inside the curd. Drain well and place in a large bowl.

Finely chop the basil and add it to a small bowl with the garlic, sesame oil, MSG, and ½ teaspoon salt, stirring to fully combine and incorporate the ingredients. It should be very fragrant and resemble coarse pesto. Add this sauce to the blanched tofu and fold gently with a spatula until the tofu cubes are evenly coated. Taste and add more salt if needed. At this point, my mom always adds extra nutritional yeast for a delicious boost of savoriness (she loves the stuff). Enjoy immediately or place in the refrigerator to chill before serving.

(recipe continues)

14 to 16 ounces (390 to 450 grams) medium-firm or firm tofu

Kosher salt

2 cups (38 grams) loosely packed fresh basil leaves, preferably Thai basil

2 garlic cloves, minced, or to taste

1 tablespoon toasted sesame oil

¼ teaspoon MSG, or 1 tablespoon nutritional yeast

Variations

TOFU WITH SCALLIONS

Xiǎocōng bàn dòufu

小蔥拌豆腐

This variation is called "little onion mixed with cubed tofu." My parents ate this frequently growing up, and it's cheap, easy, and supremely tasty. Simply omit the basil and garlic in the recipe on page 139 and instead use 3 finely chopped scallions, both white and green parts. My mom will often add a drizzle of soy sauce and scallion oil.

TOFU WITH TOON

Xiāngchūn bàn dòufu

香椿拌豆腐

Toon is a fresh herb that's beloved in Taiwan and southern China. Like curry leaves, it comes from a tree. If you have a Chinese mahogany (*Toona sinensis*) tree growing in your backyard or are lucky enough to find fresh toon in your area (some Asian supermarkets, especially in California, carry it in the springtime), here's the original dish that inspired this recipe.

In the spring, when the leaves are tender, pick the reddish-green shoots and leaves (aim for about 2 packed cups) and wash them thoroughly, removing the woody stems. Blanch them in the same pot of water you used to blanch the tofu. After 1 to 2 minutes, when the leaves are slightly wilted but still vibrant green—you'll start to smell their oniony aroma as they cook—transfer the leaves to a bowl of cold water, then drain them well, squeezing out as much water as you can. Finely chop the toon and use it in place of the basil in the recipe on page 139.

TOFU
FAQ

HOW DO I FREEZE TOFU?

To freeze a pack of tofu, cut the tofu into roughly 2-inch cubes. Place the cubes on a parchment-lined tray and freeze until hardened, then transfer to a zip-top bag or airtight container.

Transfer the bag or container to the refrigerator to thaw slowly overnight, or place on a plate on the counter to thaw quickly at room temperature (about 30 minutes). Gently press the tofu pieces between your palms over the sink or a bowl to break down any remaining ice crystals and drain out the liquid. Use the thawed tofu immediately, or transfer to an airtight container, cover with water, and refrigerate for up to 3 days.

DO I NEED TO PRESS TOFU?

Maybe you've heard you need to press the water out of tofu before cooking with it, to make it firmer and easier to brown in the pan. But I've never seen anyone press tofu in China—weighing the tofu down compresses the curds and makes the tofu less tender, which is undesirable to Chinese cooks. To drain tofu without compressing it, I was taught to soak the tofu in well-salted boiling water for 10 to 15 minutes (if using cut tofu) or simmer it in this water for 3 to 5 minutes (if using a whole block). This seems counterintuitive, but the hot salted water draws the cold water deep inside the tofu's curds to the surface, and after draining, you'll notice the tofu is firmer, too. Removing the cold water is particularly important for pan-fried and fried tofu, as wet tofu will splatter dangerously when you fry it in hot oil. But unlike pressing, this method simultaneously warms up the tofu so that it cooks more evenly, seasons the tofu, and refreshes its flavor by reducing any stale "beany" tastes (豆腥味 dòuxīngwèi). After the tofu is warmed through, simply use a towel to blot the surface dry, and when it feels dry to the touch, it's ready to use.

DO I NEED TO MARINATE TOFU?

Contrary to popular belief, tofu is not very porous.* It is composed mostly of water, and the curds are often too dense to allow marinades to permeate deeper than a few millimeters. You can certainly marinate tofu if you want—it'll probably retain *some* flavor—but it's pretty ineffective, and I've never seen it done in China. Instead, Chinese cooks use heat to infuse tofu with flavor. You'll notice in all tofu dishes that tofu is either soaked or simmered in hot salted water first, or cooked in the marinade or sauce as it bubbles away, so the tofu ends up saturated with all those delicious flavors. Tofu absorbs flavor when it's hot, not when it's cold.

HOW DO I STORE TOFU?

Always store tofu submerged in water to prevent it from drying out. Transfer any leftover fresh tofu from an opened package into an airtight container with enough water to completely cover, and place it in the fridge. Change the water every other day to ensure freshness. You can keep tofu stored like this for up to a week.

The exception to this is tofu that's been frozen, allowing ice crystals to develop, and then thawed, which does have a sponge-like, absorbent interior (see "How Do I Freeze Tofu?" at left).

SHREDDED TOFU SALAD

Liángbàn gāndòufusī

涼拌幹豆腐絲

SERVES 4 TO 6

Back when my parents regularly bought *gandoufu* (fresh tofu sheets), my siblings and I would sneak them out of the fridge and eat the chewy, lightly seasoned sheets straight from the package. They're packed with protein and sturdy enough to slice into thin noodles, and in northeast China, you'll find them tossed in a vibrant salad, laced with a bit of chili oil for heat. This is a great dish any time of year, but it's especially fantastic in the summer.

Separate the tofu sheets and cut them into wide, 4-inch strips (if they're the standard 8-inch-square sheets, just cut them in half). Then cut those strips crosswise into ⅛-inch-thick noodle-like strips—I usually roll them up like a cinnamon roll and slice all the sheets together.

Bring a saucepan of water to a rolling boil. Toss in the tofu noodles and blanch for about 2 minutes, or just until the water returns to a boil, then remove and rinse them under cold water. This will improve the tofu's texture and reduce its beany flavors. Drain in a colander, then squeeze out the water between your hands.

Place the tofu noodles in a large bowl and add the cucumber and cilantro. Place the scallion whites, dried chiles, and garlic on top of the pile of tofu noodles. In a small saucepan, heat the vegetable oil over medium heat until nearly smoking, about 2 minutes. Pour the hot oil over the aromatics to release their fragrance with a loud sizzle. Season with soy sauce, vinegar, salt, sugar, chili oil, and sesame oil and toss well to combine. Taste and adjust the seasoning as desired, adding more vinegar for acidity, sugar for sweetness, and salt as needed. Sprinkle with some sesame seeds and serve immediately.

4 ounces (110 grams) pressed tofu sheets (*gandoufu*)

1 small (4 ounces / 110 grams) Persian cucumber, julienned

Handful of fresh cilantro, stems and leaves cut into 1-inch segments (about ⅓ cup)

2 scallions, white parts only, thinly sliced

3 dried red chiles, snipped into ½-inch segments and seeds shaken out

2 garlic cloves, minced

2 tablespoons vegetable oil

1 tablespoon soy sauce

1 tablespoon pale rice vinegar

½ teaspoon kosher salt

½ teaspoon sugar

1 tablespoon chili oil

1 teaspoon toasted sesame oil

Toasted sesame seeds, for garnish

BRAISED TOFU SHEETS WITH GREEN PEPPER

Jiānjiāo gāndòufu

尖椒乾豆腐

SERVES 4 TO 6

This glossy tangle of chewy tofu ribbons and peppers braised in a velvety, garlic-fragrant sauce is so beloved in the northeast region that it's been dubbed the *guocai*, "national food." Although it looks tame, it's always made with hot green peppers, which lend mouthwatering spiciness. In the wintertime in Harbin, friends will gather in restaurants to gossip and keep warm, and this dish is bound to be on the table. Cooks first blanch the tofu sheets in alkaline water, which tenderizes them and gives them a distinct flavor; you can mimic the effect at home by adding a spoonful of baking soda to the boiling water.

Stack the tofu sheets and cut them into 1-inch-wide strips. Stack the strips, then angle the knife and cut them on the diagonal into diamond-shaped pieces. Cut the pepper into matching-size pieces. Bring a quart of water to a boil in a large wok or pan. Add the baking soda (if using) and blanch the tofu sheets for 2 minutes, stirring as the water turns cloudy. When the water returns to a boil, drain the tofu sheets in a colander.

Meanwhile, make a slurry by combining the starch with 3 tablespoons cold water in a small bowl. Stir until smooth and set aside.

Heat a wok or skillet over medium heat until a drop of water evaporates immediately upon contact, then add the vegetable oil and swirl to coat the sides of the wok. Add the scallion and half the garlic and stir-fry until the garlic is fragrant but not yet browned, about 30 seconds. Swirl in the soy sauce along the sides of the wok to release its flavor, then pour in the stock and increase the heat to high. Once the liquid is bubbling, add the blanched tofu and green pepper and cook for 2 minutes, stirring and folding continuously.

Add the MSG, five-spice powder (if using), and salt to taste and cook until the liquid has reduced by half, 2 to 3 minutes. Give the starch slurry a stir and add it gradually to the wok, stirring until the sauce is thickened and clings to the tofu sheets. Remove from the heat, stir in the remaining garlic and the sesame oil, and serve immediately.

10 ounces (280 grams) pressed tofu sheets (*gandoufu*), thawed if frozen

1 teaspoon baking soda (optional)

2 teaspoons potato starch

2 tablespoons vegetable oil

1 scallion, white part only, smacked with the flat side of a knife and minced

4 garlic cloves, minced, divided

1 tablespoon soy sauce

1½ cups (360 mL) unsalted stock of any kind or water

3 ounces (80 grams) Anaheim, jalapeño, or other hot green pepper (1 long pepper)

¼ teaspoon MSG

¼ teaspoon five-spice powder (optional)

¼ teaspoon kosher salt, plus more to taste

½ teaspoon toasted sesame oil

PAN-FRIED TOFU WITH PICKLED TOPPING

Xiāngjiān dòufu

香煎豆腐

SERVES 4 TO 6

Although simple, there's really nothing better than perfectly pan-fried tofu slices, with their crisp, golden crusts flanking a tender, custardy interior. At the Su Mao restaurant in Guangzhou, Chef Song garnishes the seared slices with spoonfuls of black-green olive preserved mustard greens and seeps a savory sauce in along the sides, darkening the tofu with flavor. Out on the table, this dish is always gone first, snatched up by eager chopsticks. If you don't have the olive preserved greens, you can replace them with pickled salted mustard greens, which brighten each bite with delicious acidic crunch.

MAKE THE SAUCE: In a small bowl, stir together all the sauce ingredients. Set aside.

PREPARE THE TOFU: Halve the block of tofu crosswise, then cut each half into 6 equal slices about ¾ inch thick, for 12 pieces total. In a wok or saucepan, bring 4 cups (960 mL) water and the salt to a rapid boil. Remove from the heat, slide the tofu slices gently into the water—they should be completely submerged—and soak for 3 minutes to heat through. This will expel the cold water from the tofu and firm up its texture.

Place the starch in a shallow bowl or plate.

Transfer the tofu to a clean tea towel to drain. Blot each piece on both sides to make it as dry as possible. Heat a well-seasoned skillet or wok over medium heat. Add 2 tablespoons of the oil and swirl to coat the skillet evenly. When the oil is shimmering, dip each tofu slice in the starch to coat both sides and place them in a single layer in the skillet. Fry, undisturbed, for about 4 minutes, until the bottom has developed a deep-golden crust. Flip each piece to cook the other side, adding a touch more oil if necessary. Depending on your burner, some pieces may brown more quickly than others; move the pieces around in the pan so they get an equal amount of heat. When the tofu is beautifully seared, remove it from the skillet and arrange it in two overlapping rows on a shallow serving dish.

Spoon the preserved vegetables on top of the tofu and finish with the cilantro and red chile slices. Give the sauce a stir and pour it carefully into the bottom of the dish, letting it seep in from the sides of the tofu to avoid staining the tops. You could also serve it on the side as a dip. Serve immediately.

THE SAUCE

2 tablespoons soy sauce

2 tablespoons hot water

1 teaspoon sugar

½ teaspoon toasted sesame oil

¼ teaspoon ground white pepper

THE TOFU

14 to 16 ounces (390 to 450 grams) medium or medium-firm tofu

1 tablespoon kosher salt

¼ cup potato starch or cornstarch, for coating

4 tablespoons vegetable oil, for pan-frying

2 tablespoons olive preserved greens (*ganlancai*) or Pickled Mustard Greens (page 306)

A few sprigs of fresh cilantro, for garnish

1 small red chile, seeded and thinly sliced, for garnish

HOMESTYLE BRAISED TOFU

Jiācháng dòufu

家常豆腐

SERVES 4 TO 6

Before stir-frying tofu, Chinese cooks will often pan-fry or shallow-fry it to develop a golden skin—the puckered surface makes it more flavorful, and the interior becomes spongier, soaking up the sauces in the wok. The Sichuan version of this homestyle dish uses spicy chili bean paste (*doubanjiang*) to lend a spicy aroma and coat the tofu in a deep-red slick of flavor, but an equal amount of fermented soybean paste, vegetarian oyster sauce, or preserved black beans serve the same savory-boosting function. Feel free to replace the dried wood ear or shiitake mushrooms with a handful of thinly sliced fresh mushrooms.

In a small bowl, soak the shiitake mushrooms in boiling water for 30 minutes. Drain, snip off and discard the stems, and halve the caps.

In a wok or saucepan, bring a few cups of generously salted water to a boil. Add the tofu slices and let soak for 3 to 5 minutes, then remove and blot dry with a clean tea towel.

Combine the starch with 1 tablespoon cold water in a small bowl.

Heat ½ cup oil in a wok or skillet, or enough to cover the pan's bottom by about ½ inch. When the oil is hot and shimmering, slide in as many tofu pieces as will fit in a single layer on the surface. Don't move the tofu until a golden crust develops on one side, about 4 minutes. Flip and cook on the other side for about 3 minutes, transfer to a paper towel–lined plate, and repeat until all the tofu is golden brown, crispy, and slightly puffy. Transfer the frying oil to a heatproof container for another use, reserving 1 tablespoon in the wok.

Return the wok to medium-high heat. Stir-fry the shiitake mushrooms, garlic, ginger, and scallion whites until fragrant, about 2 minutes. Push the aromatics to one side of the wok, then add the chili bean paste and stir-fry briefly to release its flavor. Add the soy sauce, stock, and sugar, and stir to combine. When the liquid is bubbling, add the fried tofu and carrot. Cover the wok and cook gently for 3 to 4 minutes to allow the tofu to absorb the flavors.

Uncover and add the snow peas. Return the heat to high and cook, stirring, until the liquid has reduced. Taste and adjust the flavors, adding more salt as needed. Give the starch slurry a stir and add it gradually to the wok, stirring continuously for 30 seconds, until the sauce is slightly thickened and clings to the tofu. Remove from the heat and stir in the scallion greens. Transfer to a dish and serve.

---

3 large dried shiitake mushrooms, or ¼ ounce (7 grams) dried wood ear mushrooms

Boiling water

Kosher salt

14 to 16 ounces (390 to 450 grams) medium-firm tofu, cut into ½-inch-thick slices

½ teaspoon potato starch or cornstarch

Vegetable oil, for frying

1 tablespoon finely chopped garlic

1 tablespoon finely chopped fresh ginger

2 scallions, white parts cut into 1-inch segments, green parts thinly sliced and reserved for garnish

1½ tablespoons Sichuan chili bean paste

1 teaspoon soy sauce

1¼ cups (300 mL) unsalted stock of any kind or water

½ teaspoon sugar

½ cup thinly sliced (¼-inch) carrot (cut into semicircles or diamonds)

½ cup snow peas or green pepper, cut to match the carrot

SOFT TOFU *W*ITH BLACK BEAN SAUCE

Dòuchǐ nèndòufu

豆豉嫩豆腐

SERVES 4 TO 6

I taught English for a year in Tamsui, a northern port town outside Taipei, and if I managed to commute there early I would grab a quick lunch at a vegetarian lunch canteen across the street. It was tucked into the back of a produce market and you'd miss it passing by, but show up at lunchtime, and the place would be packed, noisy with the clinking of stainless-steel chopsticks and the chatty elderly Buddhist vegetarians. For about three US dollars, you could pick five stir-fries from behind the counter, and they heaped a round pat of steamed mixed purple rice on the plate (and handed you a bowl for unlimited self-serve seaweed soup, to boot).

Out of all their dishes, my favorite was this stew with soft cubes of tofu swimming in a soothing, glossy, thickened sauce, dotted with savory bits of fermented black soybeans. If Mapo Tofu (page 159) is the fun, fiery one, then this is her low-key and cozy sister. Be sure to use soft tofu for this dish. Underrated in a world where firmness is supreme, it's delicate and breaks easily, but in a scoopable, bubbling stew like this, that's exactly what you want.

Cut the tofu into ¾-inch cubes and set aside.

Make a slurry by combining the starch with 3 tablespoons cold water in a small bowl. Stir until smooth and set aside

Heat a wok over medium heat until a drop of water evaporates immediately upon contact, then add the oil and swirl to coat the sides. Add the scallion whites, ginger, and garlic and stir-fry until the garlic is fragrant but not yet browned, about 30 seconds.

Add the fermented black beans and stir-fry briefly to sizzle and release their flavor.

Add the stock, soy sauce, salt, and sugar. When the liquid is bubbling, gently add the tofu and reduce the heat to medium-low.

Cook the tofu for about 2 minutes, gently moving the wok under the tofu instead of stirring. Give the slurry a stir and add half to the wok, using a spatula to fold it into the sauce until it thickens, then repeat with the remaining slurry. Remove from the heat and garnish with the sesame oil, white pepper, and scallion greens.

14 to 16 ounces (390 to 450 grams) soft tofu or firm silken tofu

1 tablespoon potato starch

2 tablespoons vegetable oil

2 scallions, thinly sliced, white and green parts kept separate

1 tablespoon finely chopped ginger

1 tablespoon finely chopped fresh garlic

2 tablespoons fermented black beans, rinsed, drained, and coarsely chopped

1 cup unsalted stock of any kind or water

1 teaspoon soy sauce

½ teaspoon kosher salt

1 teaspoon sugar

½ teaspoon toasted sesame oil

Dash of ground white pepper

FROZEN TOFU & SOUR NAPA CABBAGE STEW

Suāncài dùn dòngdòufu

酸菜燉凍豆腐

SERVES 4 TO 6

I first learned to freeze tofu from the internet—the process makes it porous and delightfully spongy (see box on page 141)—but my mom told me frozen tofu has been a mainstay of northern China for centuries. Most people didn't have freezers at home, so they had to buy it frozen from tofu vendors or set tofu outside during the winter. Once thawed, the sauce-absorbing chunks would be used in hot pots and stews.

My sister says this is her favorite recipe in the whole book. There's just something so cozy about a stew filled with chewy glass noodles with the big hunks of tofu soaked heavy with hot, savory broth, the acidity from the sour cabbage balanced by the sweetness of the cooked onions, and a slight warming heat from the chiles and ginger.

Soak the noodles in a bowl of warm water to soften, about 30 minutes.

Lay the sour Chinese cabbage leaves flat on the cutting board and, with the blade parallel to the cutting board, slice each thick stem in half. Cut the stems and leaves into ⅛-inch shreds against the grain.

Heat a seasoned wok over medium-high heat and add the oil, swirling to coat the sides. When the oil is shimmering, add the onion, scallions, ginger, and star anise and stir-fry until the spices have released their aromas and the onion is softening and becoming translucent, 4 to 5 minutes.

Add the red chiles and sour cabbage and stir-fry briefly to release the sour flavors of the cabbage. Add the soy sauce and five-spice powder and stir to incorporate.

Transfer everything from the wok into a large clay pot and set it over medium-low heat. (If you don't have one, keep everything in the wok.) Tip in the stock and add the tofu.

When the liquid comes to a boil, reduce the heat to maintain a gentle simmer and cook, stirring occasionally, for 20 minutes until the sour cabbage has softened.

Drain the glass noodles, add to the pot, and simmer for 10 minutes, until the noodles are tender but still slightly chewy. Taste and add salt if needed. Serve immediately.

3 ounces (85 grams) sweet potato vermicelli

10 ounces (280 grams) pickled sour Chinese cabbage, either homemade (page 309) or store-bought

3 tablespoons Shallot Oil (page 302) or vegetable oil

1 small yellow onion, diced

3 scallions, white parts only, finely chopped

1 (2-inch) piece (15 grams) unpeeled fresh ginger, thinly sliced

1 star anise pod

4 dried red chiles, seeded and halved lengthwise

1 tablespoon soy sauce

½ teaspoon five-spice powder

4 cups (960 mL) unsalted stock of any kind or water

14 to 16 ounces (390 to 420 grams) frozen medium or firm tofu, thawed, cut into 3-inch cubes, then halved into triangles

1 teaspoon kosher salt, plus more to taste

STICKY SESAME SPONGY TOFU

Zhīmá bǎiyè dòufu

芝麻百頁豆腐

SERVES 4 TO 6

Spongy tofu (see page 131) is a tofu made of soy protein with a delicious bouncy, fish-cake-like texture. Although it's little known in the States, it is available at most Asian supermarkets—look for it in the refrigerated or frozen soy-product section. At the Liansu Kongjian vegetarian restaurant in Harbin, the chefs cut the tofu into thick batons and toss it in a barbecue-style sauce that's slightly sweet and a bit spicy, with nutty sesame and fragrant cumin. The batons are arranged in a beautiful stack, and the irresistible flavors coating the chewy, soft, bouncy tofu fingers make this one of their most popular offerings. If you can't find spongy tofu, substitute firm tofu instead.

MAKE THE SAUCE: In a small bowl, combine all the ingredients for the sauce, stirring until smooth and the sesame paste is fully incorporated. Set aside.

MAKE THE SPICE MIXTURE: In another small bowl, combine all the ingredients for the spice mixture. Set aside.

PREPARE THE STIR-FRY: Cut the tofu into batons about ½ inch wide, ½ inch thick, and 3 inches long.

Heat the oil in a wok over high heat. Fry the tofu in batches until golden brown—each baton will expand and become puffy but will deflate when removed from the oil. Drain the fried tofu on a paper towel–lined plate. Pour the oil into a heatproof container for another use, reserving 2 tablespoons oil in the wok.

Return the wok to medium heat. Add the garlic and briefly stir-fry it in the reserved oil until fragrant but not yet darkened, about 30 seconds. Reduce the heat to low, then add the sauce mixture and stir as it comes to a boil. Add the fried tofu and the spice mixture and toss until each baton is evenly coated. Stir in the cilantro, arrange on a plate, and serve immediately.

THE SAUCE

2 tablespoons Chinese sesame paste, homemade (page 305) or store-bought

2 tablespoons soy sauce

1 tablespoon vegetarian oyster sauce

1 tablespoon Shaoxing wine

1 tablespoon sugar

THE SPICE MIXTURE

2 tablespoons toasted sesame seeds

2 teaspoons ground cumin

½ teaspoon five-spice powder

¼ teaspoon ground red chile or cayenne pepper

THE STIR-FRY

14 to 16 ounces (390 to 450 grams) spongy tofu (*qianye doufu*) or firm or extra-firm tofu

1 cup (240 mL) vegetable oil, for frying

2 garlic cloves, minced

3 tablespoons finely chopped fresh cilantro, for garnish

SWEET & SOUR TOFU

Gūlu dòufu

咕噜豆腐

SERVES 4 TO 6

The Cantonese technique of frying an ingredient until crispy and tossing it in a sweet-and-sour sauce has been popularized in Chinese restaurants in the States, but the dish originated in Guangzhou, where it was beloved among the first foreign guests and diplomats during the Qing dynasty. In addition to sweet-and-sour tofu, you'll often see lotus root, fried gluten, and even battered potato balls sauced this way in vegetarian restaurants. And don't be surprised by the ketchup—this Western import caught on in the 1960s in Hong Kong, when chefs enthusiastically adopted ketchup into their *tángcù* dishes, making use of the condiment's sweetness, glossy red color, and natural umami.

The flavors here should be a balance of vinegary and sweet, the sauce just thick enough to glaze each piece of tofu yet keep each piece's sheath crispy. The pineapple is optional, but it adds delightful bites of juicy sweetness. At the Yi Xin vegetarian restaurant in Guangzhou's Tianhe district, they serve the morsels tumbling out of a hollowed-out pineapple. It's addictively delicious, and the chewy tofu cubes, coated in a sweet-sharp, tangy sauce, have converted many tofu-skeptical friends.

MAKE THE SAUCE: Combine all the sauce ingredients in a small bowl and stir until smooth.

PREPARE THE STIR-FRY: Fill a heatproof bowl with a couple cups of boiling water, generously salt the water, and soak the tofu in it for 10 minutes. Remove the tofu, blot it dry with a clean tea towel, and cut it into ¾-inch cubes.

Heat the oil in a wok over medium-high heat to 370°F (195°C), or until the tip of a wooden chopstick forms a merry stream of bubbles when inserted. In the meantime, put the starch in a shallow bowl and coat each piece of tofu with the starch, tapping them to shake off the excess, then set the pieces on a plate near the stove.

When the oil is ready, add half the tofu and fry until each cube has puffed up and developed a deep golden skin, 5 to 6 minutes. Drain the fried tofu on a paper towel–lined plate. Allow the oil to come back up to temperature and repeat with the remaining tofu.

(recipe and ingredients continue)

THE SAUCE

3 tablespoons ketchup

1 tablespoon pale rice vinegar

2 tablespoons Shaoxing wine

2 tablespoons sugar

1 teaspoon soy sauce

THE STIR-FRY

Boiling water

Kosher salt

14 to 16 ounces (390 to 450 grams) firm or extra-firm tofu

2 cups (480 mL) vegetable oil, for frying

½ cup potato starch or cornstarch, for coating

½ cup (50 grams) 1-inch pieces red or green bell pepper

After all the tofu is fried, add the bell pepper and carrot to the hot oil and fry briefly to parcook, lifting them out after 10 seconds. Pour the oil into a heatproof container and reserve for another use, leaving 1 tablespoon in the wok.

Heat the wok again over medium heat until the oil is shimmering. Add the scallions, ginger, and garlic and stir-fry briefly until fragrant, about 30 seconds. Add the pineapple chunks and fry until the edges soften, about 30 seconds. Pour in the sauce mixture and stock. Bring the liquid to a boil.

Return the fried tofu cubes, carrot, and bell pepper to the wok and fold a few times to incorporate and absorb the sauce, about 2 minutes. Taste and add salt, if needed. If there is still some liquid left in the bottom of the wok, turn the heat up to high and reduce the sauce to a glaze that clings to the tofu. Immediately transfer to a serving dish and serve.

½ cup (60 grams) thinly sliced carrot (cut into ¼-inch-thick semicircles or diamonds)

2 scallions, white parts only, thinly sliced

1 tablespoon peeled and minced fresh ginger

1 tablespoon minced fresh garlic

¾ cup pineapple chunks, drained if canned, cut into bite-size pieces

¼ cup unsalted stock of any kind or water

MAPO TOFU

Mápó dòufu

麻婆豆腐

SERVES 4 TO 6

After grad school, I traveled to Sichuan Province, where my friend's mom insisted that I taste mapo tofu in Chengdu, its place of origin. The spicy, numbing braised dish of soft tofu was created in 1862 by a woman surnamed Chen. She was called Mapo, or "pockmarked elderly woman," due to the smallpox scars on her face, and she operated a stand outside the northern gates of Chengdu that catered to local workers. Her tofu dish was a sensation, soon imitated by other chefs in the city.

At culinary school, I learned how to make the vegetarian version of the dish from Chef Li, a Sichuanese chef, who explained that the four essential ingredients are the fermented black beans, chili bean paste, ground Sichuan peppercorns, and ground red chiles—everything else was negotiable. He used minced shiitake mushrooms in place of the ground beef and taught me to thicken the dish with three rounds of starch slurry, until the tofu was suspended in a silky, viscous sauce. We toasted fresh red peppercorns in oil and ground up more peppercorns to sprinkle on the dish for the famous numbing sensation, and suddenly all the elusive, seductive aromas were effortlessly alive. It tasted exactly as I'd remembered.

Soak the mushrooms in hot water for 30 minutes to rehydrate, then drain, stem, and finely chop them.

Bring a pot of salted water to a boil. Reduce the heat to low, add the tofu cubes, and simmer gently for 10 minutes to refresh the tofu's flavors and firm it up.

Make a slurry by combining the starch with ¼ cup cold water in a small bowl. Stir until smooth and set aside.

Heat a wok over medium heat until a bead of water evaporates immediately upon contact. Add the oil, swirling to the coat sides of the wok. Reduce the heat to low. Add the whole Sichuan peppercorns and dried chiles and stir-fry for 1 to 2 minutes to infuse the oil with flavor, until the chiles are slightly darkened in color and aromatic. Do not burn them. Remove from the heat. Using a slotted spoon, remove and discard the spices, leaving behind the aromatic oil.

Return the wok to medium-high heat and add the mushrooms, ginger, and garlic. Fry for 1 minute, until the mushrooms are beginning to brown. Scoot them up one side of the wok.

(recipe and ingredients continue)

4 or 5 dried shiitake mushrooms

Kosher salt

14 to 16 ounces (390 to 450 grams) firm tofu, cut into ¾-inch cubes

1 tablespoon potato starch

3 tablespoons vegetable oil

2 teaspoons whole Sichuan peppercorns

5 dried red chiles, cut into ¾-inch segments and seeds shaken out

1 tablespoon peeled and minced fresh ginger

1 tablespoon minced fresh garlic

1 tablespoon fermented black beans, coarsely chopped

2½ tablespoons Sichuan chili bean paste

Add the fermented black beans, chili bean paste, and ground chile and stir-fry briefly for 10 seconds to release their fragrance. Pour in the stock, then add sugar and soy sauce. Bring the liquid to a boil.

Lift the tofu cubes from the hot water with a slotted spoon and place them gently in the wok. To keep them from breaking, don't stir; instead, move the wok in a swirling motion, shifting the sauce as it bubbles under the tofu. Bring to a full boil.

Give the starch slurry a stir and drizzle about a third of it into the wok, swirling the wok gently to mix in the slurry as the liquid thickens. Repeat this two more times, until the sauce is glossy and clings to the tofu, then remove the wok from the heat and transfer everything to a serving dish. Sprinkle with the scallions and the ground peppercorns (these provide the tingly mouthfeel) and serve.

1 teaspoon ground Sichuan chile or chili flakes

1 cup unsalted stock of any kind or water

½ teaspoon sugar

1 teaspoon soy sauce

2 scallions, green parts only, thinly sliced, for garnish

½ teaspoon ground Sichuan peppercorns

TOFU SKIN

Tofu skins, also called soy milk skins or soy skins, are delicate sheets of soy milk protein that have become an indispensable part of the Chinese kitchen. They were once considered an annoyance to tofu makers, who had to stir the milk constantly to prevent a skin from forming, but soon discovered that when the film was lifted off the simmering soy milk, it became a flexible and creamy sheet of protein that could be eaten fresh or dried in the sun. First recorded in *Bencao gangmu* (1596) by Li Shizhen, the father of traditional Chinese medicine during the Ming dynasty, the skins are considered sweet and neutral in nature and rich in fat and protein, and they contain eighteen trace minerals. Buddhist monks layered and steamed the chewy, meaty skins, molding them into vegetarian chicken, duck, and ham in temple and banquet cuisine.

Both tofu and tofu skin are birthed from soy milk, but tofu is coagulated with the addition of minerals or acid, whereas the skins are formed simply by heat and contact with air. Since the skins are not made of curds and do not break easily, their ability to stay distinct in layers and structure even after cooking makes them endlessly versatile as a vegan protein. With their creamy, pale-yellow folds, they can be "scrambled" like eggs for stir-fries (Stir-Fried Tofu Skin and Tomato, page 175) or bun fillings (Chive-Stuffed Boxes, page 272), chopped finely and browned into crispy golden patties (Pan-Fried Tofu Skin Cakes, page 171), or braised in a spicy broth until they soften into juicy, meaty segments with a chewy edge (Braised Tofu Skins in Chili Bean Sauce, page 189).

VARIETIES OF TOFU SKIN

Also known as *yuba*, its Japanese name, tofu skin has numerous Chinese names and even more English translations, so it can be confusing to locate it in the Asian grocery store. I usually refer to it as tofu skin or soy skin, but it's also called bean curd skin, bean packets or bean bags, thousand sheets, soy sheets or soy chips, bean curd spring roll skins, oil skin, tofu bamboo or bean curd sticks, and even bean curd robes or lingerie!

Sometimes, tofu sheets (*gandoufu*, see page 131) are mislabeled as tofu skins. This is confusing, but the former is usually dry-textured like cloth and opaque in color with a thick, leathery sturdiness, whereas tofu skin is yellowish with a smooth wetness, resembling a wrinkly wad of very thin folds.

FRESH OR FROZEN TOFU SKIN
豆腐皮，豆皮，豆包 dòufupí, dòupí, dòubāo

Because they dry out almost immediately, freshly pulled soy milk skins are folded several times into compact wads or rolled into sausage-like batons to preserve their moisture. Fresh tofu skin is often sold by Asian supermarkets or local tofu vendors that already make tofu and soy milk, so if you see fresh tofu, ask if they also carry tofu skin. In many Asian grocery stores, tofu skin is most often available frozen in 10- or 12-ounce packs and resembles dark-yellow, sturdy flat chips—soak them in a bowl of warm water for an hour and they'll soften and regain their creamy ivory color.

SEMI-DRIED TOFU SKIN SHEETS
豆腐皮，千張 dòufupí, qiānzhāng

Often called bean curd sheets or bean curd spring roll skins, these giant, semitranslucent sheets come as circles, semicircles, or squares, usually laid flat in the frozen section. Each one is a single film that has been lifted off soy milk and then partially dried. They resemble oilcloth, but when brushed with liquid, they rehydrate into a thin skin that's flexible enough to wrap, roll, and stack in layers. When left out, the tofu skin sheets will dry out and crack easily, so store them in their bag in the freezer. The sheets have tough, bunched edges that should be trimmed off like string.

DRIED TOFU SKIN STICKS
腐竹 fǔzhú

When bunched and hung over a line to dry, the skins become brittle, rigid, and U-shaped and are called "tofu bamboo." You can find these dried sticks in the shelf-stable section of Asian supermarkets. These are hard and snap easily, but when rehydrated, they become chewier than fresh tofu skin. Save the leftover broken bits in the bag to make Mushroom Congee with Tofu Skin and Greens (page 286).

FRIED TOFU SKIN
油豆皮，炸豆皮，油皮

yóudòupí, zhàdòupí, yóupí

There are two kinds of fried tofu skin. When you deep-fry fresh tofu skins, the flexible, rectangular wads become crispy and dimpled, with a rich golden crust. These are sold with fresh tofu skin and can be shredded or chopped up for stir-fries. When you fry dried tofu skin sticks directly, they puff up into bubbly, brittle, Styrofoam-like sheets that soften in hot pots and soups, adding lovely richness. You'll find them in the shelf-stable section.

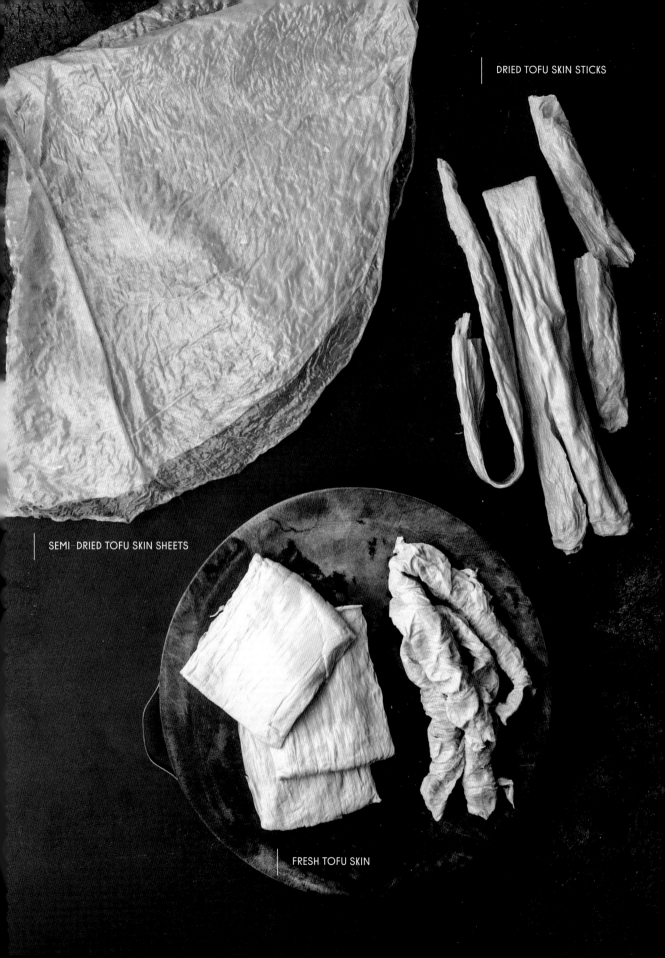

DRIED TOFU SKIN STICKS

SEMI-DRIED TOFU SKIN SHEETS

FRESH TOFU SKIN

TRADITION

傳統

THE Yongshun Tofu Skin Factory, situated between a small fruit shop and a secondhand furniture store, is in an unassuming neighborhood in the Yingge district outside Taipei. When I visited, plumes of steam rose from the roof into the 4 a.m. sky. I peered through the door and saw 蘇水木 Master Su Shuimu bent over a steaming wok, wearing a T-shirt and sandals. A portable radio was playing music from a Hokkien station. *"Zao-an,"* I greeted him. "You startled me," he said, laughing. "Come in, come in."

Inside the workshop, the air was warm and humid, and a low light illuminated the corner where the woks stood, shrouding the rest of the room in darkness like a cave. Shuimu was standing over two giant woks of fresh soy milk that his brother had made. Each wok was about three feet in diameter, set into a brick stove and lit underneath by a low gas flame. Shuimu had been making soy skins for the past three hours. He switched on a whirring mini fan, and the top of the milk shimmered and thickened, radiating outward from the center until the full surface of the liquid formed a thin membrane. "We used to wave a bamboo fan over the milk to cool it by hand, before these electric fans," he said. When the skin became wrinkly, thickened into a creamy tan color, Shuimu switched off the fan and ran a small knife around the edge of the skin, detaching it from the wok. Quickly selecting a flexible bamboo branch from a barrel, he slid the stick underneath the center of the skin and began pulling it toward the left of the wok, up and off the surface. A giant quivering sheet rose from the pot, perfectly round like a moon, immediately adhering onto itself into a semicircle. Shuimu set it across a rack to cool.

Su Shuimu recently turned seventy-three, and he's a second-generation tofu-skin maker in the family. Together with his brother 蘇鴻義 Su Hongyi, he's taken over the family business. Making these skins is a nocturnal occupation, and he enjoys the solitude of working at midnight. "The weather is cooler and more humid, and the *doupi* is less likely to break or shrink," he said. As he talked, he continued pulling skins off the pots of milk, switching between right and left hands with practiced ease. "Sometimes a bubble will form and the skin will crack," Shuimu said. "But that does not happen very often. I have had sixty years of practice." Hongyi, his younger brother, appeared at five. "As you can see, this old man has been here long before me," Hongyi said, clapping him on the back. He reached over and silenced the loud music from his brother's radio. Shuimu grunted, still hovering over his two woks like a watchful guard, his eyes fixed on the forming skins.

Shuimu said their father used to be just one of many tofu-skin makers in the village. "It was a flourishing industry, but then factories came and started producing tofu skin at a fraction of the cost," Hongyi said. Today, the Su brothers' shop is one of the few handcrafted tofu-skin shops left in Taiwan. I watched as Shuimu topped off the pot with soy milk from a nearby bucket. "Making soy milk skins is a kind of practice, it requires patience," he said. "In the summer, I will be soaked in sweat since I am standing for ten to twelve hours over steaming woks. But I enjoy it. Because it takes so long to form each skin, they are precious to eat." Although the skins were traditionally used to make mock meats in banquet cuisine, Shuimu said they were also good for everyday cooking—most of their customers cut up the skins and use the sheets in stir-fries and soups. He cracked off a piece from a sheet and handed it to me. It was dried and translucent, but as I chewed, the strip softened in my mouth, melting into a silky, tender chewiness. "Usually machine-made tofu skin is very thin, but ours is more Q [chewy] and has a better taste," Shuimu said.

Unexpectedly, the business has actually grown in the last few years in response to an expanding market for artisan traditional foods—both from consumers and vegetarian restaurants—and the brothers are trying to keep up with the demand. They were recently profiled in a documentary for Taiwan's arts and culture department. "Last week, a class of third or fourth graders came on a field trip to watch us, to learn about traditional Chinese handicraft," Hongyi said, chuckling.

"This business has kept our family together," Shuimu said. Outside, the sky over the river was lightening into a grayish blue with a streak of magenta red. His grandson came in, ducking his tall head through the door, and took two bamboo trays piled with tofu skins out into the house, laying them on a table. I watched as he stacked eight at a time and used a sharp knife to release the skins onto the table, in one swift, slicing motion. He said he works at an internet company but tries to come by every morning he can to help prepare the skins for delivery.

In the shop, they also sell sheets wrapped into seasoned vegetarian chicken rolls and fried *doupi* snacks, sweet crispy sticks dotted with sesame seeds. I bought one for the bike ride back to Taipei and went back out to the shed, where Shuimu was still pulling skins away. He was almost halfway done—he'd made nearly 200 tofu skins already and planned to stop at 400 that day. He told me about one of his granddaughters, whom he'd taught to make tofu skins every time she visited. After college, she began working at a company, but a year later realized she loved the family craft better. "She has just opened her own shop, in Taipei City," Shuimu said, smiling. He set the skin he'd just made on a beam above, to join a row of nearly a hundred skins hanging under the low rafters, half-moons drying in the warm glow of the ceiling light.

HANNAH CHE

PAN-FRIED TOFU SKIN CAKES

Dòupí bǐng

豆皮餅

SERVES 4

This oddly delicious creation of minced and mashed tofu skin, shaped and pan-fried into savory little cakes, always reminds me of Korean *pajeon* seafood pancakes, with their hot, crisply browned exterior and pleasantly soft, slightly gooey center. The diced carrot, cilantro, pickled greens, and pearly jicama stud the chewy tofu skin batter with bits of crunch and color, but you can use chopped scallions, fresh mushrooms, or whatever you have in your fridge. With a dip of chili oil and vegetarian oyster sauce, these cakes make a fantastic snack or appetizer.

Soak the dried mushrooms in boiling water for 30 minutes, or until softened. Drain, snip off and discard the stems, and finely chop the caps.

Bring a pot of well-salted water to a boil and blanch the carrot, jicama, and mushroom for 1 to 2 minutes, until they're slightly softened. Remove with a slotted spoon and drain.

Chop the tofu skins as finely as you can. If you have a food processor, pulse them a few times until they form a loose, cream-colored batter. Using your hands, gently squeeze out any excess liquid. Transfer the tofu skins to a bowl and stir in the blanched carrot, jicama, mushrooms, pickled mustard greens, and cilantro. Season with vegetarian oyster sauce, sugar, white pepper, and ½ teaspoon salt, tasting and adjusting the seasonings as necessary; the cakes should be quite flavorful.

Add the flour and potato starch to the batter, squeezing the dry ingredients into the tofu skin mixture and incorporating everything with your fingers until the dough comes together and can be formed into balls. Add additional flour, if necessary, for the dough to hold together. Roll the dough into balls roughly 2 inches in diameter and press them gently between your palms to flatten each into a pancake about ¾ inch thick.

Heat a skillet over medium-high heat until a drop of water evaporates instantly on contact. Add the oil and swirl to coat the surface. Working in batches, place the pancakes in a single layer, lower the heat to medium-low, and fry, flipping once, until both sides are golden brown and the edges are crisp, about 4 minutes per side. Transfer to a plate and serve as is, or with chili oil and soy sauce, hoisin sauce, or vegetarian oyster sauce for dipping.

½ ounce (14 grams) **dried shiitake mushrooms** (about 3 medium)

Boiling water

Kosher salt

¼ cup (30 grams) finely diced **carrot**

¼ cup (30 grams) peeled and finely diced **jicama or water chestnuts**

8 ounces (230 grams) fresh or thawed frozen **tofu skin**

¼ cup (35 grams) finely chopped **Pickled Mustard Greens** (page 306)

¼ cup (20 grams) finely chopped fresh **cilantro stems and leaves or scallion greens** (or a mix)

1 tablespoon **vegetarian oyster sauce** or stir-fry sauce

½ teaspoon **sugar**

¼ teaspoon ground **white pepper**

½ cup (70 grams) **all-purpose flour**

2 tablespoons **potato starch** or cornstarch

2 tablespoons **vegetable oil**

Chili oil and **soy sauce, hoisin sauce,** or **vegetarian oyster sauce,** for serving (optional)

STEAMED TOFU SKIN WITH GINGER, BLACK BEANS & FRIZZLED SCALLIONS

Qīngzhēng fǔzhú

清蒸腐竹

SERVES 4 TO 6

Tofu skin tastes so good by itself that a simple steam is all you need, and the gentle heat also preserves its layered structure, mild flavor, and light chewiness. Fragrance is especially important for steamed dishes—toasted sesame oil is a must, of course, but I also like a few pinches of ground sand ginger (沙薑 *shājiāng*) for a musky, peppery savoriness and slightly piney aroma. (You'll find sand ginger in powdered form in your Asian supermarket spice aisle, but if you don't have it, feel free to substitute regular ground ginger or leave it out.) For the simplest version, just serve the steamed tofu skin with a dash of finishing oil, but if you want an extra savory topping, try this variation, with fermented black beans, garlic, and crisped scallions.

Squeeze each piece of the tofu skin to remove as much water as possible. Cut the tofu skin into 4-inch segments.

In a bowl, combine the tofu skin with the sand ginger, salt, ¼ teaspoon of the sugar, the white pepper, and the sesame oil. Squeeze gently to allow the tofu skin to absorb the flavors—you can also prep this in advance and let it marinate in the refrigerator until you're ready to steam. Arrange the segments in a single layer on a heatproof plate that will fit inside a wide pan (with a lid).

Set a wire rack inside the wide pan, add water, and bring to a boil. When you can see the steam beginning to rise, place the plate on top. Cover and steam the tofu skin over medium-high heat for 8 minutes.

Meanwhile, in a small bowl, whisk together the soy sauce, remaining 1 teaspoon sugar, the MSG, and 2 tablespoons hot water until the sugar dissolves.

Remove the plate from the steamer, tip it slightly to drain off any accumulated liquid, and transfer the tofu skins to a serving dish.

Scatter the slivers of scallion and chile on top and then the black bean topping (if using). Pour the soy sauce mixture on both sides of the tofu skin to form a shallow puddle at the bottom of the serving dish. If not using the black bean topping, in a small saucepan, heat the oil over high heat until it is almost smoking. Pour the hot oil over the scallion and chile to release their fragrances. Serve immediately.

(recipe continues)

10 ounces (280 grams) fresh or thawed frozen tofu skin

½ teaspoon ground sand ginger or ground ginger

½ teaspoon kosher salt

1¼ teaspoons sugar, divided

¼ teaspoon ground white pepper

½ teaspoon toasted sesame oil

1 tablespoon soy sauce

¼ teaspoon MSG

1 scallion, white part only, thinly julienned

1 small fresh red chile, thinly julienned to match the scallion

Black Bean Topping (recipe follows; optional)

1 tablespoon vegetable oil (optional)

BLACK BEAN TOPPING

1 tablespoon vegetable oil

2 tablespoons fermented black beans, coarsely chopped

1 tablespoon peeled and minced fresh ginger

1 tablespoon minced fresh garlic

2 scallions, white parts only, thinly sliced

This topping was inspired by Cantonese "black bean steamed fish" with a topping of finely chopped scallions and fermented black beans.

In a small saucepan, heat the oil over medium-high heat until shimmering, then add the black beans, ginger, garlic, and scallions and stir-fry until aromatic and the scallion bits are starting to get crispy, about 2 minutes. Remove from the pan and scatter over the tofu skin before serving.

HANNAH CHE

STIR-FRIED TOFU SKIN & TOMATO

Fānqié chǎo fǔzhú

番茄炒腐竹

SERVES 3 OR 4

One of the easiest and most universally beloved Chinese stir-fried dishes is *fanqie chao dan*, stir-fried tomato and egg. The gentle, jammy tomatoes and rich scrambled eggs are a satisfying marriage of sweetness, acidity, and natural umami. After I went vegan, I thought I'd have to give up my beloved tomato-egg stir-fry forever, but on a trip to Suzhou to visit my uncle, I spotted it on the menu at a vegetarian restaurant. Instead of eggs, they used fried tofu skin, and it was a revelation. I ladled it over my rice and ate blissfully, feeling like I was reuniting with a long-lost friend. At home, I usually toss in a few Fried Gluten Puffs (page 199), which lend a chewy richness like egg yolk (the tofu skin is comparable to egg white), but feel free to leave them out if you don't have them.

Like all comfort foods, this dish is highly personal. Tweak the flavors until it's how you like it. Chinese chefs will tell you the secret ingredient is ketchup, which concentrates the tomato flavor in the dish—especially important if your tomatoes aren't completely ripe and sweet. If you prefer a soupier dish with more juices, add more stock; for a thicker consistency, stir in a light starch slurry.

For a smoother texture, peel the tomatoes: Score the bottom of each tomato with an X. Bring 4 cups (1 L) water to a boil in a large saucepan. Fill a bowl with cold water and set it nearby. Blanch the tomatoes briefly, about 15 seconds. Lift the tomatoes out with a slotted spoon and immerse immediately in cold water. Peel and discard the skins—they should slide off easily. You can skip this step if visible tomato peels don't bother you.

Cut the tomatoes into bite-size pieces and set aside. Unroll the tofu skins as much as possible and tear them into 3-inch pieces.

If you prefer a thicker sauce, make a slurry by combining the starch with 1 tablespoon cold water in a small bowl. Stir until smooth and set aside.

Heat a wok or skillet over high heat and add 2 tablespoons of the vegetable oil, swirling to coat sides. Add the tofu skin and stir-fry until it's puffed up slightly and turned golden. Transfer to a bowl and set aside.

(recipe continues)

1 pound (450 grams) fresh ripe tomatoes

5 ounces (120 grams) fresh or thawed frozen tofu skin

½ teaspoon potato starch (optional)

3 tablespoons vegetable oil

2 or 3 garlic cloves, thinly sliced

1 scallion, thinly sliced, green and white parts kept separate

2 teaspoons soy sauce

½ cup unsalted stock of any kind or water

2 tablespoons ketchup

2 teaspoons sugar

½ teaspoon kosher salt, plus more to taste

½ teaspoon toasted sesame oil

Add the remaining 1 tablespoon vegetable oil to the wok and heat over medium-high until shimmering. Add the garlic and scallion whites and stir-fry until they smell delicious. Tip in the tomatoes and cook for 1 minute, stirring continuously as the tomatoes soften and release their juices.

Add the fried tofu skin, soy sauce, stock, ketchup, sugar, and salt. Cook, stirring, until the mixture is bubbling, about 2 minutes. Reduce the heat to low and simmer for 2 to 3 minutes. Taste the liquid and add more salt, if needed.

Increase the heat to high, give the starch slurry a whisk (if using), and add it gradually to the wok, stirring until the sauce thickens. Garnish with the scallion greens and a drizzle of sesame oil before serving.

HANNAH CHE

VEGETARIAN ROAST GOOSE

Sù shāo'é

素燒鵝

SERVES 4 TO 6

Home to one of the oldest and largest Buddhist populations in China, Jiangnan Province was a hub of vegetarian cuisine during the Song dynasty. One of its classic dishes is vegetarian roast goose, a remarkable creation of semi-dried tofu skin. The delicate sheets are layered, filled with mushrooms and vegetables, rolled into a packet, steamed, and then fried to a shatteringly crisp exterior, in imitation of crispy goose skin. Yuan Mei, the legendary Chinese poet and gastronome, even included this dish in his classic treatise and cookbook *Recipes from the Garden of Contentment* from the Qing dynasty. You'll find variations across regional cuisines, and some chefs leave out the filling entirely, trying to replicate the actual texture of the goose, but my favorite is a version I ate in Shanghai, prettily stuffed with thin slivers of bamboo shoots, carrot, and shiitake mushrooms. Something crunchy, sweet, and savory in each bite. Nowadays, mock meats and the old imitation-style dishes are considered outdated in modern vegetarian restaurants in China, which are focused on vegetables and tofu, but this dish is enduringly popular on menus, probably because it's delicious in its own right.

MAKE THE SAUCE: Combine all the sauce ingredients in a small bowl. Set aside.

MAKE THE FILLING: Soak the mushrooms in the boiling water for 30 minutes, until plump. Snip off and discard the mushroom stems and cut the caps into thin slivers. Reserve the soaking liquid.

Heat a seasoned wok over medium heat and add the vegetable oil, swirling to coat the sides. Add the ginger and stir-fry until aromatic, about 30 seconds. Add the mushroom caps, bamboo shoots, and carrot. Stir-fry to combine. Pour in about 2 tablespoons of the sauce and stir-fry until the sauce has been absorbed, then season with salt to taste. Scrape into a bowl and let the filling cool.

In the meantime, trim off the string-like edges of the tofu skin sheets. Discard or use as a "brush." On a flat surface, lay out one tofu skin sheet with the straight edge toward you. Using the trimmed edges, a spoon, or a pastry brush, rub a light layer of the remaining sauce over the first sheet. Top with a second sheet and brush again. Repeat with one more skin.

(recipe and ingredients continue)

THE SAUCE

2 tablespoons Shaoxing wine

2 tablespoons soy sauce

2 tablespoons sugar

1 teaspoon dark soy sauce

1 teaspoon toasted sesame oil

THE FILLING

¾ ounce (20 grams) dried shiitake mushrooms (about 4 large)

1 cup (240 mL) boiling water

2 tablespoons vegetable oil

1 (2-inch) piece (15 grams) fresh ginger, peeled and thinly slivered

½ cup (70 grams) thinly julienned fresh or thawed frozen winter bamboo shoots

Pile half the filling in the center of the stacked tofu skin sheets, about 3 inches from the straight bottom edge. Fold the left and right sides of the stack toward the center, then press down gently. Brush a thin layer of the sauce on the bottom edge to help seal it. Fold the bottom up and over the filling, then roll it into a packet about 4 × 8 inches in size. Set on a plate and cover so it doesn't dry out. Stack and fill the remaining 3 tofu skins to make a second packet.

Line a bamboo steamer with a muslin cloth or perforated parchment paper. Place the rolls seam-side down in the steamer, cover, and steam over medium-high heat for 6 to 7 minutes, until the tofu skin is wrinkled and darkened. Remove from the steamer and let cool to room temperature. It may be served as is, but for the full effect, fry it.

If desired, heat about 3 inches of oil in a wok over medium-high heat to 350°F (175°C). Gently slide the steamed rolls into the wok and deep-fry, turning the rolls once, until both sides are golden brown, about 3 minutes on each side. Remove and let cool on a paper towel–lined plate. With a sharp knife, cut the rolls into 1-inch-wide pieces and serve immediately.

1 medium carrot, julienned

½ teaspoon kosher salt, plus more to taste

3 (24-inch) circular semi-dried tofu skin sheets, halved to make 6 semicircles (5 ounces / 135 grams)

Vegetable oil, for frying (optional)

Note: The tofu skin sheets dry out and crack very easily, so be sure to keep them in an airtight bag and freeze them after opening.

VEGETARIAN FISH IN SWEET & SOUR SAUCE

Tángcù sùyú

糖醋素鱼

SERVES 6 TO 8

This "fish" is made with sheets of tofu skin that are finely chopped and wrapped in nori seaweed and dried tofu skin, then steamed and deep-fried for an exterior that resembles crispy skin. My mom says it tastes just like the sweet-and-sour carp she ate at banquets, and she can't get enough of the sauce. Make this for Lunar New Year, and it'll be a showstopper. Sometimes, I skip the deep-frying and sauce presentation and make this for a sturdy protein I can slice up and use in other dishes. To make vegetarian "eels," divide the batter among four nori sheets, roll them tightly into skinny rolls, and, after steaming, slice them crosswise into 1-inch segments. Tofu skin and mushrooms are delicious ingredients on their own, so any shape will taste good even if it doesn't look pretty.

MAKE THE "FISH": In a food processor, combine the torn tofu skin and mushrooms and pulse several times until everything is shredded and resembles a coarse batter. Transfer to a large bowl. (If you don't have a food processor, finely chop these ingredients by hand.)

Add the dulse, ginger, sugar, and salt and stir to combine. Gradually mix in the flour and cornstarch, a little at a time, and knead with your hands to release the moisture and help everything stick together. You may not have to use all the starch and flour, or you may need more—it depends on the moisture content of the tofu skin and mushrooms you're using. As soon as the batter holds together when you squeeze it in your palm, set the bowl aside and wash your hands.

On a clean surface, lay out the first semicircle of tofu skin, with the straight edge toward you. Trim any tough, stringlike ends with scissors. Smear a thin layer of the batter in the center of the tofu skin, just enough to hold the nori sheet, like glue. Press the nori sheet on top of the batter, shiny-side down.

Place slightly less than half the remaining batter in the center of the nori. Shape it into an oblong mound about 6 inches long and 2 inches wide. Thinly spread more of the batter on top of the remaining sides of the nori sheet and on the areas of tofu skin not covered by the nori.

Fold the tofu skin and nori sheet tightly around the mounded batter like wrapping a package, enclosing the mound completely. Shape the whole thing into a fishlike form, tapering the ends and using more batter as

(recipe and ingredients continue)

THE "FISH"

1 pound (450 grams) fresh or thawed frozen tofu skin, drained and torn into large pieces

2½ ounces (80 grams) king oyster mushrooms, cut into thin slivers, or enoki mushrooms, ends trimmed and separated

½ teaspoon dulse powder or kelp granules (optional)

1 tablespoon minced fresh ginger

½ teaspoon sugar

1 teaspoon kosher salt, plus more as needed

3 tablespoons all-purpose flour

1½ teaspoons potato starch or cornstarch

1 circular semi-dried tofu skin sheet, halved to make 2 semicircles

2 nori sheets

Vegetable oil, for frying

Potato starch or cornstarch, for dusting

needed to help everything stick together. You will likely have more tofu skin than you need, so trim the excess. Repeat with the remaining semicircle of tofu skin, nori sheet, and batter.

Line the bottom of a steamer with two 4 × 8-inch squares of parchment paper to prevent the "fish" from sticking to each other or the bottom of the steamer. Place each fish on a piece of the parchment, cover, and steam over high heat for 10 to 12 minutes, counting from when the steam visibly rises from the steamer.

BEGIN THE SAUCE: In the meantime, soak the ginger and scallion slivers in a bowl of cold water—this will make them curl up prettily. In a small bowl, make a slurry by combining the starch with 3 tablespoons cold water. Stir until smooth and set aside.

When the "fish" are done, remove them from the pot and let cool slightly on a cutting board. Using a sharp knife, make a series of shallow (½-inch-deep) slashes vertically on each fish, holding your knife at a 45-degree angle to the cutting board surface. Don't cut all the way to the bottom—the fish should still be intact.

Heat about 3 inches of oil in a wok over medium heat to 350°F (177°C). Coat the fish with a light layer of potato starch.

Hold one fish over the wok, slashes facing down. Lower it gently into the oil—the slashes should open wider and slightly curl the fish downward. Fry the first fish, ladling hot oil over it, until one side is a golden brown, about 30 seconds. Gently turn it over and fry until the second side is completely golden brown, about 1 minute, then carefully lift it out of the oil and drain on a paper towel–lined plate. Repeat with the second fish.

Pour the oil into a heatproof container for another use, reserving 2 tablespoons in the wok. Return the wok to medium-low heat and briefly stir-fry half the curled slivered scallions and ginger, about 15 seconds, until aromatic. Finish the sweet-and-sour sauce by adding the stock, sugar, vinegar, soy sauce, and salt and bringing it to to a boil. Taste and adjust the seasoning as necessary.

Give the starch slurry a stir and add it gradually to the liquid, stirring until it bubbles and thickens, about 30 seconds. Pour the sauce evenly over the fish and garnish with the remaining curled ginger and scallion slivers. Serve immediately.

THE SWEET & SOUR SAUCE

1 (2-inch) piece (15 grams) fresh ginger, peeled and cut into fine slivers

2 scallions, cut into fine slivers, both white and green parts

1¼ teaspoons potato starch

5 tablespoons unsalted stock of any kind or water

¼ cup sugar

2 tablespoons Chinkiang black vinegar

½ tablespoon soy sauce

¾ teaspoon kosher salt, plus more to taste

FIVE-SPICE VEGETARIAN CHICKEN

Sùjī

素雞

**MAKES 1 ROLL
(ABOUT 1½ POUNDS);
SERVES 6**

When simmered in broth, tightly wrapped in cloth, and steamed, tofu skin sheets develop an intricate muscle-like layering and a tender, chewy texture similar to that of meat. Compared to store-bought products that often contain lots of ingredients and potentially unhealthy additives, *suji* is breathtakingly simple. You can slice it up to use in sandwiches or cook it as the protein in dishes like three-cup chicken and kung pao chicken. Sometimes I just eat it straight from the fridge with a dip of soy sauce and some chili oil. The finished texture will depend on the type of tofu skin—tofu skin sticks will result in a chewier roll with distinct layers, while semi-dried tofu skin sheets create a softer and more cohesive texture. Feel free to play around with the flavors. If you want to make an American-style roast, for example, instead of the soy sauce and five-spice you can add fresh thyme, rosemary, sage, and black pepper to the broth.

If you're using semi-dried tofu skin sheets, cut the circles first in half and then into quarters, stacking them on top of each other. Roll into a log and cut into 1-inch strips. If you're using dried tofu skins, soak them first in hot water (or in cold water overnight in the refrigerator) until they are white and completely softened, then drain and snip them into 2-inch-wide strips.

In a large stockpot, combine 6 cups (1.4 L) water, the cut tofu skins, soy sauce, five-spice powder, salt, sugar, and white pepper. Bring to a boil over medium-high heat, reduce the heat to maintain a simmer, and simmer, uncovered, for 45 minutes, stirring occasionally to nudge the darkened layer on top back into the brine.

Drain the tofu skins in a colander, discarding the broth. When cool enough to handle, squeeze the tofu skins gently between your palms to extract any liquid.

Place the tofu skins in a muslin cloth or fine-woven cheesecloth on a rimmed plate or baking pan to catch any liquid. Fold in both sides of the cloth and roll tightly from the long end to form a log about a foot long and 4 inches in diameter. Tie it with kitchen twine (or cotton cord), squeezing out any remaining liquid as you wrap the twine around the length of the roll to the other end. The compressed tofu skin should feel as firm as a flexed biceps—the tighter the cloth is tied, the firmer the "chicken" will be. Knot the end of the twine securely.

(recipe continues)

12 ounces (336 grams) circular semi-dried tofu skin sheets, or 12 ounces dried tofu skin sticks

¼ cup soy sauce

2 teaspoons five-spice powder

2 teaspoons kosher salt

1 teaspoon sugar

¼ teaspoon ground white pepper

Chinkiang black vinegar and chili sauce or chili oil, for serving (optional)

Note: This is different from Shanghai-style vegetarian chicken (上海素雞 *Shànghǎi sùjī*), which is compressed from *gandoufu,* tofu sheets.

Place the roll on a steamer rack and bring the water underneath to
a boil. Steam for 45 minutes, until the roll is compact and the tofu
skins have adhered to each other. Immediately unwrap the cloth and
remove the roll to prevent it from sticking to the cloth as it cools. Let
the roll cool before slicing.

Cut into ½-inch-thick slices and serve immediately with a dipping
sauce of vinegar and chili sauce or chili oil. Alternatively, cut it into
pieces to use in other recipes or in place of pressed tofu. Store in an
airtight container in the refrigerator for up to 4 days or freeze for up
to a month.

HANNAH CHE

THE CHINESE TRADITION OF MOCK MEAT

I always wondered about the whole point of mock meats. Why call something pork, chicken, or fish if as a vegetarian or Buddhist you are opposed to eating those animals in the first place? And if you aren't, why make something "fake" to resemble meat or fish if you can eat the actual thing?

It turns out that the symbolism of these dishes is often more important than the dish itself, especially in a Chinese banquet for Lunar New Year. Auspicious meanings are based on homophones: for example, 雞 *jī*, "chicken," is a homophone of 吉 *jí*, "luck," so having a chicken dish ensures good fortune, as in the saying 吉祥如意 *jíxiáng rúyì*, "good fortune to you/may everything go smoothly." 魚 *yú*, "fish," is a homophone of 餘 *yú*, "surplus," so fish on the table represents the expression 年年有餘 *niánnián yǒuyú*, "may you have a surplus every year."

Even the presentation and appearance of the food matters: my dad says the fish has to be served whole on the plate, to maximize prosperity, with its head pointing toward the host or guest, and that flipping it over with your chopsticks is bad luck. Meatballs symbolize good luck, roundness, and unity of family. Shrimp, arranged in a half-moon shape, represent golden ingots, bringing prosperity, as do dumplings. Lettuce, 生菜 *shēngcài*, is a homophone for "increasing wealth," 生財 *shēngcái*. For weddings, entertaining guests, and holidays, there are certain standards and patterns in a proper banquet, and meat and fish play a central role in these rituals.

Simultaneously, an entire cuisine developed using vegetarian ingredients to imitate these animal foods, giving rise to many creative uses of tofu skin and tofu over the centuries in palaces and monasteries (see "The History of Vegetarian Eating in China," page 33). At these banquets, nonvegetarians eat dishes they are familiar with, and vegetarians feel equally part of important symbolic rituals. A lot of it is quite playful, too, such as the Vegetarian Fish in Sweet-and-Sour Sauce (page 181).

BRAISED TOFU SKINS IN CHILI BEAN SAUCE

Xiānglà fǔzhú

香辣腐竹

SERVES 4

Dried tofu skin sticks, also called "tofu bamboo," need to be soaked before cooking, but the resulting texture is completely different from fresh tofu skin. The segments are sturdy, with a pleasing chewiness and layered folds that trap liquid and sauces for a juicy bite. Typically, people blanch them and toss them into a mixed salad with wood ears, boiled peanuts, celery, soy sauce, and chili oil. My favorite method is to braise them in a red broth infused with Sichuan peppercorns and chili bean paste—they'll take the extended cooking time without falling apart. Just like the name implies, this dish is both *xiāng*, aromatic and *là*, spicy.

Break the U-shaped tofu skin sticks in half and then into quarters and place them in a large bowl. Cover completely with salted warm water and weigh them down with a plate to keep them submerged. They will turn white as they soak. When they are completely softened—this will take between 1 to 2 hours—squeeze each stick dry and use a sharp knife or pair of scissors to cut it into 2-inch pieces, discarding any remaining hard bits.

Heat a seasoned wok over medium-high heat and add the oil, swirling to coat the surface. Add the garlic, star anise, and peppercorns. Stir-fry briefly, toasting them in the oil to coax out their flavors and aromas, about 1 minute. Add the chili bean paste and ground chile and stir-fry for another 30 seconds. Add the stock, soy sauce, cumin, and sugar.

Add the rehydrated tofu skins and bring the liquid to a boil. Reduce the heat to maintain a gentle simmer. Cook, uncovered, for 6 to 7 minutes to allow the tofu skin to soften and absorb the flavors.

Meanwhile, make a slurry by combining the starch with 2 tablespoons cold water in a small bowl. Stir until smooth.

Turn the heat to high and cook until the liquid at the bottom of the wok has reduced. Give the starch slurry a whisk and gradually add it to the wok, stirring continuously until the sauce has thickened and clings to the tofu skins. Transfer to a dish and garnish with the scallion greens before serving.

6 ounces (170 grams) dried tofu skin sticks

Kosher salt

2 tablespoons vegetable oil

3 garlic cloves, minced

1 star anise pod

1 teaspoon whole Sichuan peppercorns

1 tablespoon Sichuan chili bean paste

1 tablespoon ground Sichuan chile or coarse red chile flakes

1½ cups (360 mL) unsalted stock of any kind or water

1 tablespoon soy sauce

¼ teaspoon ground cumin

½ teaspoon sugar

1 teaspoon potato starch

Thinly sliced scallion greens, for garnish

GLUTEN

The craft of separating gluten from flour dates back roughly 1,500 years to sixth-century China. Noodle makers discovered that rinsing flour dough with water would drain its starch in a silky, cloudy liquid, leaving behind a wobbly, stretchy mass of protein, which today is commonly known in the West as seitan. Monks called the new ingredient *mianjin*, or "wheat's tendon."

Gluten is essentially the "muscle" of wheat, and it became a main ingredient in Buddhist vegetarian cooking—monks stretched out the gluten into rolls, added leavening, steamed it, and fried it, using these imitation meats in banquet dishes. By the Song dynasty, gluten was well established in the cuisine and held in high esteem by the Song literati. "It has the color of fermented milk, and a flavor superior to chicken or pork," said poet Wang Yan, while Ge Changgeng, the famous Taoist monk, admitted that he enjoyed it more than tofu: "Soft tofu is delectable, but it is gluten that has the cleanest taste."

Gluten is inherently bland, lending itself well to Chinese cooking techniques. Gao Lian (1574–1624) records the earliest written recipes for gluten in his compendium *Yinzhuan fushijian* (Essays on drinks and delicacies for medicinal eating), and includes pan-fried gluten slices (*jianfu*), deep-fried gluten (*zhafu*), and smoked gluten (*yanfu*). With a meaty texture and an ability to absorb flavor, gluten's versatility is highlighted in thousands of ways in Chinese cuisine.

VARIETIES OF GLUTEN PRODUCTS

Increasingly, seitan products like sausages, roasts, burgers, and nuggets are becoming more popular as meat alternatives in the States, but gluten products have been used in Chinese cuisine for a long time and typically come unseasoned, since they're used in stir-fries or cooked in hot pots. They come prepped in a few main ways, and you can find most of the following in Asian supermarkets, usually in the frozen section, but they are also easy to make at home.

FRIED GLUTEN PUFFS
油面筋 yóumiànjīn

These puffy golden balls are made by frying pieces of gluten in hot oil. They are light and fragile, with hollow interiors, and are sometimes stuffed with fillings. They can be found dried, sold in shelf-stable bags in Asian supermarkets.

MARINATED FRIED GLUTEN PUFFS
麵筋罐頭 miànjīn guàntou

In Asian supermarket aisles, you'll find small 3½-ounce cans of gluten puffs soaked in liquid with different flavorings, like gluten with peanuts, spicy gluten, and gluten with sesame oil. These are ready to eat and do not need additional seasoning.

POACHED GLUTEN ROLL
麵腸 miàncháng

Also called boiled gluten or "wheat sausages," these are strips of raw gluten wrapped around chopsticks to form long, lumpy batons. They have a chewy springiness and are delicious stir-fried or braised. They're available in Asian grocery stores in the frozen section and need to be thawed before using.

GLUTEN WHEELS
麵輪 miànlún

These are gluten rolls that have been sliced, fried, and dried into hard, shelf-stable "wheels." They must be soaked in warm water for at least 4 hours to fully rehydrate. They are typically added to noodle soups or stews.

RAISED GLUTEN
烤麩 kǎofū

When you add yeast to a mass of wheat gluten, it rises like dough and forms a springy, spongy loaf with an intricate structure of air bubbles. This leavened gluten is not only more easily digested but also more porous, and during cooking it soaks up sauces readily like a sponge. In traditional markets in China and Taiwan, you'll find it in trays, steamed together like pull-apart rolls. In supermarkets, it's sold frozen or dried. The dried cubes should be soaked to rehydrate in cool water for at least 2 hours.

POACHED GLUTEN ROLL

GLUTEN WHEELS

RAISED GLUTEN

FRIED GLUTEN PUFFS

FRESH GLUTEN

Zìzhì miànjīn

自制面筋

**MAKES ABOUT 1 POUND
(450 GRAMS)**

It's easy to make gluten or seitan at home and requires just flour, water, and a pinch of salt. Most washed seitan recipes call for a firm kneaded dough, but I've found that using a wetter dough and stirring it vigorously instead of kneading forms a more tender gluten and won't result in that rubbery, spongy texture typical of overkneaded gluten. Washing the gluten is the fun part, and it's oddly therapeutic, like playing with slippery, silky clay. If your gluten separates into little scraggly bits, don't worry; keep washing and it will eventually form a single elastic mass. Keep the starch-clouded liquid to water plants or to make *liangpi* (cold skin noodles; see page 211).

For quicker and easier results, you can also make it by simply mixing vital wheat gluten with water. This forms the gluten mass immediately, essentially skipping to the last rinse in the previous method. Vital wheat gluten is available at health food stores and in the flour or bulk section of most supermarkets.

Once you've made the gluten, continue with one of the prep methods that follow—poached or fried—to use in the recipes in this chapter.

USING FLOUR (TRADITIONAL WASHING METHOD): Place the flour in a large bowl. In a separate bowl, dissolve the salt in the lukewarm water. Pour the salt water into the flour and use a pair of chopsticks to stir it in one direction until you can't see any dry flour remaining. Continue to stir vigorously to allow the gluten strands to form, folding and scraping the sides with a spatula, for about 4 minutes. The dough will be very tacky and sticky.

Cover and let the dough rest for 2 hours to develop its gluten. You can also prep this the night before—just cover and pop the dough into the refrigerator.

Prepare a large bowl for washing the gluten—to prevent splashing, you can set it in your kitchen sink. Set a fine-mesh sieve or fine colander over another empty bowl on the counter—you'll pour the starch water into here.

Give the rested dough a good stir with chopsticks. It should be very stretchy, smooth, and satiny. Scrape the mass of dough into the large bowl. Cover with about 3 cups (720 mL) lukewarm water, either from the tap or from a pitcher. Do not use cold water, as it makes it noticeably more difficult to break down the starch.

(recipe continues)

9 cups (1,125 grams) all-purpose flour (see Note)

¾ teaspoon kosher salt

3¾ cups (840 mL) lukewarm water, plus more as needed

Note: You can also use bread flour, which has a higher protein content. This will yield more gluten (about a 34 percent gluten yield with bread flour as opposed to 28 percent from all-purpose flour), but since bread flour is significantly more expensive, I usually stick to all-purpose.

HANNAH CHE

Knead the slippery mass in the bowl with your fingers. As the starch separates from the gluten, it will cloud the water. Continue to "wash" the dough, stretching out the strands under the water and squishing them to release more starch.

After 1 minute, lift the dough from the water and pour the water through the sieve into the empty container, catching any dough bits and recombining them with the dough.

Repeat by adding new water to the bowl to again wash the dough. The dough will become looser and stretchier as the starch washes away. Continue kneading the dough, then repeat the process with new water. By the third or fourth wash, the dough will feel less slimy, and any loose bits should come together to form a cohesive, stretchy ball. By the fifth wash, you can just discard all the water—it will have very little starch left. At the end, you should have a stretchy, beige-colored mass of dough. It should have a clean, rubbery feeling, a bit like chewing gum. Don't worry if the water doesn't run clear; it will be a lot more translucent than when you started but still murky.

Place the gluten mass in a clean large bowl and cover with cool water. Leave uncovered to rest for at least 1 hour, then pour off the water and prepare it with one of the methods that follow. It's best to use it on the same day, but you can also refrigerate it, covered in water, overnight.

USING VITAL WHEAT GLUTEN (QUICK METHOD): Combine the vital wheat gluten and salt in a large bowl. Gradually add the water and stir with chopsticks to combine. Mix until there is no more dry gluten and the dough forms a cohesive mass.

Using your hands, knead the gluten lightly in the bowl for about 30 seconds. After a certain point the dough will be too elastic to knead; pick it up and massage it between your fingers, helping the gluten strands form and kneading out any remaining dry spots.

Cover the dough with cool water. Leave uncovered to rest for at least 1 hour, then pour off the water and prepare it with one of the methods that follow. It's best to use it the same day, but you can also refrigerate it, covered in water, overnight.

7 ounces (200 grams; 1½ cups) vital wheat gluten

½ teaspoon kosher salt

1 cup plus 2 tablespoons (270 mL) lukewarm water

IS GLUTEN/SEITAN UNHEALTHY?

Gluten hasn't been embraced like other plant protein sources due to sometimes unfounded gluten fears and a greater awareness of celiac disease and non-celiac gluten sensitivity. Up to 20 percent of Americans say they try to avoid gluten, and seitan isn't very common outside of exclusively vegan and vegetarian restaurants.

However, gluten is an excellent source of lean protein, low in saturated fat and carbohydrates, and a single modest serving (2½ ounces / 70 grams) contains 45 percent of the recommended daily value of iron.

Most people who report non-celiac gluten sensitivity actually react to glyphosate, the main chemical used in pesticides for growing wheat, especially among GMO sources. To avoid this chemical, simply use an organic brand of vital wheat gluten or make your own gluten using organic flour.

POACHED GLUTEN ROLLS

Miàncháng

麵腸

MAKES 8 ROLLS

Buddhist monks first wrapped strips of gluten around chopsticks and boiled them until they were firmed up and delightfully chewy. The intention was to imitate the look and texture of tripe, but it's a brilliant way to shape gluten: the layered rolls cook more evenly than chunks or pieces and have a better mouthfeel and distinct "grain," due to the stretching and wrapping. They resemble plump individual sausages, and once cooled, they can be cut into slices or slivers for stir-frying.

If the gluten cooks rapidly in boiling water, it will become rubbery and grainy. Be sure to keep the heat at a low, gentle simmer.

Using your hands, stretch, pull, and flatten the mass of gluten into a roughly 6 × 10-inch rectangle. Lay it on a cutting board. Using a sharp knife, divide it lengthwise into 8 long strips.

Hold two chopsticks together in your nondominant hand. (Simply hold them with tips up—not as if you're eating with them.) Take the strip of gluten and, starting from the tip ends, pinch it tightly between the two chopsticks. Stretch the gluten downward with your dominant hand and begin to turn the chopsticks as you tightly wind the gluten around itself, forming a plump, 8-inch-long baton. Each layer should overlap the other, so that there are no gaps.

Tuck the end of the gluten strip beneath the last fold and press the entire roll firmly with your palm for about 15 seconds to allow it to adhere to itself. Slip the gluten roll off the chopsticks and let it rest in a bowl of cool water as you repeat the process with the remaining strips.

Bring 6 cups (1.4 liters) water to a boil over high heat. You can also use a vegetarian or chicken-flavored stock to infuse these with more flavor, but traditionally they're bland, meant to be seasoned and flavored when added to dishes. Lower the heat to maintain a simmer and place the gluten rolls in the water. Keep the water at a gentle simmer—the goal is to have no surface disturbance at all, just tiny bubbles. Simmer, uncovered, for 30 minutes, until the gluten is firm and holds its shape when pressed, then remove the pan from the heat and allow the rolls to cool completely in the water.

Place the cooled rolls in a container and cover with fresh cool water. Store in the refrigerator. You can also use them immediately, but the gluten will be quite soft; chilling overnight will firm them up.

Poached gluten is highly perishable, so use it within 2 days. Alternatively, shake it dry, pack in a zip-top bag, and freeze for up to 3 months.

1 pound (450 grams) Fresh Gluten (page 194)

FRIED
GLUTEN PUFFS

Yóumiànjin

油麵筋

MAKES ABOUT 24 BALLS

When you drop a piece of gluten in hot oil, it slowly puffs up into a hollow, airy sphere. These puffs deflate when stir-fried with vegetables, shrinking into wrinkly, golden morsels that add texture and richness. They're called "oil gluten." When cooked in soup or dropped into a bubbling hot pot, they collapse and soak up the flavors of the broth and can be eaten with the broth or fished out and dipped into sauces. You can also chop up the gluten puffs and use them in fillings for buns and dumplings.

Using your hands, stretch, pull, and flatten the gluten into a roughly 4 × 6-inch rectangle, then cut it into strips and snip each into pieces the size of a cherry, 8 to 10 grams in weight. Working with one piece at a time, stretch out the gluten, tuck each of the four corners into the center, and roll it in your palm to form a round shape. Repeat with the remaining gluten. Let the balls rest on a plate while you heat the oil. Be careful that the pieces don't touch; gluten adheres onto itself very easily.

In a wok, heat about 2 cups (480 mL) oil over medium heat to 300°F (150°C)—the lower frying temperature allows the gluten balls to puff up and keep their shape.

Fry the gluten balls in batches, dropping each piece separately into the oil so they don't stick to each other. You should see bubbles form around the gluten balls as they fry. Turn each ball continuously so it evenly takes on color. To make the balls puff up more, gently press them under the oil with a slotted spoon or chopsticks—you will feel them inflate as they try to pop back up.

After 5 to 6 minutes, or when the balls are round, hollow, and golden in color, remove them and place on paper towel–lined plate to drain. Repeat with the remaining gluten balls. The gluten puffs will slowly deflate and collapse as they cool.

Store the fried gluten puffs in an airtight container or zip-top bag in the refrigerator for up to 4 days, or freeze them for up to 3 months. Thaw them in a bowl of water until you can separate them with your fingers.

**6 ounces (170 grams)
Fresh Gluten (page 194)**

Vegetable oil, for frying

RAISED GLUTEN

Kăofū

烤麸

**MAKES ABOUT 20 OUNCES,
ENOUGH FOR 2 DISHES**

Adding a leavener to gluten and steaming it transforms rubbery protein into a soft and springy loaf called *kăofū*. This uniquely porous, spongelike protein is meaty and versatile, and it can be eaten cold in salads, fried, and braised in thick, juicy hunks, or added to soups like frozen tofu. Although you can buy *kaofu* dried or frozen in Chinese supermarkets, fresh *kaofu* is easy to steam at home, tastes infinitely better, and doesn't contain any suspect preservatives. Like all forms of fresh gluten, it's highly perishable, so use within 2 days, or cut it into cubes and freeze in an airtight container or bag for up to 2 months.

Combine the warm water, yeast, and sugar in a bowl and stir to dissolve. Let rest for 5 minutes, until bubbles form on the surface.

Whisk together the vital wheat gluten and salt in a large bowl. Gradually add the liquid mixture to the dry ingredients and stir with chopsticks to combine. Mix until it's too thick to stir, then knead it in the bowl until it comes together into a soft, rubbery mass. After a certain point, the dough will be too elastic to knead; pick it up

1¾ cups (420 mL) warm water

1 teaspoon (4 grams) active dry yeast

¼ teaspoon sugar

2 cups (280 grams) vital wheat gluten

1 teaspoon kosher salt

Vegetable oil, for greasing

and massage it between your fingers, helping the gluten strands form and kneading out any remaining dry spots.

Line the bottom of a 9-inch round or square pan with a piece of parchment paper. Grease the bottom and sides with a thin coating of oil. Gently remove the gluten from the bowl and place it in the pan. Spread it out and flatten it as much as you can. Cover and let rise in a warm place for 2 to 4 hours, until it's nearly doubled in size, soft, and pillowy.

Place the pan into a steamer set over water. Cover and bring the water to a boil over high heat. Once you see steam start to rise, steam for 15 to 18 minutes, until a toothpick inserted into the center of the gluten comes out clean. Transfer the pan to a wire rack and let the gluten cool completely. The loaf will start to collapse and deflate; don't be

alarmed! When the gluten is at room temperature, cut it into long strips and either tear it into 1-inch pieces or cut into 1-inch cubes.

Use the steamed gluten immediately or store it in a zip-top bag or airtight container in the refrigerator for up to 2 days. You can also freeze the cubes in a zip-top bag for up to 2 months.

Alternatively, if you're using traditional washed gluten (see page 194), combine 1 teaspoon (4 grams) active dry yeast and ½ teaspoon sugar in ¼ cup warm water. Allow the yeast to activate and form bubbles on the surface. Add the yeast solution to the washed gluten mass and slowly knead it in until all the liquid is fully incorporated. Follow the instructions above to place it in a pan, allow it to rise, and steam it.

STIR-FRIED GLUTEN *WITH* GINGER & SCALLIONS

Jiāngshāo miàncháng

姜燒麵腸

SERVES 4 TO 6

My dad says that the texture of the gluten in this dish has the richness of *wǔhuāròu*, fatty pork, and the chewiness of chicken. Unlike seitan products in the West, Chinese gluten is typically unseasoned because it's used as a blank-canvas ingredient, like plain tofu, and it simply needs a combination of aromatics and seasonings to taste wonderful. In this case—my favorite—it's stir-fried with the explosively fragrant flavors of ginger and scallions. To prep the gluten, you can cut it into either sausage-like coins or strips.

MAKE THE SAUCE: Whisk together all the sauce ingredients in a small bowl until combined. Set aside.

MAKE THE STIR-FRY: Heat the oil in a wok over high heat until shimmering, then add half the gluten slivers and fry, stirring continuously to prevent them from sticking to the wok. When the edges are a light golden brown, remove the gluten with a skimmer and drain on a paper towel–lined plate. Repeat with the remaining gluten. Pour the oil into a heatproof container for another use, reserving about 2 teaspoons in the wok.

Return the wok to medium-low heat. Add the ginger and the scallion whites and stir-fry until aromatic, 1 minute. Increase the heat to high and add the gluten and chiles. Give the sauce mixture a stir and pour it into the wok, letting it roll down the sides and sizzle.

Cook, stirring continuously, until everything is piping hot and coated in the seasonings, a few seconds. Taste and season with salt, if needed.

Add the scallion greens. Remove from the heat and let the residual heat wilt the scallions. Serve immediately.

THE SAUCE

2 teaspoons soy sauce

2 teaspoons vegetarian oyster sauce

2 teaspoons Shaoxing wine

½ teaspoon sugar

⅛ teaspoon ground white pepper

THE STIR-FRY

½ cup vegetable oil, for frying

10 ounces (280 grams) Poached Gluten Rolls (page 198), cut into ¼-inch-thick slivers or slices

1 (2-inch) piece (15 grams) fresh ginger, cut into thin slivers

3 scallions, smacked lightly and cut into 2-inch sections, white and green parts kept separate

2 fresh red chiles, seeded and thinly julienned (about ¼ cup)

Kosher salt

MALA–SPICED GLUTEN SKEWERS

Málà kǎomiànjīn

麻辣烤麵筋

MAKES 5 SKEWERS

Gluten is widely eaten as street food in many parts of China. From glowing food carts and braziers in night markets in Xi'an, Langfang, Shenyang, Zhengzhou, and other northern cities, vendors sell tantalizing spirals of chewy-crisp gluten skewered on sticks and grilled over smoky hot coals, and people walk around snacking on them like barbecued meat. They're brushed with various seasonings like five-spice, seafood-flavor, curry, and Sichuan *mala* spice.

You can roast these at home in the oven or use a grill. If you're grilling, be sure to soak the wood or bamboo skewers in cold water first.

MAKE THE MALA SPICE OIL: In a small bowl, combine the red chiles, peppercorns, five-spice powder, cumin, sesame seeds, oyster sauce, chili bean paste, sugar, and salt, stirring to form a fragrant paste.

Heat the scallion oil in a wok over medium-low heat until shimmering, add the prepared spice paste, and stir to incorporate it into the oil. Keep the temperature just hot enough that the oil is fizzing rapidly around the spices, drawing out their aromas, but not so hot that they burn. When the oil smells very fragrant, about 2 minutes, remove from the heat and transfer the oil to a bowl.

To cook the skewers, first line a baking sheet with parchment paper. Spear each gluten roll on its own skewer, leaving it at the top like a marshmallow ready for the campfire. Hold one skewer in front of you, tip facing up, and angle a small, sharp knife at the top of the gluten roll, perpendicular to the skewer. Turn the roll while cutting into the gluten down to the skewer in a sawing motion to form a spiral. Stretch out the spiral-cut gluten so that it's evenly dispersed along the skewer. Place it on the prepared baking sheet and repeat with the remaining rolls.

Preheat a grill to medium-high or the oven to 425°F (220°C). Brush the skewers on both sides with a generous amount of the spice oil, making sure to coat inside the crannies of each spiral. Lay the skewers on the grill or on the baking sheet and cook until golden, 3 to 4 minutes if grilling, or 8 to 10 minutes if roasting, flipping them once halfway through. Transfer the skewers to a plate and serve immediately.

THE MALA SPICE OIL

1 tablespoon ground red chiles or chile flakes

½ teaspoon ground Sichuan peppercorns

½ teaspoon five-spice powder

2 teaspoons ground cumin

1 teaspoon sesame seeds

1 tablespoon vegetarian oyster sauce

1 tablespoon Sichuan chili bean paste

1 teaspoon sugar

½ teaspoon salt

¼ cup Scallion Oil (page 301), Shallot Oil (page 302), or neutral-flavored oil

10 ounces (280 grams; 5 rolls) Poached Gluten Rolls (page 198), chilled overnight

EQUIPMENT

5 bamboo or wooden skewers, soaked for 30 minutes in cold water if grilling

GLUTEN PUFFS WITH NAPA CABBAGE

Miànjīn shāo báicài

麵筋燒白菜

SERVES 6

Although they're great stir-fried with mushrooms, silk gourd, and other high-moisture vegetables, fried gluten puffs have a particular affinity with napa cabbage. The gluten readily soaks up all the juices released by the cabbage and adds its own richness. This homestyle dish is a gorgeous study in textures: the silky, tender cabbage, the gentle chew of the gluten puffs, and the slippery, savory shiitake mushrooms. This is one of those dishes that makes a satisfying meal with just a bowl of rice.

Soak the mushrooms in a bowl of hot water for about 30 minutes to rehydrate. Remove and discard the stems and cut the caps in half.

Meanwhile, make a slurry by combining the starch with 1½ tablespoons cold water in a small bowl. Stir until smooth and set aside.

Heat a wok or skillet over medium heat until a drop of water evaporates immediately upon contact. Add the vegetable oil and swirl to coat the sides of the wok. Fry the mushrooms, pressing them down to sear the edges for more flavor, until they are slightly browned, about 1 minute. Add the scallion whites, ginger, and garlic and stir-fry until aromatic, about 30 seconds.

Increase the heat to high, add the napa cabbage stems and salt, and cook, folding continuously, until the stems are slightly softened, about 2 minutes. Add the cabbage leaves, stock, and gluten puffs and season with the sugar and MSG. Reduce the heat to low, cover, and simmer for 5 to 6 minutes.

Uncover and stir in the vegetarian oyster sauce. Taste and add additional salt if needed. Turn the heat to high, give the starch slurry a whisk, and add it to the wok, stirring continuously as the sauce thickens enough to coat the cabbage, about 30 seconds. Remove from the heat and stir in the sesame oil, then transfer to a dish, scatter on the scallion greens, and serve.

4 dried shiitake mushrooms

1 teaspoon potato starch

2 tablespoons vegetable oil

2 scallions, cut into 3-inch lengths, white and green parts kept separate

4 or 5 thin slices (15 grams) peeled fresh ginger

2 garlic cloves, thinly sliced

13 ounces (360 grams) napa cabbage, cut into 1-inch lengths, stems and leaves kept separate

½ teaspoon kosher salt, plus more to taste

1 cup unsalted stock of any kind or water

3 ounces (84 grams) Fried Gluten Puffs (page 199; about 15)

½ teaspoon sugar

¼ teaspoon MSG

1 tablespoon vegetarian oyster sauce

½ teaspoon toasted sesame oil

FOUR DELIGHTS

Sìxǐ kǎofū

四喜烤麸

SERVES 6

This is a classic Shanghai dish often served at banquets and offered as a cold appetizer at many vegetarian restaurants. The name describes *rensheng sixi,* the "four happinesses" or "four delights" of life from an ancient Chinese poem: lighting the candle on your wedding night, finding your name on the royal enrollment list, receiving rain after a long drought, and running into a friend in a distant land.

But the literal four delights in this dish are the peanuts, slinky wood ears, colorful strands of lily flowers, and cubes of chewy fried gluten, which soak up the sweet sauce and become glossy and moist, laden with the spiced aromas. Sometimes the dish will include sliced bamboo shoots, and you can swap in cashews, chestnuts, or shelled edamame for the peanuts. And if you can't find the dried daylily flowers, replace them with half a carrot, thinly julienned, for a comparable effect.

One hour before cooking, soak the wood ears and peanuts in a small bowl of boiling water to generously cover. Soak the shiitake mushrooms and daylily flowers in another bowl with at least 1½ cups (360 mL) boiling water (you will reserve this liquid).

Heat about 2 inches of vegetable oil in a wok over medium heat to 360°F (180°C). Drop in a cube of gluten to test—it should immediately rise to the surface in a vigorous, bubbling sizzle. Fry the gluten cubes in batches until they are golden and crisp on the edges, about 3 minutes. Remove and drain on a paper towel–lined plate. Pour the oil into a heatproof container for another use, reserving 2 teaspoons in the wok.

Squeeze out the water from the shiitake mushrooms and daylily flowers (reserve the soaking liquid). Trim off and discard the mushroom stems, and cut the caps into 2 or 3 pieces each. Tear the soaked wood ears into bite-size pieces, discarding any knobby ends.

Return the wok to medium-high heat. Add the ginger and scallions and stir-fry briefly to release their fragrance, then add the wood ear and shiitake mushrooms. Stir-fry for 2 minutes, until the mushrooms start to brown, then add the star anise, both types of soy sauce, the Shaoxing wine, sugar, and 1½ cups (360 mL) of the reserved mushroom soaking liquid.

¼ ounce (7 grams) dried wood ear mushrooms

¼ cup (40 grams) raw peanuts

Boiling water

4 dried shiitake mushrooms

10 to 12 dried daylily flowers

Boiling water

Vegetable oil, for frying

10 ounces (280 grams) Raised Gluten (page 200), cut into 1-inch cubes

4 or 5 thin slices (15 grams) unpeeled fresh ginger

2 scallions, both white and green parts, cut into 1-inch pieces

1 star anise pod

3 tablespoons soy sauce

1 teaspoon dark soy sauce

2 tablespoons Shaoxing wine

2 tablespoons rock sugar or Chinese brown sugar, plus more to taste

½ teaspoon kosher salt, plus more to taste

½ teaspoon toasted sesame oil

Bring to a boil, add the fried gluten and drained peanuts, and lower
the heat to maintain a simmer. Cover and cook for about 15 minutes,
until the gluten is soft and soaked with flavor. There will seem to
be too much liquid at first, but it will gradually be absorbed. Add
the daylily flowers. Turn the heat to high and cook until the liquid is
reduced to a depth of ½ inch and starting to thicken into a glossy
sauce, 8 to 10 more minutes. Taste and add salt to taste. Stir in the
sesame oil and remove from the heat. Serve immediately or let cool
and serve at room temperature or chilled.

THE VEGAN CHINESE KITCHEN

COLD SKIN NOODLES

Liángpí

涼皮

SERVES 2

Instead of discarding the silky, clouded water left over from washing gluten by hand, cooks in northern China traditionally leave the wheat starch to settle and then steam it in pans over hot water to make *liangpi*, or "cold skin" noodles. Like any homemade noodle, it's time-consuming but completely worth it: the freshly steamed, translucent white skins are soft and tender to the bite but have a bouncy tug and chew unlike anything you'll get from store-bought glass noodles or rice noodles.

Place the leftover gluten-washing water in a large transparent container, cover, and refrigerate for at least 4 hours or up to overnight. The water will separate from the starch, forming two distinct layers. Pour off as much of the clear water from the top as you can, leaving the starchy liquid at the bottom. Measure out 2½ cups (600 mL) of the starchy liquid, place it in a large bowl, and whisk it with the salt to make the batter (see Note).

Fill a wok with a tight-fitting lid with 3 inches of water, enough that a cake pan can sit on the water, and bring to a boil over high heat. Fill a wide basin with cold water and set it nearby.

Meanwhile, pull out two 9-inch cake pans or shallow rimmed plates and lightly coat one of the pans with oil. This is a crucial step to prevent the batter from sticking. When the water in the wok comes to a boil, place the oiled pan on the water's surface.

Give the batter a whisk and add just enough batter to the greased pan to cover the bottom evenly (tilt the pan to help it spread). Cover the wok and steam for 3 to 4 minutes. When the skin is translucent and rising up in large, swelled bubbles, it's done. If you don't see bubbles yet, you need to cook the batter longer.

Carefully remove the pan with tongs and set it in the basin of cool water. Grease the second pan and place it in the wok. Ladle in more batter, cover, and steam.

When the first pan has cooled, run a knife or chopstick around the perimeter of the pan, then peel the skin noodle off with your hands and set it aside on an oiled plate. Wash the first pan and lightly grease it again. Continue until there is no batter remaining.

Slice the cooled skins into 1-inch-wide noodles.

About 10 cups (2.4 L) of starchy liquid left from making washed gluten (see page 194)

½ teaspoon kosher salt

Vegetable oil, for coating

Note: After the first batch, feel free to adjust the batter. It's hard to predict the consistency of the noodle, since everyone's starch liquid is different, but if the noodle is too opaque or chewy for your liking, you can add more water in ¼-cup (60 mL) increments to thin it. A thinner batter will result in more tender and translucent noodles.

COLD SKIN NOODLES OR RAISED GLUTEN SALAD *WITH* SESAME SAUCE

Liángbàn kǎofū liángpí

涼拌烤麩涼皮

SERVES 4

Whenever my family went to a northeastern Chinese restaurant, we'd order a big platter of chilled "cold skin" noodles (*liangpi*, page 211) as a refreshing starter. They'd slice the cold, chewy noodles into ribbons and anoint the glossy pile with bright vinegar, hot chili oil, creamy sesame paste, and a hint of nose-tickling wasabi, and add julienned cucumber and cilantro for a layer of juicy crunch. You can also dress cubes of raised gluten in the same way—they soak up the sauce like sponges—and many restaurants will combine both the gluten cubes and the *liangpi* in one dish. Feel free to add sliced red onion or sliced fresh chiles for some heat.

MAKE THE SAUCE: In a small bowl, combine all the sauce ingredients and whisk to incorporate until smooth—it should be thin but creamy.

MAKE THE SALAD: In a separate bowl, toss the salt with the julienned cucumber and let it sit for a few minutes for the salt to draw out moisture.

Place the noodles and/or raised gluten cubes in a serving bowl. Drain the cucumber and place it on top, then add the cilantro and scallion. Pour in the sauce and stir everything together to incorporate. Taste and adjust the seasoning if needed. Enjoy immediately.

THE SAUCE

1 tablespoon Chinese sesame paste, homemade (page 305) or store-bought

3 garlic cloves, minced

2 tablespoons soy sauce

1 tablespoon pale rice vinegar

1 tablespoon Chinkiang black vinegar

½ teaspoon sugar

1 teaspoon toasted sesame oil

1 tablespoon Red Chili Oil with sediment (page 301)

½ teaspoon wasabi paste (optional)

THE SALAD

½ teaspoon kosher salt

1 medium Persian cucumber, julienned

1 batch Cold Skin Noodles (page 211), or 8 ounces (224 grams) fresh Raised Gluten (page 200), cut into cubes; or a combination of both

½ cup roughly chopped fresh cilantro

1 scallion, white and green parts, thinly sliced on the diagonal

MUSHROOMS

山珍燴 • MOUNTAIN TREASURE
MEDLEY

雪豆秀珍菇 • STIR-FRIED
OYSTER MUSHROOMS WITH
SNOW PEAS

涼拌金針菇 • COLD-DRESSED
ENOKI MUSHROOM &
CUCUMBER SALAD

酸辣木耳 • HOT & SOUR
WOOD EAR

美滋杏包條 • SPICY SESAME
KING OYSTER MUSHROOMS

宮保菇丁 • KUNG PAO
MUSHROOMS

猴菇串 • SPICY CUMIN LION'S
MANE MUSHROOM SKEWERS

脆香茶樹菇 • CRISPY FRIED
MUSHROOMS WITH
FIVE-SPICE SALT

山珍 • DELICACY

健體蓮藕湯 • LOTUS ROOT
SOUP WITH DRIED
MUSHROOMS & PEANUTS

Mushrooms play a multifaceted role in Chinese cooking—they're cooked fresh in dishes, dried and used as flavoring ingredients, and steeped in teas and broths for their medicinal properties. Beyond the common cultivated varieties like the oyster and shiitake family, you'll find more than 800 wild species across various regions in China, like the matsutake or "pine antlers" foraged in the high forests of Yunnan, the spongy bamboo pith fungus that grows in the humid warmth of Sichuan's bamboo groves, and the intensely fragrant, dark hazel mushrooms from the mountains of Heilongjiang.

Fresh mushrooms are deemed the "meat and fish among plants" and cooked to bring out their umami and satisfying textures—tender, seafood-like mushrooms are tastiest stir-fried in a hot wok with ginger and scallions (Stir-Fried Oyster Mushrooms with Snow Peas, page 218), while crunchy and slippery varieties can be blanched and dressed in a spicy vinegary dressing (Hot-and-Sour Wood Ear, page 222, and Cold-Dressed Enoki Mushroom and Cucumber Salad, page 221). Sturdier varieties like king oyster mushrooms are delicious glazed in a spicy sweet-and-sour sauce (Kung Pao Mushrooms, page 226) or battered and fried into an irresistible finger food (Crispy Fried Mushrooms with Five-Spice Salt, page 233).

In Chinese cuisine, dried shiitake mushrooms are more commonly used than fresh mushrooms, treasured for their deep fragrance and potent savoriness, which intensifies during the drying process. Often the amber-tinged soaking water is reserved to use as a stock. When rehydrated, they are more intense in flavor and chewier than their fresh counterparts and can be braised with soy sauce or simmered into wonderfully nourishing soups (Lotus Root Soup with Dried Mushrooms and Peanuts, page 237).

MOUNTAIN TREASURE MEDLEY

Shānzhēn huì

山珍燴

SERVES 4

This recipe is perfect for mixing and matching different mushrooms. When I lived in Portland, Oregon, I loved to bike to the downtown farmers' market on Saturdays to feast my eyes on all the local mushrooms—in the late summer and fall, tables and baskets would be piled high with delicate morels, lacy maitake (hen-of-the-woods), fresh shiitake, chanterelle, and lobster mushrooms. I'd get just a few varieties and stir-fry them with some scallions and garlic; in the wok they became luxuriously soft and tender but still springy, bathed in a gently thickened broth. The fried gluten puffs are optional, but they lend richness and soak up the potent flavors of the mushrooms. On a cold and drizzly evening, there's nothing better than huddling over a bowl of this stew with some rice.

If you're using the gluten puffs, soak them in warm water to soften for 5 minutes. Clean the fresh mushrooms with a dry cloth and trim off any tough bits. Tear them into bite-size segments or, if you're using king oyster mushrooms, cut them into ½-inch-thick coins (I like to score them with crosshatching cuts).

Make a slurry by combining the starch with 1½ tablespoons cold water in a small bowl. Stir until smooth and set aside.

Heat the scallion oil in a wok or skillet over medium-low heat. Stir-fry the scallion whites and ginger for about 1 minute, until fragrant. Add the garlic and stir-fry briefly, until it just starts to color.

Increase the heat to medium-high. Add the mushrooms and stir them around to pick up all the fragrant oil, then sear until they're slightly browned, about 3 minutes. Pour in the stock and add the gluten puffs, if using.

Reduce the heat to maintain a simmer and cook, uncovered, for about 3 minutes, stirring occasionally. There may not seem to be enough liquid at first, but the mushrooms will soon start to release their liquid.

While the mushrooms are bubbling away, taste the liquid with a spoon and add salt to taste. If you want a soupier dish, you can add more stock. When the mushrooms are softened and have a slightly jellied texture, give the starch slurry a whisk and add it gradually to the wok, stirring to incorporate, until the sauce is thickened. Remove from the heat, drizzle the sesame oil on top, and add a dash of white pepper. Garnish with the scallion greens and serve.

6 or 7 fried gluten puffs, homemade (page 199) or store-bought (optional)

12 ounces (340 grams) assorted fresh mushrooms, a mix of light and dark varieties

1 teaspoon potato starch

2 tablespoons Scallion Oil (page 301) or vegetable oil

2 scallions, thinly sliced, white and green parts kept separate

1 (2-inch) piece (15 grams) unpeeled fresh ginger, thinly sliced

3 garlic cloves, thinly sliced

1 cup unsalted stock of any kind, plus more as needed

¾ teaspoon kosher salt, plus more to taste

½ teaspoon toasted sesame oil

¼ teaspoon ground white pepper

STIR-FRIED OYSTER MUSHROOMS WITH SNOW PEAS

Xuědòu xiùzhēngū

雪豆秀珍菇

SERVES 4

When my sister first tasted this dish, she was convinced it contained seafood. Gilled, fan-shaped oyster mushrooms are fittingly named: coaxed to soften in a hot wok with garlic until their juices are released, they become velvety smooth and mildly chewy, with a delicious seafood-like umami and a subtle woodsy earthiness. The aroma of Sichuan peppercorns pairs well with oyster mushrooms; if you bloom the peppercorns in the oil and then remove them, you can infuse the dish without having to chew on or pick out the little peppercorns as you're eating. I also add a handful of snappy snow peas for contrasting crispness and a pop of color.

When looking for oyster mushrooms, pick those with a springy texture and no bitter dark spots. A white coating of fuzz on the stalks is fine—that's the mushroom's mycelium, not mold, and the mushrooms are perfectly edible after you rinse it off.

Clean the oyster mushrooms and trim off any hard stalk bits. Keep bite-size mushrooms intact; pull bigger mushrooms apart at the stem to split them into wedge-shaped pieces.

Add the oil and the peppercorns to a cold wok. Heat over medium-high heat until the peppercorns are bubbling and fizzing. When they start to float but before they turn very dark, reduce the heat to low and fry for 5 to 6 minutes to infuse the oil with flavor. Remove the peppercorns with a slotted spoon or strainer and discard.

Increase the heat to high. Stir-fry the scallion and garlic in the fragrant oil until aromatic but not yet browned, about 30 seconds. Add the mushrooms and stir-fry briefly to absorb all the oil, about 30 seconds, then toss in the snow peas. Stir-fry until the peas are brightened in color but still crisp and the mushrooms have released their liquid, about 2 minutes. Add salt and white pepper. Swirl in the Shaoxing wine until you can smell its fragrance and stir-fry until the liquid is mostly evaporated, just a second or two. Serve immediately.

10 ounces (280 grams) fresh oyster mushrooms

2 tablespoons vegetable oil

1 teaspoon whole Sichuan peppercorns

1 scallion, both white and green parts, thinly sliced on a diagonal

2 garlic cloves, thinly sliced

1 cup (2 ounces / 50 grams) snow peas, ends trimmed

½ teaspoon kosher salt

¼ teaspoon ground white pepper

1 tablespoon Shaoxing wine

COLD-DRESSED ENOKI MUSHROOM & CUCUMBER SALAD

Liángbàn jīnzhēngū

涼拌金針菇

SERVES 4

In Chinese, enoki mushrooms are called *zhen gu*, needle mushrooms, but sometimes I think of them as "noodle mushrooms," because of their svelte white stems and strand-like, slippery appearance. They are pleasantly chewy, almost crunchy, and it's hard to overcook them. Usually cooked in stews and soups, enoki mushrooms are also delicious blanched for a cold-dressed dish—I pair them here with julienned cucumber for crunch and slivers of carrot for color and sweetness. This vibrant, joyful, and juicy tangle has lots of interesting textures going on, and with the sharp, zingy vinaigrette made with chili oil, it's very refreshing.

This will make a good amount for a side dish or appetizer, but if you want a bigger salad (or leftovers to enjoy cold during the week), pick up two packs of mushrooms at the store and double the recipe.

Trim off the root end of the enoki mushroom bunch. Tear it into smaller clusters, each about as thick as a pencil.

In a medium bowl, toss the cucumber with ½ teaspoon salt and let it sit for 10 minutes to draw out moisture.

In the meanwhile, bring a pot of water to a boil and blanch the mushrooms until you can smell their earthy fragrance and the water's surface starts to foam, about 2 minutes. Remove the mushrooms with a slotted spoon, rinse them under cold water, and squeeze dry. Place in a large bowl. Bring the water back to a boil and blanch the carrots for 30 seconds, just until they lose their raw crunch. Drain the carrots, rinse them under cold water, shake dry, and transfer to the bowl.

Gently squeeze the liquid from the cucumber without rinsing off the salt and place in the bowl with the mushrooms and carrot. Add the scallion (if using) and garlic. Season with the soy sauce, vinegar, sugar, MSG, chili oil, sesame oil, and more salt to taste, adjusting and adding more as needed. Add the cilantro and mix thoroughly to coat. Enjoy immediately or chill before serving.

1 bundle (7 ounces / 200 grams) enoki mushrooms

½ large hothouse cucumber, peeled and thinly julienned

Kosher salt

½ medium carrot, thinly julienned

1 scallion, white part only, thinly julienned (optional)

2 garlic cloves, finely chopped

1 tablespoon soy sauce

1 tablespoon pale rice vinegar

1 teaspoon sugar

¼ teaspoon MSG, or ½ teaspoon mushroom bouillon powder

1 tablespoon Red Chili Oil with sediment (page 301)

1 teaspoon toasted sesame oil

½ cup roughly chopped fresh cilantro stems and leaves

HOT & SOUR WOOD EAR

Suānlà mùěr

酸辣木耳

SERVES 2 OR 3 AS AN APPETIZER

Every time my parents visited their hometown of Harbin, they would come back with pounds of dried black wood ear mushrooms, the regional specialty that old friends and colleagues pressed into their hands as farewell gifts. My parents stowed the red-wrapped boxes in their carry-on luggage, and back in the States, the dried wood ears lasted for months or even years in our pantry. Just a spoonful of the curly, paper-light pieces, soaked in hot water, would blossom into a glistening handful that my mom would add to stir-fries, the taste from a thousand miles away rebirthed in every dish.

Wood ears are used extensively in Chinese cooking, but unlike other fungi, they don't have much flavor and are treasured instead for their slippery, crunchy texture and health benefits—eating wood ears is said to nourish the body and "clean out the lungs." Different versions of this quick cold dish are found across China, and you can add thinly sliced onions and even cucumber for a juicy crunch, but I always come back to my mom's recipe, which has a warm glow of heat and a vinegary, bold sauce to complement the cool, slick mushrooms.

Place the dried wood ears in a large bowl, cover with 2 cups (480 mL) warm water, and soak for 30 minutes—they will expand dramatically, so make sure the bowl can hold at least 4 cups in volume. After soaking, rub the softened wood ears under cool water, washing away any grit, and pinch off and discard any tough, knobby ends. Tear larger ears into bite-size pieces; you should have about 2 cups.

Bring a medium pot of water to a boil. Add the wood ears and blanch for 2 to 3 minutes, until you see foamy bubbles appear on the surface and start to smell a mildly fishy, earthy aroma. Drain in a colander and rinse under cold water. Squeeze out as much water as you can and transfer the wood ears to a bowl. Add the garlic, chiles (if using), vinegar, soy sauce, salt, sugar, MSG, sesame oil, and chili oil. Stir well, taste, and adjust, adding additional vinegar for brightness and more salt as needed. Transfer to a serving dish and enjoy at room temperature, or cover and marinate in the refrigerator for a couple hours, then and serve chilled.

½ ounce (14 grams) dried wood ear mushrooms

2 garlic cloves, minced

4 fresh Thai red bird's-eye chiles, seeded and thinly sliced (optional)

1 tablespoon Chinkiang black vinegar

2 teaspoons soy sauce

½ teaspoon kosher salt

¼ teaspoon sugar

⅛ teaspoon MSG

½ teaspoon toasted sesame oil

1 tablespoon Red Chili Oil with sediment (page 301)

¼ cup finely chopped fresh cilantro

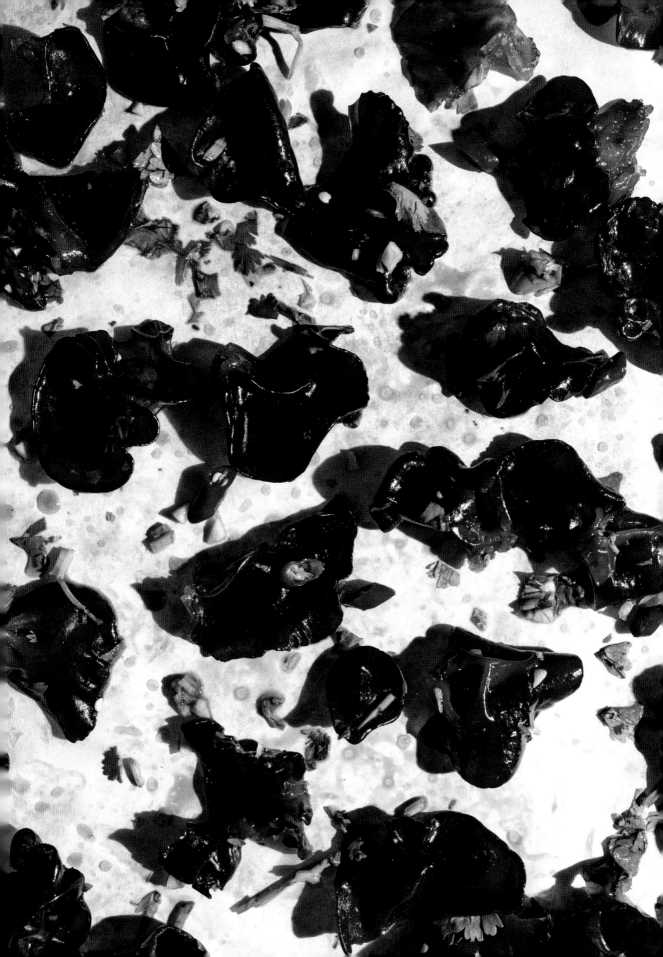

SPICY SESAME KING OYSTER MUSHROOMS

Měizī xìngbāotiáo

美滋杏包條

SERVES 4

King oyster mushrooms are the big "bois," the hunks of the mushroom world, and one of the most versatile due to their thick, mild-flavored, and spongy white stalks, which can be cut into all sorts of shapes. In one of my favorite transformations, you score thin round slices with crosshatched cuts, roll and fasten them with toothpicks, and fry them into mock squid slices. You can also cut them into cubes (Kung Pao Mushrooms, page 226) or tear them into strips. Like all mushrooms, king oyster mushrooms release water when they're cooked, so to prevent sogginess, I blanch them and gently squeeze out their liquid before stir-frying. Tumbled in the hot wok, the ivory mushroom shreds take on color and grow chewier as they caramelize in the sweet-and-sour sauce, laced with ground chiles and cumin, rich sesame paste, and a nutty fragrance from the Shaoxing wine.

MAKE THE SAUCE: In a small bowl, whisk together all the sauce ingredients until smooth. Set aside.

Wipe the mushrooms clean with a damp cloth and trim off any tough bits on the root end. Cut them crosswise into 3-inch segments, then tear each into ¼-inch shreds with your fingers.

Bring a pot of water to a boil and blanch the shredded mushrooms for 2 minutes, until the water comes to a boil again and you can smell the mushroom's woodsy fragrance. Rinse the shreds under cold water and drain them well, then squeeze out the water between your hands.

Heat a seasoned wok over medium-high heat until a bead of water evaporates on its surface within 1 second of contact. Add the vegetable oil and swirl to coat the sides of the wok. Sizzle the minced garlic briefly until fragrant but not yet colored, 30 seconds.

Tip in the mushrooms and stir a few times to pick up the fragrant oil, then let them sear for 30 seconds, until they just start to brown. Add the chiles, cumin, and sesame seeds. Stir in the sauce, coating the mushrooms, and cook until they are piping hot and glazed, a few seconds. Taste and season with salt. Transfer the mushrooms to a dish, garnish with scallion greens, and serve.

THE SAUCE

1 tablespoon vegetarian oyster sauce

1 tablespoon Chinese sesame paste, homemade (page 305) or store-bought

1 teaspoon soy sauce

1 teaspoon pale rice vinegar

1 tablespoon sugar

1 tablespoon Shaoxing wine

12 ounces (336 grams) king oyster mushrooms

2 tablespoons vegetable oil

2 garlic cloves, minced

2 teaspoons ground chiles or chili flakes

½ teaspoon ground cumin

2 teaspoons toasted sesame seeds

Kosher salt

Thinly sliced scallion greens or finely chopped fresh cilantro, for garnish

KUNG PAO MUSHROOMS

Gōngbǎo gūdīng

宮保菇丁

SERVES 4

Kung pao is a Sichuanese flavor profile combining a sweet, hot, and vinegary glaze with crisp golden peanuts and blistered dried red chiles that generously pepper the dish and lend more nose-tingling, smoky aroma than overwhelming heat. Although traditionally made with chicken, I've seen the kung pao glaze used to cook everything from fried oyster and lion's mane mushrooms, tofu, and gluten cubes to tender cabbage and crunchy cubes of lotus root. The ingredients are quickly tossed in the wok, with nubs of scallion and sizzled ginger and garlic, until piping hot with aroma and coated in a light, glistening layer of seasonings (no gloopy sauce here). I prefer king oyster mushrooms because they are pale in color, mild-flavored, and large enough to cut into uniform cubes, but you can also substitute an equivalent amount of fresh shiitake or portobello mushrooms. I've included a few other kung pao possibilities below.

MAKE THE SAUCE: Whisk together all the sauce ingredients in a small bowl until smooth and blended.

MAKE THE STIR-FRY: In a large bowl, toss the mushroom cubes with the soy sauce, salt, and sesame oil, then let them rest for 5 minutes to release their liquid.

(recipe and ingredients continue)

THE SAUCE

2 teaspoons Chinkiang black vinegar

1 tablespoon Shaoxing wine

1 tablespoon soy sauce

2 teaspoons sugar

¼ teaspoon kosher salt

¼ teaspoon ground white pepper

¼ teaspoon potato starch

TWO WORDS FOR SAVORY

The Chinese language contains two words for savory: 鲜 *xiān* and 香 *xiāng*. *Xian*, written with a "fish" radical, is associated with seafood or the bright, clean flavor of a light chicken broth, a savoriness tasted on the tongue, while *xiang* means "fragrant" or "aromatic" and describes a deeper, full-bodied savoriness experienced in the nose and palate. Cantonese chefs often say that *xian* is highest in light-colored mushrooms, like hen-of-the-woods, enoki, and oyster mushrooms, while darker-colored varieties, such as tea tree, porcini, brown beech, and shiitake mushrooms, are rich in *xiang*.

Heat the vegetable oil in a wok over medium-high heat to 360°F (185°C), or until a wooden chopstick forms a merry stream of bubbles when inserted. While the oil is heating, check on the mushroom cubes—they should be damp. Add ½ cup of the starch to the bowl and squeeze the mushroom cubes to allow the starch to be absorbed. The mushroom cubes should still be slightly damp. Add the remaining starch and toss again, until each cube is coated with a generous amount. This will prevent them from sticking to each other when frying.

Fry the mushroom cubes in batches. Separate the cubes with your fingers as you drop them in to prevent them from clumping up. After about 15 seconds in the oil, the mushrooms will begin to sizzle and splatter as their internal water comes out. Stand back and wait until the splattering slows, then stir the cubes with a skimmer or spider until they are golden brown and crisp, about 2 minutes. Remove the cubes and transfer to a paper towel–lined dish. Bring the oil back up to temperature and repeat with the remaining mushrooms. Pour the oil into a heatproof container for another use, reserving 2 teaspoons in the wok.

Return the wok to medium heat. Stir-fry the ginger and garlic until fragrant, about 30 seconds. Add the dried chiles and peppercorns and stir-fry until the chiles start to darken, about 30 seconds. (Make sure your kitchen is well ventilated, as this will give off a stinging smoke.)

Add the scallions, chile, and mushroom cubes, then increase the heat to high and pour the sauce down the side of the wok, so that it sizzles on the way to the bottom. Toss for 30 seconds, just until the sauce coats the mushroom cubes and everything is piping hot. Stir in the peanuts, remove from the heat, and serve.

THE STIR-FRY

2 medium king oyster mushrooms (10 ounces / 280 grams), cut into ½-inch cubes (about 3 cups)

½ teaspoon soy sauce

½ teaspoon kosher salt

½ teaspoon toasted sesame oil

2 cups (480 mL) vegetable oil, for frying

¾ cup potato starch or cornstarch

1 (2-inch) piece (15 grams) fresh ginger, peeled and thinly sliced

2 garlic cloves, thinly sliced

⅓ cup dried red chiles (about 15), snipped into ½-inch segments and seeds shaken out

1 teaspoon whole Sichuan peppercorns

2 scallions, white parts only, cut into ¼-inch pieces

½ cup green chile pepper or bell pepper, cut into 1-inch pieces

½ cup dry-roasted peanuts or Fried Peanuts (page 304)

SPICY CUMIN LION'S MANE MUSHROOM SKEWERS

Hóugū chuàn

猴菇串

MAKES 10 SKEWERS

Before the 2014 ban on open-air grilling on the streets in Beijing, you could smell the smoky aroma of lamb skewers grilling over charcoal before you even saw the vendors. The meaty kebabs, introduced first by Uighur vendors from Xinjiang, have become a ubiquitous street food. Whenever my siblings and I visited Beijing when younger, we always found a chance to buy skewers off the street and sit on the roadside, contentedly gnawing on the salty skewered pieces of meat seasoned with a dry rub of ground chile, ground cumin, and garlic. I first encountered this vegan version at the Yi Xin vegetarian restaurant in Guangzhou, and I couldn't believe I wasn't eating meat. The lion's mane mushroom is so uncanny in its resemblance to meat in appearance and taste, it even appears to have tender "fatty" bits interspersed with chewier "lean" portions. It's mind-blowing.

While fresh lion's mane mushrooms are wonderful, I recommend using only dried for this, as its rehydrated texture is much meatier and it absorbs less oil than fresh. In Asian supermarkets, you can usually find it next to the dried shiitake mushrooms.

MAKE THE MARINADE: In a small bowl, combine all the ingredients for the marinade, mixing until smooth.

PREPARE THE SKEWERS: Soak the dried mushrooms in a large bowl of cold water for 30 minutes (place a bowl or plate on top to weigh the mushrooms down and keep them submerged). Gently squeeze the mushrooms to press out the bitter amber-colored liquid. Drain the water, add fresh water, and soak again for 5 minutes. Squeeze out the liquid and repeat two more times, soaking for 5 minutes each time, or until the water runs clear. Tear the rehydrated mushrooms into bite-size ½-inch chunks and place them in a large bowl.

Pour the marinade mixture over the mushrooms, squeezing the mushrooms gently so the marinade is fully absorbed. Add the starch and squeeze so that it sticks to the mushroom pieces. Add more starch as needed so that each piece is generously coated.

Thread the mushroom pieces on the bamboo skewers, roughly 6 or 7 pieces per skewer, and squeeze them with your palm to tightly shape them together.

(recipe and ingredients continue)

THE MARINADE

½ teaspoon kosher salt

1½ tablespoons soy sauce

1 tablespoon vegetarian oyster sauce

2 teaspoons Red Chili Oil (page 301)

½ teaspoon ground red chile

1½ teaspoons ground cumin

1 teaspoon whole cumin seeds

½ teaspoon sugar

¼ teaspoon five-spice powder

½ teaspoon garlic powder

⅛ teaspoon ground black pepper

Heat the oil in a wok or large skillet to 355°F (180°C) or until a wooden chopstick forms a steady stream of bubbles when inserted. Lay 4 of the skewers in the oil and fry for 2 minutes, turning every 20 seconds so that all sides cook evenly.

With the skewers still in the oil, increase the oil temperature to 375°F (190°C) and continue frying until the mushrooms are deep golden brown and very crispy, about 1 minute more. Remove the skewers with a skimmer or tongs and transfer them to a paper towel–lined plate to drain. Sprinkle immediately with salt, ground cumin, and cayenne. Repeat with the remaining skewers in batches of 3. Serve immediately.

THE SKEWERS

3½ ounces (100 grams) dried lion's mane mushrooms (about 3 large heads)

½ cup potato starch or cornstarch, or as needed

3 cups (720 mL) vegetable oil, for frying

Kosher salt

Ground cumin

Cayenne pepper

EQUIPMENT

10 bamboo or wooden skewers, trimmed to 9 inches in length

LION'S MANE MUSHROOMS

One of the most exciting ingredients in the vegetarian culinary world is lion's mane mushroom or 猴頭菇 *hóutóugū*, which translates to "monkey's head mushroom" in Chinese. This furry and shaggy white mushroom is one of China's 四大名菜 *sìdà míngcài*, "four famous specialties" (the others being bear's paw, sea cucumber, and shark fin), and it's often called the "meat among plants" (素中葷 *sù zhōng hūn*) due to its meatlike texture and savory flavor.

In traditional Chinese cuisine, lion's mane mushrooms were used in soups. In contemporary restaurants, fresh lion's mane mushrooms are steamed or blanched to eliminate bitterness, sliced into "steaks" and marinated, and often served with a black pepper sauce. When dried and rehydrated, lion's mane mushrooms become chewy and sinewy and pull apart like beef or chicken. They are frequently used to replace the meat in dishes like kung pao chicken, three-cup chicken, or cumin lamb kebabs.

You can find fresh lion's mane mushrooms at many farmers' markets and local grocery stores these days, and bags of dried lion's manes are available at larger Asian supermarkets or in traditional Chinese herbal shops, where they're sold for medicinal properties. The mushrooms are believed to have potent curative effects and are said to lower cholesterol, aid the digestive tract, boost immunity, and provide antiaging properties.

CRISPY FRIED MUSHROOMS WITH FIVE-SPICE SALT

Cuìxiāng cháshùgū

脆香茶樹菇

SERVES 4 AS AN APPETIZER OR SNACK

With their light, crunchy exterior and addictive dusting of ground Sichuan peppercorn and five-spice powder, it's impossible to have just one of these crispy fried mushrooms. Though it's optional, I usually serve them on a nest of puffed vermicelli threads, an edible, absorbent base, and scatter some fresh lily bulb petals on top, which offer a sweet, floral crunch in contrast to the salty mushrooms. This is great as finger food for a party, or as a snack to nibble on with drinks. The best mushrooms for this are brown beech mushrooms (*bunashimeji*) or tea tree mushrooms (also called velvet pioppini), both of which have slender, sturdy stems and a mild woodsy flavor.

Trim the root ends of the mushrooms and wipe off any visible dirt with a damp cloth; do not wash them. Pull the mushrooms apart into bite-size pieces and tear any thicker stalks lengthwise into 2 or 3 strips, creating rough surfaces for the starch to stick to.

Place the mushrooms in a bowl and add the soy sauce, peppercorn oil, ground chile, and ¼ teaspoon of the five-spice powder. Toss to coat, then set aside for 5 minutes.

Heat the vegetable oil in a wok over medium-high heat to 340°F (170°C). If you'd like to make the vermicelli nest, place the bundle of vermicelli into the wok—it will puff up immediately. While the threads are still white, immediately lift it out with a skimmer. Arrange the dry, crispy threads on the serving dish as a nest.

The mushrooms should feel damp to the touch after marinating. Prepare a separate bowl of the starch. Grab a handful of the mushrooms and toss them in the starch. Lightly squeeze them and toss with more starch to ensure a generous coating.

Fry the mushrooms in batches, dropping them individually into the oil to prevent them from sticking together. Turn the pieces continuously for even coloring and fry until golden and crisp, about 1 minute. Transfer the fried mushrooms immediately to the bed of vermicelli, then fry the remaining mushrooms, working quickly so you can serve them hot.

Sprinkle the fried mushrooms with the remaining ½ teaspoon five-spice powder, the ground Sichuan peppercorns, and salt to taste. Garnish with a few chile slivers or a sprig of cilantro, and scatter the fresh lily bulbs (if using) on top. Enjoy immediately.

6 ounces (170 grams) fresh brown beech mushrooms or tea tree mushrooms

1 teaspoon soy sauce

½ teaspoon Sichuan peppercorn oil or toasted sesame oil

½ teaspoon ground chile or chile flakes

¾ teaspoon five-spice powder, divided

3 cups (720 mL) vegetable oil, for frying

½ bundle (1 ounce / 28 grams) bean thread vermicelli (optional)

½ cup potato starch or cornstarch

½ teaspoon ground Sichuan peppercorns

Kosher salt

Fresh red chili slivers or cilantro sprigs, for garnish

8 to 10 fresh lily bulb petals (optional)

DELICACY

CULTURALLY, Chinese people often express their love and affection not with words but with food. Every time we visited China when I was growing up, relatives took us out to dinner and ordered lavish spreads of duck, pork, beef, lamb, and fish, and expensive delicacies like sea cucumbers, abalone, and crab when it was someone's birthday. My mom brought us handfuls of dried red dates and walnuts when we were studying for tests to boost our flagging energy and replenish our brains.

Wild foods, mostly game, have been long treasured for their almost magically tonic properties, and although now illegal, these delicacies are still discreetly sold and consumed across China today. Their rarity and high prices magnify the demand—having these foods on the table is a chance to show off wealth. Serving shark fin at wedding banquets and business dinners, until the environmental pushback of the recent decade, was a mark of hospitality but also a symbol of status. One might argue that it has the same luxurious connotation as foods like white truffle, beluga caviar, Wagyu beef, and foie gras in the West.

"Mushrooms are the only foods in the plant world that can replace these expensive delicacies," Chef Wen, my cooking teacher, said one day. Our class was in the storeroom, sorting through a delivery of matsutake mushrooms, recently arrived from Yunnan Province. They are one of the most expensive wild mushrooms in China, and each was individually wrapped, dirt still clinging to its roots. A bowl of matsutake soup, simmered in a simple white radish broth, could sell for 150 yuan, the equivalent price of five vegetable dishes from the same menu. Many mushrooms already had counterparts among seafood and other animals: in Chinese, beech mushrooms are called "crab-flavored mushroom" (蟹味菇 *xièwèigū*), porcini are "cow's liver mushroom" (牛肝菌 *niúgānjùn*), and morels are "sheep's stomach mushrooms" (羊肚菌 *yángdǔjùn*). But today, Wen said, chefs are using coveted mushrooms to replace old luxuries: in Hong Kong, for instance, a high-end restaurant began swapping maitake and *bailing* mushrooms for shark fin—the gentle slippery crunch, the springy chewiness, the rubbery slitheriness so treasured by the Chinese palate can all be found in the fascinating, vast world of edible fungi.

Most of the wild mushroom varieties in China come from Yunnan Province. During the summer and autumn, the local markets overflow with wild mushrooms that are carried down from cloud-topped mountains in baskets and piled high on tarps and carts in orange, brown, and yellow heaps. Yunnan's high forests are home to a mesmerizing variety of more than 800 edible mushrooms, from prized, well-known varieties like porcini, matsutake, chanterelle, and truffles to unusual local fungus like 虎掌菌 *hǔzhǎngjùn* (tiger's paw mushroom), 青頭菌 *qīngtóujùn* (green head mushroom), and 黑頭雞樅菌 *hēitóujīcōngjùn* (black chicken-head mushroom). The mushrooms sustain communities in the mountains, where villagers supplement subsistence farming by foraging and selling the mushrooms either in local markets or to sellers for international distributors.

In China, I once visited a former chicken farm that had been converted to grow lion's mane mushrooms. In the greenhouses covered with thick sheeting, the fluffy clumps were peeking out of their bags of sawdust and bran substrate. It was peaceful and quiet, save for the gentle drone of the ventilation fans, and the air was cool and heavy with moisture. Mushrooms excrete enzymes that break down whatever they're latching onto, whether sawdust, straw, peat moss, rice husks, or leaf litter, a worker explained. In nature, fungi have an unparalleled ability to manage decay and to restore fertile environments. In farms, the mushrooms are cultivated on agricultural waste—perfectly good substrate that was otherwise going to be sitting in a landfill somewhere. The worker said they only took a few liters of water throughout their whole life cycle, misted in carefully monitored amounts, and I thought about how many livestock could fit into the same space, and the thousands of gallons of water needed to produce a few pounds of meat. I watched as the workers walked between the rows, snipping off clusters of mushrooms with scissors and dropping them into a small box. It was so quiet I could hear each gentle plunk onto the lining paper.

At a vegetarian hot pot restaurant in Guangzhou, I sat under a trellis of vines, enjoying the opening course of dried mushrooms, ginseng root, fox nuts, lily bulbs, and goji berries simmered into a dark, earthy broth. *Drink this in eighteen sips*, an accompanying slip of paper instructed. *On the first sip, breathe in the aroma. On the second, you'll taste a returning sweetness. Drink the third mouthful as slowly as possible, and feel your throat, esophagus, and stomach slowly warm up. On the fifth, your palms will emanate heat.* Later, as we dipped peanut sprouts and chanterelles in the burbling hot pot, the restaurant's owner stopped by for a chat. She was a Chinese medicine practitioner, and she said that mushrooms, though they had been used medicinally for hundreds of years, are gaining revived attention. "They are the only foods apart from animal sources high in vitamin D and vitamin B_{12}," she said. She listed their immunity-boosting properties and anti-inflammatory antioxidants—reishi mushrooms, in particular, she said, are powerful in fighting pulmonary cancer and traditionally eaten for longevity since they are one of the longest-growing mushrooms. She handed us pamphlets and urged us to eat more mushrooms. At the end of the meal, as the hot pot bubbled down, we ladled the broth into our bowls. It was richly fragrant and full-bodied, enriched by the rare and wild mushrooms we'd cooked in it, and I sipped the powerful broth slowly, wondering if this is what drinking longevity felt like.

LOTUS ROOT SOUP *WITH* DRIED MUSHROOMS & PEANUTS

Jiàntǐ liánǒutāng

健體蓮藕湯

SERVES 6 TO 8

In Guangzhou, vegetarian chefs have perfected the method of coaxing savory, full-bodied soups from dried mushrooms and legumes like mung beans and peanuts. It's best to use a pressure cooker for this recipe, which cuts down on the cooking time and minimizes flavor loss. This is a wonderfully soothing soup: the lotus root chunks are cooked until tender, each bite drawing out glistening fibers, surrounded with soft, starchy chunks of Chinese yam, shelled mung beans, and tender peanuts. Drinking the hot, silky broth feels richly nourishing, and each sip gradually warms you up, like an enveloping hug.

Soak the raw peanuts and dried beans in a bowl of cold water for at least 6 hours or overnight. Rinse the dried tea tree mushrooms to wash off any dust, then soak them with the shiitake mushrooms in warm water for at least 30 minutes (it's okay if the centers of the shiitake aren't fully hydrated). Squeeze dry and reserve the soaking liquid.

Rinse the mung beans and drain (they don't need to be soaked). Peel the Chinese yam and cut it crosswise into 4-inch segments, then lengthwise into quarters (or leave it whole if the yam is less than 1 inch in thickness), and place them in a bowl of cold water to prevent browning. Split the lotus root in half lengthwise, then cut it into half-circle slices, about ¾ inch thick.

In a wok or skillet, heat 2 tablespoons of the oil over low heat until shimmering. Fry the ginger slices and peppercorns. When the ginger is browned on the edges and the peppercorns are starting to pop, about 2 minutes, pick them out with a strainer and place them in a small muslin spice bag (you can add them directly to the pot as well, but using the spice bag makes the finished soup look cleaner). Place the bag in a large soup pot or pressure cooker.

Turn the heat under the wok up to medium-high. Add all the mushrooms and fry them briefly in the fragrant oil, pressing each one down onto the surface of the wok to brown, about 2 minutes. Transfer them to the soup pot.

(recipe continues)

¼ cup (40 grams) raw shelled peanuts

¼ cup (50 grams) dried black-eyed peas or pinto beans

⅓ ounce (10 grams) dried tea tree mushrooms (茶樹菇 *cháshùgū*; 7 mushrooms)

4 medium dried shiitake mushrooms (½ ounce / 15 grams)

3 tablespoons (40 grams) shelled mung beans

6 ounces (170 grams) Chinese mountain yam (*shanyao*; substitute 1 medium potato)

9 ounces (250 grams) lotus root (about 1 medium segment), peeled

3 tablespoons vegetable oil, divided

1 (2-inch) piece (15 grams) unpeeled fresh ginger, sliced

2 teaspoons whole white peppercorns

4 candied jujube dates or dried jujube dates

2½ teaspoons kosher salt, more to taste

Add the remaining 1 tablespoon oil to the wok. Arrange the lotus root slices in a single layer and sear them, flipping halfway through, until both sides are browned and smell delicious, about 2 minutes per side. Transfer to the soup pot.

Measure the mushroom soaking liquid and add enough water to make a total of 8 cups (1.9 L) liquid. Add it to the pot along with the peanuts, black-eyed peas, mung beans, yam, and jujube. If you're using a pressure cooker, set it to cook on manual for 25 minutes, then let the pressure release naturally. If you're cooking on the stovetop, first bring the soup to a boil, then lower the heat and simmer gently, partially covered, for about 1½ hours, until the peanuts and beans are tender. Season with salt, ladle the soup into bowls, and serve.

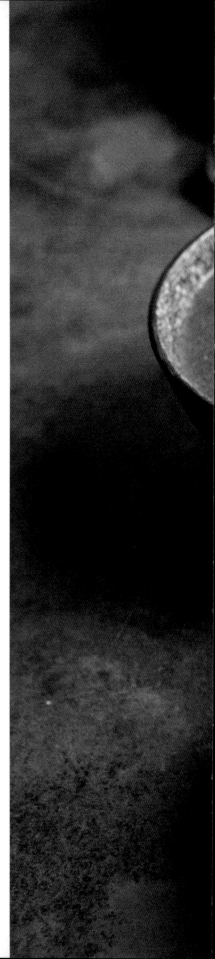

HANNAH CHE

RICE, WHEAT & NOODLES

白米飯 • STEAMED WHITE RICE

紫米飯 • MULTIGRAIN
PURPLE RICE

香菇炒飯 • MUSHROOM
FRIED RICE

包菜粉絲 • STIR-FRIED
VERMICELLI NOODLES

麻醬麵 • SESAME NOODLES

蔥油拌麵 • SCALLION OIL
NOODLES

蕃茄湯麵 • TOMATO NOODLE
SOUP

麵糰 • STEAMED BUN DOUGH

饅頭 • MANTOU

花卷 • SCALLION FLOWER BUNS

素包子 • STEAMED STUFFED
BUNS (BAOZI)

VEGETARIAN FILLINGS, FIVE WAYS

水餃 • BOILED DUMPLINGS
(JIAOZI)

韭菜盒子 • CHIVE-STUFFED BOXES

蔥油餅 • SCALLION PANCAKES

芝麻燒餅 • SESAME FLATBREADS
(SHAOBING)

Rice and wheat are foundational foods in the Chinese diet. Rice is steamed in a tightly covered pot or rice cooker, with no salt or oil, and served plain, since it acts as the neutral background to the other dishes. A stir-fry feels incomplete without rice to eat with it, and particularly delicious dishes are praised as effective to "send down the rice." At home, we gather around the table, each with our individual bowl of rice and a pair of chopsticks, and eat by transferring morsels from the shared dishes to our rice. The rice in China is identifiable by its origin and tied to a specific terroir: jasmine rice or "fragrant rice," grown in lush, terraced rice paddies in the south, is loose and fine-grained and perfumes the house with aroma as it cooks, while round short-grain rice, cultivated in fields in the north, is plumper and softer, with a huggy stickiness.

Wheat plays a greater role in the diet of northern China, along with millet and corn. Breads, noodles, and dumplings are staple foods, and a big, plain steamed bun (Mantou, page 255) was traditionally the main starch for a meal, eaten with stir-fried dishes just like a bowl of rice.

Noodles, made of rice or wheat, are enjoyed in every regional cuisine, and they are casual by nature and reliably quick—you order noodles for lunch at a street stall, or rustle them up at home; most of the recipes here come together in about 15 minutes. Vermicelli noodles are neither rice nor wheat, but transparent threads made of mung bean starch, and they're often finely chopped up for savory vegetarian bun fillings or stir-fried.

STEAMED WHITE RICE

Bái mǐfàn

白米飯

MAKES 5½ CUPS; SERVES 4

When a kid graduates college, Chinese relatives often gift them a rice cooker, assuming that as long as they can make rice for a meal, they'll be able to survive. A rice cooker has become, at this point, the traditional way to cook rice, but you certainly don't need one.

Depending on the brand and how old the crop of rice is, the water required for cooking may vary slightly. Short-grain rice benefits from a presoak, while long-grain jasmine rice or Thai fragrant rice doesn't need soaking and won't absorb as much water. For brown rice and short-grain rice, try to soak the rice in the pot for at least 30 minutes (or up to 8 hours) before cooking it—this will kick-start the absorption of water for fluffier, more evenly cooked grains. If you're eyeballing, aim for the water level to be ½ to ¾ inch above the rice, about the length of your pointer fingernail. You can also control the texture of your rice with the quantity of water; use more water for softer, stickier rice.

This recipe makes 5½ cups cooked rice, or 4 servings. You can halve it and use just 1 cup of rice, but rice tastes better when you steam at least 2 cups, so I usually make more than I can eat in one meal and save the rest for fried rice. Or freeze the leftover rice in individual portions for a future meal.

Place the rice in a deep bowl or in the insert pot of the rice cooker or pressure cooker. Cover with cool tap water.

Wash the rice by swirling and rubbing the grains between your hands. The water will become cloudy with starch; swish and drain the rice, then repeat until the rinsing water runs clearer, two or three times. Drain in a large fine-mesh sieve or colander after the final rinsing.

RICE COOKER: Add the drained rice back to the pot with 2 cups water. If you're using short-grain rice, allow the rice to soak for at least 30 minutes. When you're ready to cook, close the lid, then press the start button. After the timer beeps, wait 8 to 10 minutes before opening. If you use the keep warm function, you can let the rice sit there for a few hours before serving. Open the lid and use a fork or spatula to gently separate the rice grains and fluff them up before serving.

2 cups (370 grams) jasmine rice or short-grain rice

2 cups (480 mL) water for a rice cooker or electric pressure cooker, or 3 cups (720 mL) for the stovetop

242

HANNAH CHE

PRESSURE COOKER: Add the drained rice back to the pot with 2 cups water. If you're using short-grain rice, allow the rice to soak for at least 30 minutes. When you're ready to cook, close the lid and seal the valve, and set to manual mode for 5 minutes on high pressure. After the timer counts down, allow the pressure to release naturally for 10 minutes, followed by a quick release. Open the lid and give the rice a good stir to fluff it up before serving.

STOVETOP: Transfer the drained rice to a medium, heavy-bottomed pot with a tight-fitting lid. If you're using short-grain rice, allow the rice to soak for at least 30 minutes. Add 3 cups water and place the pot over high heat. Bring to a rolling boil and stir the rice a few times to dislodge the grains at the bottom of the pot. Continue boiling for about 5 minutes, stirring the bottom occasionally, until most of the water has been absorbed and you see small, craterlike depressions on the surface of the rice.

Immediately cover the pot and reduce the heat to the lowest possible setting. Allow the rice to steam, covered, for 13 to 15 minutes—do not lift the lid at this point, or the rice will fail to cook evenly (this ruined rice is called 夾生 *jiáshēng*, "partly done," and must be finished in a steamer). Remove the lid and check that the grains are tender and fluffy. If you can still see water, cover the pot and keep cooking for another minute or so. Remove from the heat. Use a fork or spatula to gently separate the rice grains and fluff them up before serving.

To freeze the cooked rice, scoop it into small airtight containers (or zip-top bags) in 1-cup or single-meal portions. Cool the containers or steaming bags to room temperature, then label the containers with the date, close, and stash them in the freezer. To reheat, open the lid, sprinkle some water on top, and loosely cover with a paper towel, then microwave for 3 to 4 minutes, until the rice is hot all the way through. Or transfer the rice to a steamer basket over simmering water and steam for 5 minutes. Frozen rice tastes just as good as fresh rice when reheated and will keep in the freezer for up to 1 month.

(recipe continues)

Variations
BROWN RICE

Cāo mǐfàn

糙米飯

Makes 5½ cups; serves 4

2 cups long- or short-grain brown rice

2½ cups (600 mL) water for a rice cooker or pressure cooker, or 3¾ cups (900 mL) for the stovetop

Follow the instructions for Steamed White Rice (page 242), but increase the cooking time:

RICE COOKER: Use the brown rice setting.

PRESSURE COOKER: Set to 20 minutes on high pressure (or 10 minutes if it soaked overnight). Allow the pressure to release naturally for 10 minutes, followed by a quick release.

STOVETOP: Bring to a boil, continue cooking over high heat until you see craters, then cover and steam for 30 minutes, or 20 minutes if it was soaked overnight. Remove the lid and check that the grains are tender and cooked through. If the grains are too chewy, add about ¼ cup extra water, cover, and steam for another minute or so. Otherwise, let the rice rest for an additional 15 minutes before serving to allow it to continue steaming over residual heat.

QUINOA RICE

Límài fàn

藜麥飯

Makes 5½ cups; serves 4

1 cup (185 grams) jasmine rice or short-grain white rice

1 cup (180 grams) quinoa

2 cups (480 mL) water for a pressure cooker, or 3 cups (720 mL) for the stovetop

At home, my mom rarely cooks white rice, unless we have guests coming over. She always finds a way to mix in millet, quinoa, or other grains for more fiber and nutritional heft. Quinoa (藜麥 límài) is our favorite, since the nutty grains speckle the white rice with flavor and texture and add protein.

It's important to wash the quinoa well to remove any bitterness caused by naturally occurring saponins; wash it as instructed for rice on page 242, then follow the instructions for Steamed White Rice.

HANNAH CHE

MULTIGRAIN PURPLE RICE

Zǐmǐ fàn

紫米飯

**MAKES 5½ CUPS;
SERVES 4**

You can cook white rice with black rice and other interesting-textured grains and legumes like sorghum, pearled barley, lentils, adzuki beans, mung beans, and even chickpeas, as long as they're soaked in advance. Mixed rice, now a fashionable choice in vegetarian and health-centered restaurants in China, was considered inferior in the past and a food for the impoverished, since adding other grains was a way of stretching the luxury of white rice, but the concept of eating *wugu zaliang*, "five cereals and multigrains," is increasingly popular as people look back to traditional ways of eating. The black rice also tints the other grains a beautiful shade of purple.

In a bowl, soak the black rice and other grains or legumes in cool water to cover by 2 inches for at least 4 hours, or overnight for best results. Wash under running water, rinsing away the discolored liquid, then drain well.

Follow the instructions for Steamed White Rice (page 242), but increase the cook time:

RICE COOKER: Use the brown rice or mixed rice setting.

PRESSURE COOKER: Set to cook on high pressure for 10 minutes. Allow the pressure to release naturally for 10 minutes, followed by a quick release.

STOVETOP: Bring to a boil, continue cooking over high heat until you see craters, then cover and steam for 20 minutes. Allow to rest for 10 minutes over residual heat before uncovering.

½ cup (108 grams) black rice or Forbidden Rice

½ cup (about 100 grams) dried black beans, mung beans, adzuki beans, lentils, or a mix

1 cup (185 grams) short- or long-grain white rice

2 cups water (480 mL) for a rice cooker or pressure cooker, or 3 cups (720 mL) water for the stovetop

MUSHROOM FRIED RICE

Xiānggū chǎofàn

香菇炒飯

SERVES 3 OR 4

Beloved in nearly every region in China, fried rice can be very humble, a fridge-cleaning meal made with leftover rice and vegetables past their prime, or served on elegant platters at the end of formal banquets.

The one rule is that you must use thoroughly cooled cooked rice, preferably left in the refrigerator overnight. Freshly cooked or hot rice results in unpleasantly soggy, heavy fried rice, while cold rice cooks into fragrant, separate grains. For vegan fried rice, it's important to have savory, umami elements apart from just rice and vegetables.

Break up any clumps of rice with a spatula or with your fingers.

Heat a wok over medium-high heat until a drop of water evaporates instantly on contact, then add 1 tablespoon of the scallion oil, swirling to coat the sides. Add the shiitake mushrooms, pressed tofu, carrot, mustard stalk, and a sprinkle of salt and stir-fry until the mushrooms are fragrant, the vegetables are vivid in color, and the tofu is heated through and starting to sear on the bottom, about 5 minutes. Transfer from the wok to a small bowl.

Heat the remaining 1 tablespoon scallion oil, then add the scallion whites and stir-fry until aromatic, about 30 seconds. Stir in the garlic, then immediately add the rice and reduce the heat to medium-low. Stir and fold the rice continuously, loosening the clumps, until the rice is heated through, about 3 minutes.

Increase the heat to medium-high. Add the mushrooms, tofu, carrot, mustard stalk, and corn to the rice and toss and fold until fully incorporated and piping hot.

Add the pickled greens. Season with soy sauce, ½ teaspoon salt, the MSG, and the white pepper, tasting and adjusting as needed. Remove from the heat and stir in the peanuts, sesame oil, and scallion greens. Serve immediately.

3 cups cooked rice (page 242), cooled completely

2 tablespoons Scallion Oil (page 301) or vegetable oil, divided

½ cup (4 large) fresh or dried shiitake mushrooms, rehydrated (see page 231) and diced

1 square (2 ounces / 56 grams) pressed tofu, cut into ⅛-inch dice

¼ cup (40 grams) carrot cut into ⅛-inch dice

¼ cup (40 grams) mustard green stalk or broccoli stem cut into ¼-inch dice

Kosher salt

3 scallions, thinly sliced, white and green parts kept separate

3 garlic cloves, minced

¼ cup (50 grams) corn, thawed

2 tablespoons finely chopped pickled napa cabbage or Pickled Mustard Greens (page 306)

½ teaspoon soy sauce

¼ teaspoon MSG or mushroom bouillon powder

¼ teaspoon ground white pepper

2 tablespoons pea-size chopped peanuts

½ teaspoon toasted sesame oil

FRIED RICE TIPS

Fried rice is a dish that is endlessly adaptable to your tastes and whatever ingredients you have on hand. When composing and cooking your own fried rice, keep these tips in mind:

- Mushrooms are wonderful in fried rice. Any kind will work, but my go-to is finely chopped stir-fried shiitake mushrooms.

- A great replacement for eggs is tofu skin (page 164), which can be scrambled and provides the same richness and protein.

- Include a pickled or preserved ingredient like Pickled Mustard Greens (page 306) or olive preserved vegetable; the acidity, saltiness, and umami give the fried rice character.

- Include a vegetable with a bit of sweetness, like carrots, corn, or peas.

- Include something with a savory crunch, like fried shallots, fried soybeans, fried peanuts, toasted pine nuts or cashews, fried taro cubes, or roasted nori shreds.

- Season with kosher salt, a pinch of mushroom bouillon powder or MSG, a generous dash of ground white pepper, and toasted sesame oil. I also add a tiny bit of soy sauce, but salt should be the primary seasoning, as too much soy sauce darkens the color of the fried rice and makes it soggy.

- At the very end, let the rice grains brown in the oil and stick slightly to the wok. This creates crispy, crunchy bits of toasted rice with a delicious aroma.

STIR-FRIED VERMICELLI NOODLES

Bāocài fěnsī

包菜粉絲

SERVES 4

This is the kind of noodle stir-fry you'd order at a street stall in a night market, tossed over a flaming burner in less time than it takes to find a seat. If cooked just right, the slick, thready noodles cling to your chopsticks and to each other in a fragrant mass, laced with the smoky aroma of the searing iron (called *wok hei*), and tangled with ribbons of cabbage, scallion, and shiitake mushrooms. I love mung bean vermicelli because they're naturally gluten-free, take on flavor easily and cook to a chewy bite. Like fried rice, this is total comfort food.

MAKE THE SAUCE: In a bowl, stir together all the sauce ingredients until combined.

PREPARE THE NOODLES: In a bowl, soak the noodles in cold water for 15 minutes, then drain them in a colander and place them in a large bowl. Cut the noodles roughly in half with clean kitchen scissors. Add the scallion oil and dark soy sauce and toss to coat—this will prevent the noodles from sticking to the wok later and add some base flavor.

Heat a wok over medium-high heat until a drop of water evaporates immediately on contact. Add the vegetable oil and swirl it around to evenly coat the sides. Add the garlic, scallion whites, shiitake mushrooms, and chiles and stir-fry briefly, about 30 seconds, until the mushrooms are beginning to brown and everything is fragrant. Add the cabbage and toss a few times, stir-frying until it is softened, about 2 minutes. Sprinkle with the salt and stir to incorporate.

Push the cabbage to one side of the wok. Give the sauce a stir and pour it into the center of the wok. It should sizzle as it hits the hot surface. Immediately add the vermicelli noodles. Stir continuously and fold the noodles to incorporate them with the vegetables and the sauce. If the noodles are cooking too quickly, reduce the heat—you don't want them to dry out and stick to the bottom. Add more liquid, if needed. When the noodles are piping hot, tender with a slight chew, and there isn't any more liquid visible at the bottom of the wok, remove it from the heat. Stir in the scallion greens, sesame oil, and white pepper (if using). Taste and add additional salt if needed. Serve immediately.

THE SAUCE

2 tablespoons soy sauce

1 teaspoon sugar

½ teaspoon salt

1 teaspoon Chinkiang black vinegar

¾ cup unsalted stock of any kind or water

THE NOODLES

3 bundles dried mung bean vermicelli (6 ounces / 170 grams)

2 teaspoons Scallion Oil (page 301) or vegetable oil

1 teaspoon dark soy sauce

2 tablespoons vegetable oil

4 garlic cloves, minced

2 scallions, white parts finely chopped, green parts cut into 3-inch segments, kept separate

4 dried shiitake mushrooms, soaked until fully rehydrated and cut into ⅛-inch strips

2 fresh small red chiles, seeded and thinly julienned

4 cups (12 ounces / 340 grams) finely shredded green cabbage

½ teaspoon kosher salt

1 teaspoon toasted sesame oil

¼ teaspoon ground white pepper (optional)

SESAME NOODLES

Májiàngmiàn

麻醬麵

SERVES 2

I came home one summer evening after a long bike ride on Yangming mountain, feeling so hungry I thought I'd keel over. Downstairs from my apartment in the crowded Beitou Market was a noodle stand, and I set my bike against the table, plunked myself on a pink plastic stool, and asked for a bowl of sesame sauce noodles. It cost about two US dollars, but to this day I still remember it as the best bowl of noodles I've ever eaten. The magic is all in the sauce—nutty sesame paste, minced garlic, slightly citrusy ground Sichuan peppercorn, soy sauce, a splash of rice vinegar, and a drizzle of smoky chili oil—folded into just-cooked noodles. For a refreshing crunch to go with the noodles, add some julienned cucumber. This is another recipe that will come together in about the same amount of time as it takes to boil the water.

MAKE THE SAUCE: Combine the sauce ingredients in a small bowl until smooth and blended.

Bring a pot of water to a boil. Add the noodles and cook according to package instructions to desired doneness. When the noodles are almost done, stir 1 tablespoon of the noodle cooking water into the sauce; it should be creamy and pourable, not too thick.

Drain the noodles in a colander and divide them between two bowls. Add a few spoonfuls of the sesame sauce to each bowl and stir to coat the noodles. Taste and add more sauce if needed. Sprinkle on some sesame seeds, garnish with sliced scallion greens and cucumber (if using), and enjoy immediately.

If you have any sauce remaining, store it in an airtight container in the fridge for up to a week and use it to dress blanched or steamed vegetables.

Note: Chinese sesame paste has a deeper flavor than tahini since the sesame is well-toasted before grinding, but tahini will work as a substitute.

THE SAUCE

2 tablespoons Chinese sesame paste, homemade (page 305) or store-bought (see Note)

1 tablespoon soy sauce

1 teaspoon Chinkiang black vinegar

2 garlic cloves, minced

½ teaspoon ground Sichuan peppercorns

2 teaspoons Red Chili Oil with sediment (page 301)

¼ teaspoon ground white pepper

7 ounces (200 grams) dried Chinese wheat noodles

Toasted sesame seeds, for garnish

Thinly sliced scallion greens, for garnish

1 small Persian cucumber, thinly julienned, for garnish (optional)

SCALLION OIL NOODLES

Cōngyóu bànmiàn

蔥油拌麵

SERVES 2

I first encountered the wonder of these noodles when I was in Shanghai—almost every vendor seemed to have their own version of "scallion oil–dressed noodles," whether it was a swanky shop in a shopping mall or a street stand. The potent flavors come from the smoky, savory oil infused with slow-fried scallions, garlic, and sesame seeds. It is stupidly delicious and comes together in 15 minutes or less.

Heat a wok or skillet over medium heat. Add the oil and heat until shimmering. Add all the scallions and cook, stirring continuously, until they are very fragrant and starting to caramelize, 4 to 5 minutes. You want their flavor to slowly infuse into the oil without burning the scallions; reduce the heat if necessary.

Add the garlic and sesame seeds and cook for 1 minute, just enough to toast the sesame seeds and coax out the garlic's aroma. After the sesame seeds start to pop, add the soy sauce and sugar and stir-fry to incorporate. Spoon the scallion mixture into a bowl.

Bring a pot of water to a boil. Add the noodles and boil according to package instructions to desired doneness. Drain the noodles in a colander and divide them between 2 bowls. Put some of the fragrant scallion sauce into each bowl, then toss to coat. Taste and adjust the amount of sauce as needed and serve immediately. You will likely have some of the scallion oil remaining; store it in an airtight container in the fridge for up to a week and use over noodles or rice.

¼ cup vegetable oil

4 scallions, smacked lightly with the flat blade of a knife, then cut into 2-inch sections, both white and green parts

3 garlic cloves, minced

1 tablespoon sesame seeds

2 tablespoons soy sauce

½ teaspoon sugar

7 ounces (200 grams) dried Chinese wheat noodles

TOMATO NOODLE SOUP

Fānqié tāngmiàn

蕃茄湯麵

For soupy noodles, having a flavorful broth is key, but that doesn't mean you have to cook it for a long time. The quick stir-fried tomato here makes the dish: it adds lovely acidity and color and takes the soup to a richer level of savoriness. I also like to simmer some soft tofu in the pot and throw in leafy greens at the end for a complete meal.

SERVES 2

Bring a pot of salted water to a boil. Add the noodles and cook according to the package instructions, or to desired doneness.

While the noodles cook, heat the vegetable oil in a separate saucepan over medium heat and add the tomatoes, white parts of the scallions, and a pinch of salt. Lightly stir-fry until the tomatoes are softened, about 1 minute. Add the stock and the tofu and bring to a boil. Season with salt to taste and a pinch each of white pepper and MSG. Add the greens (if using) at the very end, so they can wilt in the pot.

When the noodles are cooked to your liking, lift them out of the pot with chopsticks or a slotted spoon and divide them between 2 bowls. Ladle the soup, greens, and tofu over the noodles. Add a few drops of sesame oil and scatter each with half of the scallion greens. Mix well and serve with a soup spoon and chopsticks.

Kosher salt

7 ounces (200 grams) dried Chinese wheat noodles

2 tablespoons vegetable oil

1 medium tomato, peeled or unpeeled, cut into ¼-inch-thick slices

2 scallions, thinly sliced, white and green parts kept separate

3 cups (720 mL) unsalted stock of any kind or water

7 ounces (200 grams) soft tofu, cut into ½-inch cubes

Ground white pepper

MSG

Handful of fresh greens, like bok choy, lettuce, pea shoots, choy sum, or spinach (optional)

½ teaspoon toasted sesame oil

TOMATO
NOODLE SOUP

SEASAME
NOODLES

SCALLION OIL
NOODLES

STEAMED BUN DOUGH

Miàntuán

麵糰

MAKES 10 BUNS, OR ENOUGH DOUGH FOR THE RECIPES IN THIS CHAPTER

Steaming gives Chinese breads their distinctive texture—lightly chewy and soft (鬆軟 *sōngruǎn*), with a moist and airy interior and uniform white color with no crust. The pillowy bread is springy; if you squeeze a bun in your palm, it'll expand right back like a sponge. You can use this dough recipe for almost all Chinese steamed breads, including plain mantou (page 255), scallion buns (page 257), and stuffed buns (page 259): the basic recipe is flour, yeast, and warm water, with a pinch of salt for elasticity, baking powder for an extra bit of lift, and a small amount of oil for a subtle luster on the bun's surface.

In a small bowl or glass liquid measuring cup, proof the yeast by stirring together the warm water and sugar and allowing it to dissolve. Sprinkle the yeast on top and let sit for 5 to 10 minutes, until the surface looks foamy. If the yeast does not foam, then start over with newer yeast.

BY HAND: In a large bowl, combine the flour, salt, and baking powder.

Make a well in the center of the dry mixture. Pour in the wet mixture and stir with a pair of chopsticks until it forms fat flakes. Clean off the chopsticks and add the oil to the dough. Knead for 5 minutes, incorporating any remaining flour on the sides of the bowl, until the dough forms a firm, shaggy ball.

Cover with a tea towel and let the ball rest in the bowl at room temperature for 10 minutes, to relax and soften the dough. Continue kneading for another 5 minutes, until the dough is smooth, supple, and elastic.

STAND MIXER: Combine the flour, salt, and baking powder in the bowl of a stand mixer fitted with the dough hook. On low speed, slowly pour in the yeast mixture, then add the oil as the dough comes together into a ball. Increase the speed to medium and knead until the dough is smooth and elastic, 6 to 8 minutes.

For either method: Clean out the bowl and place the dough back in it. Set it in a warm place, cover it with a clean tea towel, and let rise until it has doubled in size. This will take 1 to 1½ hours, depending on the room temperature. Alternatively, let it rise in the fridge, covered, for at least 8 hours or up to overnight. You may use this dough in any of the bun recipes in this chapter; to make classic northern plain steamed buns (mantou), turn the page.

(recipe continues)

1 cup (236 grams) warm water

1 tablespoon granulated sugar

1¼ teaspoons active dry yeast (see Note)

420 grams (3 cups) all-purpose flour, or 280 grams (2 cups) all-purpose flour plus 140 grams (1 cup) plain pastry flour, plus more all-purpose flour for kneading

½ teaspoon kosher salt

1 teaspoon baking powder

1 teaspoon vegetable oil

Note: If you have instant yeast instead, substitute the same amount, skip the proofing step, and simply combine the yeast with the dry ingredients.

MANTOU

Mántou

饅頭

To make mantou, scrape the risen dough onto a lightly floured surface and knead vigorously for another 5 minutes, until there are no air bubbles and the dough is very smooth. Roll the dough into a 20-inch log about 1½ inches in diameter. Using a sharp knife, cut it into 10 equal portions. Cut out the same number of 3½-inch squares of parchment paper.

Take one portion of the dough and pull and tuck the dough into a round shape, with the seams on the bottom. Place the bun on the floured surface, cup it with both palms, and shape in a circular motion to make it stand taller. Place the bun on a parchment square. Repeat with the remaining dough.

Transfer the buns (on the parchment) into two steamer baskets, making sure they're at least 1 inch apart, as they will expand. Cover with a tea towel and let them rise for 15 to 20 minutes. Fill the steamer base or a wok with water to reach just below the baskets, about 2 inches—the bottom of the basket shouldn't touch the water. Use this time to clean up your station and any remaining utensils.

Uncover and check the proofed dough—when you gently push on a bun, your finger should leave an indentation that springs back slowly.

Set the baskets with the buns over the cool water and heat over high heat until the water comes to a boil (you will see steam rising from the pot). Reduce the heat to medium and steam the buns for 12 minutes. Remove from the heat and allow the buns to sit in the steamer, covered, for 5 minutes. This will prevent a sudden change in temperature that might cause the buns to deflate or wrinkle.

Uncover the steamer and press a fingertip gently into a bun—if it feels firm and the indentation bounces back immediately, it is done. If it still feels squishy, cover and steam for 3 to 5 more minutes, then test again. Enjoy the buns hot or let them cool before serving.

If you have only one steamer basket and are making the buns in batches, place the remaining buns in the refrigerator while the others cook to slow their rising. Check the water remaining in the wok and replenish it before steaming the second batch.

Refrigerate any remaining steamed buns in zip-top plastic bags or freeze them in a single layer on a baking sheet and then transfer them to a zip-top bag. To reheat, steam them directly from the refrigerator or freezer for 6 to 8 minutes, until hot all the way through.

A NOTE
ON FLOUR

Flour sold in the United States generally has a higher amount of gluten than flour in Asia. This is because it's milled with hard wheat, high in gluten-forming protein, which makes it ideal for breads and pastas, as the gluten lends structure and makes them chewier. However, it's harder to get the same fluffy lightness and tender, spongy textures you want in Chinese breads. To make up for the difference, I use a blend of all-purpose flour and plain pastry flour when I'm making buns and dumplings. Generally, 2 parts all-purpose flour and 1 part pastry flour will approximate the "softer" wheat and lower gluten content of Chinese all-purpose flour.

Different brands of all-purpose flour also vary in gluten and protein. To find the protein content of your brand, check the nutritional label and calculate the amount of protein per 100 grams of flour. For example, if the label says ¼ cup or 34 grams flour contains 4 grams protein, then 100 grams will contain roughly 11.7 grams, making the protein percent 11.7 percent. The higher the percentage, the "stronger" the flour.

MEASURING FLOUR

Because measuring flours and starches by volume yields significant variation (one cup of flour may range from 3 to 6 ounces, depending on how you scoop or pack it), I highly recommend using a digital scale. It allows you to use a single bowl, instead of multiple measuring cups, and the precise weight measurements in these recipes (listed first) will ensure the best consistency for the dough. For the dry ingredient measurements I've provided, I used the scoop-and-level method to determine their volume equivalents.

SCALLION FLOWER BUNS

Huā juǎn

花卷

MAKES 10 BUNS

My dad's favorite steamed bread is plain *mantou*, but he'd always make scallion buns for me and my siblings—we loved them since they were flavorful on their own, dotted with bits of scallion and the savory fragrance of ground Sichuan peppercorn. After Dad rolled out the dough, I'd help him brush on the oil, sprinkle the salt, and stack the layered "flowers," and after they finished steaming, I often burned my fingers peeling back the soft, fluffy layers, eager to devour them hot. Don't be intimidated by the intricate look of the buns; they're very easy to shape. You can freeze any leftover buns and pop them directly into a steamer to reheat.

MAKE THE SCALLION OIL: Place the scallions, ground peppercorns (if using), and salt in a heatproof bowl. Heat the vegetable oil in a saucepan until it is nearly smoking, then pour it quickly over the scallions to release their fragrance.

Cut ten 4-inch parchment paper squares.

Scrape the risen dough onto a lightly floured surface and knead vigorously for 5 minutes, until there are no more air bubbles and the dough is very smooth. Divide the dough in half and cover one portion with a damp tea towel so it doesn't dry out. Using a rolling pin, roll the other half of the dough into a rectangle about 20 inches long × 12 inches wide × ¼ inch thick, with the long side facing you.

Spread a thin layer of the scallion oil on the dough using a brush or your fingers and leaving a ½-inch margin. Gently roll up the dough away from you and toward the top edge, then pinch the long edge closed to seal in the oil. Trim off both ends and slice the remaining dough crosswise into 8 equal-size pieces.

Take 2 of the pieces and stack one on top of each other, then place a chopstick across the middle of the top piece, almost as if you're going to cut it in half, and press down firmly just enough to stick the pieces together. Slide the chopstick out and place the bun on a square of parchment paper. Repeat with the remaining pieces to make 4 buns. Repeat with the remaining half of the dough. Don't discard the 4 raggedy ends— stack them together to make two smaller buns, for 10 buns total.

(recipe continues)

SCALLION OIL

6 scallions, green parts only, thinly sliced

½ teaspoon ground Sichuan peppercorns (optional)

1 teaspoon kosher salt

3 tablespoons vegetable oil

1 batch Steamed Bun Dough (page 253), risen but not shaped

All-purpose flour, for dusting

Set up a large steamer. Transfer the buns into steamer baskets, making sure they're placed at least an inch apart, as they will expand when cooking. Cover and let them rise for 15 minutes.

In the meantime, fill the steamer base or wok with water to reach just below the baskets, about 2 inches. The bottom of the basket shouldn't touch the water. Use this time to clean up your station and any remaining utensils. Uncover and check the proofed dough—when you gently push on a bun, your finger should leave an indentation that springs back slowly.

Set the baskets with the buns over the cool water and heat over high heat until the water comes to a boil (you'll see the steam rising from the pot). Reduce the heat to medium and steam the buns for 10 minutes. Remove from the heat and allow the buns to sit in the steamer, covered, for 5 minutes.

This will prevent a sudden change in temperature that might cause the buns to deflate or wrinkle. Uncover the basket and press a fingertip gently into the bun—if it feels firm and the indentation bounces back immediately, it is done. If it still feels squishy, cover and steam for 3 to 5 more minutes, then test again. Enjoy the buns hot or let them cool before serving.

If you have only one steamer basket and are making the buns in batches, place the remaining buns in the refrigerator to slow their rising while the others cook. Check the water in the wok and replenish it before steaming another batch.

Refrigerate any remaining steamed buns in zip-top plastic bags or freeze them in a single layer on a baking sheet and then transfer them to a zip-top freezer bag. To reheat, steam them directly from the refrigerator or freezer for 4 to 5 minutes.

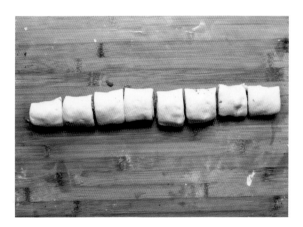

HANNAH CHE

STEAMED STUFFED BUNS (BAOZI)

Sù bāozi

素包子

MAKES 21 BUNS

There are few foods more perfect than a baozi. Each one is a self-contained package you can eat with your hands, a soft, white sphere of steamed bread wrapped around a sweet or savory filling. Typically, northern-style baozi are big and hearty, stuffed with pork, mushrooms, and cabbage or other dumpling-style fillings. Sweet versions can include red bean paste, sweet date paste, or lotus seed. In teahouses in Guangzhou, baozi come nestled in trios in stacked bamboo steamers, and they're made with a sweeter and fluffier dough and filled with sweet barbecued pork (*char siu bao*), yellow oozing custard or molten black sesame. In Taiwan, rows of baozi are tucked into a giant skillet and pan-fried into cube-shaped, crispy-bottomed buns (水煎包 *shuǐjiānbāo*), and many vendors offer vegetarian fillings with pickled mustard greens, cabbage, pressed tofu, and vermicelli.

The beauty of baozi is that you can fill them with whatever you'd like. Five of our family's favorite vegetarian stuffings are included here. You can also use the cabbage filling provided in Boiled Dumplings (page 267), or the chive and tofu skin filling provided in Chive-Stuffed Boxes (page 272).

There are different ways of forming the buns, and I include instructions for a few common methods of pleating. If you're doubling the recipe and making a larger batch with multiple fillings, mark the buns by using different methods of pleating, so people will know what to expect inside. And don't worry if you can't quite get the hang of the circular pleats—it takes lots of practice, and if all else fails, just pinch the ends at the top, or fold the two edges together and pleat it into a half-moon shape, like a steamed dumpling. They don't have to be perfect to taste good.

Follow the instructions for basic steamed bun dough. As the dough is resting, prepare your filling of choice.

Scrape the dough out of the bowl onto a clean, lightly floured surface. Knead vigorously for 5 minutes, until there are no more air bubbles and the dough is very smooth. Divide the dough in half.

(recipe continues)

1 batch Steamed Bun Dough (page 253), risen but not shaped

1 batch filling of choice (recipes follow)

All-purpose flour, for dusting

Using both palms, roll one portion of the dough into a log about a foot long and 1½ inches in diameter. Pinch off pieces of the dough and weigh them—they should be a little over 1 ounce (32 grams) each, about the size of a golf ball. Repeat so that you have 21 equal-size pieces, keeping the cut portions covered with a dampened tea towel to prevent them from drying out. Cut 21 (3½-inch) squares of parchment paper.

Lightly dust the dough pieces with flour. Flatten each piece with your palm into a flat, round disk. Using a thin rolling pin, roll the disk into a flat circle with your dominant hand, turning the disk between rolls with your other hand to make a circle about 3½ inches in diameter. As you roll the dough, leave the center alone so that you end up with a circle that's thicker in the middle and thinner toward the edges. Repeat with all the dough to make 21 wrappers and dust them lightly with flour before you stack them so they don't stick to each other. Keep covered so they don't dry out.

Hold one wrapper on your nondominant hand, cupping your palm to form the wrapper into a cup shape. Place about 3 tablespoons of the filling in the center. Press the filling down gently, leaving a ¾-inch margin of dough around the filling.

TO SHAPE ROUND BUNS: Using your dominant hand, pinch the edge of the wrapper with your thumb and index finger to make the first pleat. Rotate the wrapper with your nondominant hand as you extend your index finger and pinch another pleat, moving counterclockwise if right-handed or clockwise if left-handed around the edge. Use your non–pleating hand's thumb to press and poke down the filling as the opening closes. Your pleating hand should be relatively stationary, centered in the middle of the wrapper, while the other hand rotates—try not to pull the dough. Pinch the top of the baozi closed with 2 or 3 pleats, making a pointed tip, or leave it unsealed with a small opening. Set the filled baozi down and gently shape it so it stands upright.

TO SHAPE WHEAT BRAID BUNS: Gather opposite sides of the circle toward the center like a dumpling. With your dominant hand, use your thumb and index finger to begin pinching pleats to close the edges, one on the left side of the crease and one on the right, moving toward the top. At the very end, pinch a flat tail to seal in the filling.

TO SHAPE SPLIT CHAR SIU–STYLE BUNS: Gather the edge of the circle equidistantly in 3 places toward the center to form a triangle. Enclose and pinch the edges tightly to seal in the filling. Fold the 3 corners to meet in the center and pinch them to form 3 triangular peaks.

THE EASIEST SHAPE: Simply fold the dough over to encase the filling in a half-moon shape and pinch the edges tightly closed. You can pleat the edges a bit as well if you like.

TO COOK THE BAOZI: Place each filled baozi on a parchment paper square. Cover the shaped buns and let them rise for 15 minutes as you set up the steamer. If you're using a wok with bamboo steamer baskets, fill the wok with water to just below the baskets, about 2 inches—the bottom of the basket shouldn't touch the water. While the buns are proofing, bring the water to a boil over high heat.

Place the buns in the basket about 1½ inches apart. Put the remaining uncooked buns in the refrigerator, covered, to slow their rising while the others cook. Cover and steam the buns over high heat for 8 to 9 minutes, then remove the steamer from the heat and let the buns sit in the covered steamer for 5 minutes, to prevent them from wrinkling. Uncover and transfer the buns to a plate or wire rack. Replenish the water as needed and continue steaming the remaining buns. Serve them hot or at room temperature.

Refrigerate any cooked and cooled buns in zip-top plastic bags or freeze them in a single layer on a baking sheet and then transfer them to a zip-top freezer bag. To reheat, steam them directly from the refrigerator or freezer for 8 minutes, or until the filling is hot.

VEGETARIAN FILLINGS, FIVE WAYS

For plant-based baozi fillings, there are several tips to ensure they taste spectacular. Mushrooms and vegetables like cabbage and leafy greens lose a lot of volume and release water when they cook, but you don't want this to happen inside the dumpling wrapper or the bun. Instead, salt and briefly stir-fry them beforehand to cook out their moisture and infuse them with more flavor. Also precook pungent aromatic ingredients like scallions and onions to release their flavor.

Don't skimp on the oil in these fillings, since it's the only source of fat and richness, and it's necessary for a juicy, savory mouthfeel. I always use scallion oil for more flavor. Finally, taste the filling and season it generously before using; it should taste so good you could eat it with a spoon.

Sour Cabbage and Glass Noodle Filling

Suāncài fěntiáo

酸菜粉條

MAKES 5 CUPS, ENOUGH TO FILL 21 BUNS

The bright, sharp acidity from sour fermented cabbage always lends extra flavor, and as the cabbage cooks, its mouth-puckering acidity mellows into a rich, juicy filling. Stir-fried onions add sweetness and bulk, and the finely chopped glass noodles create a chewy, richer mouthfeel.

6 ounces (170 grams) sweet potato vermicelli noodles

1 pound (450 grams) sour fermented Chinese cabbage, homemade (page 309) or store-bought

¼ cup Scallion Oil (page 301) or vegetable oil

1 large yellow onion

3 scallions, both green and white parts

1 tablespoon minced fresh ginger

1 tablespoon soy sauce

½ teaspoon kosher salt, plus more to taste

½ teaspoon five-spice powder

1 tablespoon toasted sesame oil

Bring a pan of water to a boil. Cook the noodles according to the package instructions until tender but still chewy. Refresh them in cool water and drain well. While you're cooking the noodles, finely chop the sour cabbage (or pulse it in a food processor) and squeeze out the excess liquid; you should have at least 3 cups. Finely chop the onion and scallions. Finely chop the starch noodles when they've cooled.

Heat the scallion oil in a wok over medium-high heat until shimmering. Add the onion, ginger, and scallions and stir-fry until the onion is softened and very aromatic, about 4 minutes. Add the sour cabbage and cook, stirring continuously, until the cabbage is softened and heated through, about 3 minutes. Remove from the heat, stir in the chopped glass noodles, and season with the soy sauce, salt, five-spice powder, and sesame oil. Stir well and taste, adjusting seasonings as needed—it should be very flavorful. Transfer to a large bowl and set aside to cool as you prepare the dough. This may be prepared and stored overnight in the fridge before using.

Cabbage and Shiitake Mushroom Filling

Xiānggū gāolìcài

香菇高麗菜

**MAKES 5 CUPS,
ENOUGH TO FILL 21 BUNS**

This is a popular vegetarian combination—savory shiitake mushrooms and glistening bits of vermicelli noodles are the perfect counterpart to the tender cabbage, which I salt and briefly stir-fry to eliminate moisture and build flavor. Green cabbage will work fine, but flat-head or Taiwanese cabbage (高麗菜 *gāolìcài*) is even better—its leaves are softer and sweeter.

  8 large dried or fresh shiitake mushrooms

  Boiling water (if using dried shiitakes)

  1 pound (450 grams) cabbage, preferably flat-head cabbage

  2 teaspoons kosher salt, divided, plus more to taste

  1 bundle mung bean vermicelli (2 ounces / 56 grams)

  ¼ cup Scallion Oil (page 301) or vegetable oil

  2 scallions, halved lengthwise and finely chopped, both green and white parts

  1 tablespoon minced fresh ginger

  1 tablespoon minced fresh garlic

  1 teaspoon soy sauce

  1 tablespoon vegetarian oyster sauce

  1 tablespoon toasted sesame oil

  1½ teaspoons sugar

If you're using dried mushrooms, soak them in a couple cups of boiling water for 30 minutes.

Cut the cabbage in half. Slice out and discard the hard stem portion. Shred the leaves in a food processor or finely chop them by hand. Transfer the leaves to a bowl and toss with 1½ teaspoons of the salt. Set aside for 10 minutes, then squeeze the cabbage to remove as much water as possible.

Squeeze the soaked mushrooms dry; whether using dried or fresh, snip off and discard the stems and finely chop the caps. In the meantime, bring a pot of water to a boil. Cook the vermicelli according to the package instructions, until tender but still chewy. Rinse in cold water and drain well. Finely chop or pulse them in a food processor and place them in a large bowl.

In a seasoned wok, heat the scallion oil over medium-high heat until shimmering. Add the mushrooms and stir-fry for 2 minutes, until they are browned. Add the chopped scallions, ginger, and garlic and stir-fry until aromatic, about 30 seconds. Add the soy sauce and shredded cabbage and stir-fry for about 2 minutes, until the cabbage is slightly wilted but still crisp.

Remove the pot from the heat and stir in the chopped vermicelli to incorporate. Season with the remaining ½ teaspoon salt, the oyster sauce, sesame oil, and sugar. Add additional salt to taste—the filling should be very flavorful. Transfer the mixture back to the large bowl and set aside to cool as you prepare the dough. This may be prepared and stored overnight in the fridge before using.

Mustard Greens and Pressed Tofu Filling

Xuěcài dòugān

雪菜豆乾

**MAKES 5 CUPS,
ENOUGH TO FILL 21 BUNS**

One of my all-time favorites is the classic "snow vegetable" (雪菜 *xuěcài*) bun: the vendor in my Taipei neighborhood chops and salts mustard greens and mixes them with slinky bits of vermicelli and pressed tofu. Mustard greens have a peppery bite and pungency that mellows out into a distinct mustard aroma—it's absolutely delicious in a filling.

5 large dried or fresh shiitake mushrooms

Boiling water (if using dried shiitakes)

1 pound (450 grams) fresh leafy mustard greens

2 teaspoons kosher salt, plus more as needed

1 bundle mung bean vermicelli
(2 ounces / 56 grams)

¼ cup Shallot Oil (page 302) or vegetable oil

3 squares smoked or five-spice pressed tofu
(6 ounces / 170 grams), finely diced

1 tablespoon minced fresh ginger

1 tablespoon vegetarian oyster sauce

1 teaspoon sugar

1 teaspoon toasted sesame oil

¼ teaspoon ground white pepper

If you're using dried mushrooms, soak them in a couple cups of boiling water for 30 minutes, then squeeze dry. Whether using dried or fresh, snip off and discard the stems and finely chop the caps.

Thoroughly wash the mustard greens and shake the leaves dry. Finely chop the greens and transfer them to a large bowl. Toss with the salt and let sit for 10 minutes, then scrunch your hands through them to release any liquid. Without rinsing, squeeze out and discard as much water as you can.

Cook the vermicelli according to the package instructions, until the noodles are tender but still chewy. Rinse in cold water and drain well. Finely chop or pulse them in a food processor and place in a large bowl.

In a seasoned wok, heat the shallot oil over medium-high heat until shimmering. Add the pressed tofu pieces and fry for 3 minutes, until they are golden brown around the edges and slightly blistered. Add the ginger and mushrooms and stir-fry until aromatic, about 2 minutes. Add the mustard greens and stir-fry quickly until hot and wilted, about 1 minute.

Remove the wok from the heat and stir in the chopped vermicelli noodles, vegetarian oyster

sauce, sugar, sesame oil, and white pepper and add additional salt to taste—the filling should be very flavorful. Set the filling aside as you prepare the dough. This may be prepared and stored overnight in the fridge before using.

Dill and Fried Tofu Filling

Huíxiāng dòufu

茴香豆腐

**MAKES 5 CUPS,
ENOUGH TO FILL 21 BUNS**

Using fresh dill in dumpling and bun fillings is a longstanding tradition in the northeast of China, and I learned this recipe from my grandma, who simply fries tofu until golden and finely chops it with the feathery green dill fronds, seasoning the filling with soy sauce and sesame oil. The buttery, savory, and herbaceous aroma of the dill is the key flavor here, so if you don't like dill, I'd pick another filling. But for dill lovers, this is going to be your favorite—it's so simple that I can never quite believe how delicious it is.

14 to 16 ounces (390 to 450 grams)
extra-firm tofu

Vegetable oil, for frying

8 ounces (224 grams) fresh dill

1 tablespoon soy sauce

¾ teaspoon kosher salt, or more to taste

2 tablespoons toasted sesame oil

Soak the tofu in boiling water to cover for 15 minutes, then blot it dry and cut it into 1½-inch cubes.

Heat 2 cups (480 mL) oil in a wok over medium-high heat to 370°F (195°C), or until a wooden chopstick forms a merry stream of bubbles when inserted. Working in batches, fry the tofu until each cube has developed a crispy, golden crust,

(recipe continues)

5 to 6 minutes. Transfer to a paper towel–lined plate. Pour the oil into a heatproof container for another use.

When the tofu is cool enough to handle, finely chop and place it in a large bowl. Soak the dill in a large bowl of cold water, then rinse it well to wash off any grit or dirt, and shake dry. Trim roots and discard.

Finely chop the dill and place in the bowl with the tofu; you should have about 3½ cups. Add the soy sauce, salt, and sesame oil and blend well. Taste and add more salt as needed—the filling should be very flavorful. Set aside as you prepare the dough. This may be prepared and stored overnight in the fridge before using.

Char Siu King Oyster Mushroom Filling

Chāshāobāo

叉燒包

**MAKES 5 CUPS,
ENOUGH TO FILL 21 BUNS**

I got the inspiration for this vegetarian version of char siu barbecued pork at a teahouse in Guangzhou—the combination of fried king oyster mushrooms and pressed tofu provides both tenderness and meaty chew. The syrupy reduced mixture of vegetarian oyster sauce and hoisin sauce creates a savory and sweet dark glaze that coats the filling in a sticky, glossy coating, and as the fluffy white buns expand in the steamer, sometimes a bit of the sauce will ooze out between the cracks.

1 teaspoon potato starch

Vegetable oil, for frying

14 ounces (390 grams) king oyster mushrooms, cut into ½-inch cubes

4 squares smoked or five-spice tofu (8 ounces / 224 grams), cut into ⅛-inch dice

1 medium yellow onion, cut roughly into ½-inch pieces

2 tablespoons soy sauce

⅓ cup sugar

3 tablespoons hoisin sauce

1 tablespoon vegetarian oyster sauce

1 teaspoon toasted sesame oil

¼ teaspoon kosher salt, plus more to taste

Make a slurry by combining the starch with 1½ tablespoons cold water in a small bowl. Stir until smooth and set aside.

Heat 2 cups (480 mL) oil in a wok over high heat to 375°F (190°C). Fry the mushroom cubes until they are shrunken in size and golden brown, about 4 minutes. Remove with a slotted spoon or spider and shake dry over the wok, then transfer to a paper towel to drain.

Add the tofu cubes and fry just until golden and slightly blistered, but not so long they lose all their moisture, about 2 minutes. Drain on paper towels. Pour the oil into a heatproof container for another use, reserving 2 tablespoons in the wok.

Return the wok to medium-high heat and sauté the onion pieces until softened and becoming translucent, about 3 minutes. Add the soy sauce and stir, then pour in ¾ cup water and bring to a boil. Simmer for 4 minutes, then remove the onion pieces with a slotted spoon. The onions are there to infuse the stock with their flavor, but you don't want them in the actual filling.

Add the sugar, hoisin sauce, vegetarian oyster sauce, mushrooms, and tofu and stir to incorporate. Give the starch slurry a stir, then slowly add it to the wok, stirring continuously, until the liquid has reduced and thickened into a sauce that coats the mushrooms and tofu like a glaze. Remove from the heat, stir in the sesame oil, and add salt to taste. Set the filling aside as you prepare the dough. This may be prepared and stored overnight in the fridge before using.

HANNAH CHE

BOILED DUMPLINGS (JIAOZI)

Shuǐjiǎo

水餃

MAKES 90 TO 95 DUMPLINGS

In our family, we get an assembly line going whenever we make dumplings: my dad rolls out the wrappers, the rest of us fill and pleat them, and my mom usually runs the stove, dropping the dumplings into the boiling water and hauling them out when they float to the surface. For years, I've been making this vegetarian filling to satisfy even the meat eaters in our family; it's a take on the classic napa cabbage and pork filling that uses cabbage, shiitake mushrooms, and freshly fried tofu for a satisfying, juicy savoriness. Don't be alarmed at how many dumplings this makes; they freeze easily, and a bag of frozen homemade dumplings is the best thing to have stashed in your freezer for future meals since they cook quickly without needing to be defrosted. My mom's principle is that if you're going to take the time to make dumplings, you might as well make a big batch.

MAKE THE DOUGH: Combine the flour and salt in a large bowl. Make a well in the center and pour in the water. Stir with a pair of chopsticks until it forms large flakes. Using your hands, knead the dough in the bowl until all the flakes come together into a shaggy ball and there is no more dry flour in the bowl. Let rest for 5 minutes, then knead again until it is taut, smooth, and firm, about 7 minutes. Cover the bowl with a plate or tea towel and allow the dough to rest for 15 minutes.

MAKE THE FILLING: Soak the mushrooms in boiling water to cover for 30 minutes to rehydrate. Squeeze dry, then snip off and discard the stems and finely chop the caps.

Soak the tofu in boiling water to cover for 15 minutes, then blot it dry and cut it into 1½-inch cubes.

Finely chop the cabbage leaves and stems. Alternatively, pulse the cabbage in a food processor to shred it. Transfer to a bowl and toss with the salt. Set aside for 10 minutes to allow the cabbage to release its moisture.

(recipe and ingredients continue)

THE DOUGH

560 grams (4 cups) all-purpose flour, plus more for dusting

¾ teaspoon kosher salt

280 grams (1 cup plus 3 tablespoons) cold water

THE FILLING

4 large dried shiitake mushrooms

Boiling water

14 to 16 ounces (390 to 450 grams) extra-firm tofu

1 pound (450 grams) napa cabbage leaves

1 teaspoon kosher salt, plus more to taste

Heat 2 cups (480 mL) oil in a wok over medium-high heat to 370°F (195°C), or until a wooden chopstick forms a merry stream of bubbles when inserted. Working in batches, fry the tofu until each cube has developed a crispy, golden crust, 5 to 6 minutes. Transfer to a paper towel–lined plate. Pour the oil into a heatproof container for another use. When the tofu is cool enough to handle, finely chop and place it in a large bowl.

Squeeze the salted cabbage to remove as much water as possible. Heat the scallion oil in a wok or skillet over medium-high heat until shimmering. Stir-fry the ginger and scallions until aromatic. Add the mushrooms and soy sauce and stir-fry until the liquid is drawn out and the mushrooms start to brown, about 5 minutes. Add the squeezed cabbage and the fried tofu and cook until the cabbage is piping hot and most of the liquid is evaporated, about 2 minutes. Remove from the heat and transfer everything to the bowl that was holding the cabbage.

Add the vegetarian oyster sauce, sugar, white pepper, and sesame oil. Taste and add additional salt if needed—the saltiness and flavor of boiled dumplings will dilute as they cook, so make sure it is very flavorful. Stir in the potato starch so that the loose filling slightly clumps together, then set aside to cool as you prepare the wrappers.

MAKE THE WRAPPERS: Scrape the dough out of the bowl onto a lightly floured surface and knead briefly for 2 minutes until smooth. Cut the dough in half.

Take one portion and form it into a ball, then poke a hole in the center and shape it like a donut. Lift the dough up off the board so that gravity causes the bottom half of the donut to stretch and sag down, and gently shape the dough with your hands as it grows skinnier, forming an O-shaped rope.

When the dough is about ¾ inch in diameter, break the donut into a long rope, then grasp one end of the rope in your fist and use the other hand to tear off ¾-inch pieces with a sharp, quick snap of your wrist. Each portion should be the size of a gumball, weighing between 9 and 10 grams. Alternatively, you can use a knife or a pastry scraper to cut the rope into ¾-inch pieces. Toss the dough pieces in flour to generously dust them, and set them to one side of your floured work surface. Repeat with the remaining half of the dough.

(recipe continues)

Vegetable oil, for shallow-frying

¼ cup Scallion Oil (page 301) or vegetable oil

2 tablespoons minced fresh ginger

3 scallions, both white and green parts finely chopped

2 tablespoons soy sauce

1 tablespoon vegetarian oyster sauce

½ teaspoon sugar

½ teaspoon ground white pepper

1 tablespoon toasted sesame oil

2 tablespoons potato starch or cornstarch

Dumpling Dipping Sauce (recipe follows), for serving

Flatten the dough pieces with your palm into circular disks. Position a rolling pin on the dough and move it forward and back a few times, rolling only halfway up to the center. Turn the dough with your nondominant hand, rotating away from the rolling pin, until the wrapper is 3 inches in diameter with a quarter-size "belly" in the center. For boiled dumplings, try to roll it out as thin as possible—my parents always say the marker of a good boiled dumpling is how thin and tender the skin is, but for steamed or pan-fried dumplings, you want it to be slightly thicker so it doesn't break. Toss the wrapper onto a generously floured surface and continue with the remaining disks of dough. Keep the finished wrappers dusted with flour as you stack them to prevent them from sticking to each other.

To fill the dumplings, place a wrapper on the palm of your nondominant hand. Spoon about 2 teaspoons of the filling into the center. To make a simple dumpling, fold the wrapper in half so the edges meet, and pinch the dough all along the rim to seal in the filling. Press the bottom belly of the dumpling onto the board so that it stands upright. To make a pleated dumpling, fold the wrapper in half so the edges meet. Hold it in your nondominant hand, cradling it with your fingers. With your dominant hand, starting at the bottom corner closest to you, pinch with your index finger and thumb to form the first pleat. Grasp the closest edge of the wrapper with your thumb and fold it over on itself to make a pleat, pressing it against the back edge of the wrapper to meet your index finger. Repeat this step, pressing each pleat against the back edge, until you reach the top of the circle. Repeat from the other corner with your other hand, sealing in the filling completely. You should have 6 to 8 pleats when done. With either method, be sure to pinch the edges of the dough airtight so the filling doesn't leak out when boiling the dumplings.

Bring about 4 quarts water to a boil in a large stockpot over high heat. When the water is rapidly boiling, drop in 10 to 12 dumplings and stir gently with a wooden spoon. When the water reaches a full boil again, add 1 cup cool water (this will replenish the water that has evaporated) and bring the water back to a rolling boil. When the dumplings are floating on the surface and puffed up, they are done. This will take roughly 4 to 5 minutes. Transfer the dumplings with a large slotted spoon or strainer to a serving plate. Continue cooking as many as you'll eat in one meal and freeze the remaining uncooked dumplings. Serve the boiled dumplings immediately with the dipping sauce.

To freeze the uncooked dumplings, place them in a single layer on a baking sheet and freeze for 30 minutes. Transfer them to a zip-top bag and stash in the freezer for up to 1 month. You can cook them without defrosting: just plop a few in a pot of boiling water and cook until they're puffed up and tender, 3 to 4 minutes.

DUMPLING DIPPING SAUCE
Makes ¼ cup

2 tablespoons Chinkiang black vinegar

2 tablespoons soy sauce

½ teaspoon sugar

1 teaspoon chili garlic paste, chili oil, or sriracha

Stir the sauce ingredients together until smooth and set aside until you're ready to eat.

CHIVE-STUFFED BOXES

Jiǔcài hézi

韭菜盒子

MAKES 16 BOXES

Think of these as giant pan-fried dumplings or turnovers. They're usually filled with fragrant chives, glistening bean thread noodles, and scrambled eggs, although here I simply replace the egg with tofu skin. My dad says that the key to a good chive-stuffed box is to roll the wrapper as thin as possible so that it encloses the piping-hot, juicy filling like a delicate, slightly chewy but crisp sheath. I was always too impatient and ate mine immediately after it was fried, but my mom would patiently wait for hers to cool and then eat it with Chinkiang black vinegar, a tiny bit carefully spooned onto each bite.

MAKE THE DOUGH: Place the flours and salt in a large bowl. Make a well in the center and pour in the boiling water. Stir with a pair of chopsticks until it forms large flakes. Add the cool water and continue to stir until the flour comes together into a shaggy ball.

When it is cool enough to touch, knead the dough in the bowl until it is taut and smooth, 7 to 10 minutes.

Cover the bowl and allow the dough to rest at room temperature for at least 15 minutes. You can also make the dough in advance and refrigerate it in an airtight container or zip-top bag for up to 2 days. Allow the dough to return to room temperature before using.

MAKE THE FILLING: While the dough is resting, tear the tofu skin into large pieces. Heat a wok or skillet over medium heat and add the oil. When shimmering, add the tofu skin and stir-fry, much as you would scramble an egg, until it is lightly golden, about 2 minutes. Transfer to a cutting board. When cool enough to handle, finely chop and place it in a large bowl. Add the chives and cooled noodle bits to the bowl. Add the salt, sesame oil, and white pepper, then taste and adjust as necessary. The filling should taste a little salty; the flavor will mellow as it cooks.

To make the wrapper, uncover and knead the dough lightly on a floured surface until soft and elastic. Divide the dough in half. Keep one portion covered under a damp tea towel or plastic wrap. Cut the other half into 8 equal-size pieces.

On a lightly floured surface, press each piece into a flat disk. Use a rolling pin to roll it out into a thin wrapper about 5 inches in diameter. Repeat with the remaining disks and the other half of the dough; you should end with 16 wrappers in total. Dust the wrappers with flour to prevent them from sticking to each other.

(recipe continues)

THE HOT WATER DOUGH

250 grams (2 cups) all-purpose flour, plus more for dusting

125 grams (1 cup) pastry flour

¼ teaspoon kosher salt

207 grams (¾ cup plus 2 tablespoons) boiling water

2 tablespoons (28 grams) cool water

THE FILLING

8 ounces (225 grams) tofu skin, thawed if frozen

3 tablespoons vegetable oil

9 ounces (252 grams) Chinese garlic chives, trimmed and finely chopped

1 bundle mung bean or sweet potato vermicelli (2 ounces / 56 grams), cooked, drained, cooled, and cut into ½-inch pieces

1½ teaspoons kosher salt, plus more to taste

1 teaspoon toasted sesame oil

¼ teaspoon ground white pepper

Vegetable oil, for pan-frying

Holding a wrapper in the palm of your nondominant hand, place about 3 heaping tablespoons of the filling in the center of the wrapper. Fold the circle in half to form a half-moon shape and tightly pinch the edges flat to seal them. You can pleat the flat edge again, rolling it inward and pinching to form a braid-like border.

Heat a large skillet over medium heat. Add enough oil to lightly cover the bottom and heat until the oil is shimmering. Working in batches, arrange the chive boxes in the skillet in a single layer, spaced about ½ inch apart. Pan-fry until golden brown on one side, about 3 minutes. Flip them over.

Pour ½ cup water into the pan—it will sizzle and splatter on contact—and cover immediately with a lid to trap the steam. Let the dumplings steam for 3 minutes, until you can hear them sizzling and most of the water has evaporated.

Uncover and check the bottoms of the chive boxes. If there is still liquid remaining in the pan, or if the bottoms are not yet golden brown, continue cooking, uncovered, for another minute. Remove each chive box and allow it to drain on a paper towel. Repeat with the remaining dumplings. Allow to cool slightly before eating. Serve with Chinkiang vinegar and chili oil.

SCALLION PANCAKES

Cōngyóubǐng

蔥油餅

MAKES SIX 8-INCH PANCAKES

Scallion pancakes are simple in concept: dough, chopped scallions, salt, and oil rolled out into thin pancakes and pan-fried until crispy. But try as I might, I could never replicate the elusive flakiness of the ones I bought from vendors on the street, the kind that pull apart into sheet upon sheet of satiny layers, with a shatteringly crisp exterior but tender interior.

After talking to several scallion pancake vendors in Taipei, I realized that they had one thing in common: they made their dough in advance and refrigerated it in pre-portioned balls before rolling them out at the cart the next day. One vendor gave me a ball from her icebox to take home, and I realized it wasn't elastic like bread dough, but wet, soft, and sticky, almost too sticky to roll out. After more tinkering, I realized it really was that simple: the secret to a good scallion pancake is just a high-moisture dough that's minimally kneaded and refrigerated overnight.

I'm happy to say I can now make scallion pancakes worthy of street-vendor status in my own kitchen, and I hope you try them, too—they're delicious for breakfast and make a great appetizer, cut into wedges and served hot, either by themselves or with a dipping sauce of black vinegar, soy sauce, and a dab of chili oil or chili sauce. You can freeze the uncooked pancakes and reheat them directly from the freezer—just give them a few extra minutes in the skillet, flipping until both sides are crisp and browned.

MAKE THE DOUGH: Place the flour and salt in a large bowl. Make a well in the center and add the boiling water, stirring with a pair of chopsticks until large flakes form. Add the cool water and continue stirring until the flour forms a shaggy ball.

Knead the dough in the bowl until it just comes together into a smooth, taut ball, about 2 minutes. Do not overwork the dough; it should be sticky and hold an indentation indefinitely when pressed with a fingertip. Cover and refrigerate overnight. After chilling, it will look darker in color and be still tacky but firmer to the touch.

MAKE THE SCALLION OIL PASTE: In a heatproof bowl, combine the flour and salt and place the scallions and ground peppercorns on top. Heat the oil in a small pan over high heat until it is nearly smoking, then pour it on top of the spices and scallions in the bowl, releasing

(recipe and ingredients continue)

THE DOUGH

360 grams (2½ cups) all-purpose flour, plus more for dusting

216 grams (1½ cups) pastry flour or cake flour

½ teaspoon kosher salt

236 grams (1 cup) boiling water

148 grams (½ cup plus 2 tablespoons) cool water

their aroma. Stir well to form a thin, fragrant paste. Using an oil paste will prevent oil from leaking out onto your counter as you roll the dough and provide more distinct layers.

To make the pancakes, divide the cold rested dough into 6 equal portions. The dough should feel very malleable. Work on one portion at a time and return the remaining portions to the bowl, covering them so they don't dry out. On a lightly floured surface, roll the first portion into a 14 × 8-inch rectangle, or as thin as you can make it without the dough tearing. Dust the surface with flour to prevent the rolling pin from sticking.

Spread a thin, even layer of the oil paste onto the surface of the rectangle using a pastry brush or the back of a spoon. Roll the long side of the dough up, jelly-roll-style, to form a thin log of dough. Gently stretch out the log, then form the log into a tight spiral, rolling right to left. Tuck the end securely underneath, pat the roll lightly into a fat, 1-inch-thick disk, and allow it to rest for 10 minutes while you shape the remaining portions of dough.

When all the disks are formed, take the first disk of dough and make two or three gentle passes on its surface with the rolling pin. If the dough has rested properly, it should be relaxed and very easy to roll out without it stretching or bounding back. Rotate the dough 90 degrees and repeat until the disk is 8 to 9 inches in diameter and about ¼ inch thick.

Brush a thin layer of oil on a large nonstick pan or seasoned cast-iron skillet and heat over medium heat until the oil shimmers. Lay the pancake evenly on the surface, then cover the pan with a tight-fitting lid and cook for 3 minutes, until the bottom of the pancake is golden brown. Flip the pancake and cook, uncovered this time, until the pancake is crispy and browned on both sides, about 6 minutes total.

Before removing the pancake, take two spatulas and "zhuzh" the sides of the pancake, pushing them toward each other to loosen the layers. Cut each pancake into 8 wedges and serve hot.

To freeze, stack the uncooked but fully rolled-out pancakes on top of each other, with wax paper or parchment paper sandwiched in between. Freeze them in a large zip-top bag for up to 1 month.

THE SCALLION OIL PASTE

90 grams (½ cup plus 2 tablespoons) all-purpose flour

1½ teaspoons kosher salt

1 cup thinly sliced scallion greens (from about 6 scallions)

1 teaspoon ground Sichuan peppercorns (optional)

½ cup vegetable oil, plus more for pan-frying

SESAME FLATBREADS (SHAOBING)

Zhīmá shāobǐng

芝麻燒餅

MAKES SIX 5-INCH FLATBREADS

My great-grandfather, a migrant from Shandong Province, operated a stand selling fried yeasted breads on the streets of Harbin. My great-grandmother rose before dark to help him scoop out the proofed dough, and they shaped and stretched it gently with wet palms, dropping the pieces into the shimmering oil in a deep wok. After a few seconds, the dough would begin to puff up, turning deep golden and crispy. Pillowy and oblong like a fish, they were called *mianyu*, "bread fish," and workers bought them for breakfast, washing the mouthfuls down with steaming bowls of soy milk. My great-grandfather also made *xianbing*, "stuffed pocket" breads, and leavened scallion pancakes, each layered stack cut with a knife into wedges dotted with scallion bits. But he was most famous for his simple dough rolled with an oil paste to form a multitude of layers and baked in a hot tandoor-style oven until golden and crusty. After the breakfast rush, he'd hurry to his job rowing passengers across the Songhua River, while my great-grandmother prepared the dough for the next morning.

A *shaobing* and hot soy milk is the northeast Chinese equivalent of a croissant and espresso. The texture is best described as a cross between a yeasted flatbread and a flaky biscuit. There are lots of ways to make *shaobing* and even more fillings—sometimes vendors will sell sweet varieties with red bean paste or sweet lotus seed paste tucked inside. But this is my favorite savory version, with sesame seeds and a hint of ground Sichuan peppercorns.

MAKE THE DOUGH: In a small bowl or glass liquid measuring cup, dissolve the sugar in the warm water. Sprinkle on the yeast and let sit for 5 minutes. It will bloom into foamy bubbles on the surface of the water. If not, start over with newer yeast.

Combine the flours, baking powder, and salt in a large bowl. Make a well in the dry ingredients. Slowly pour in the wet mixture with one hand while using the other to stir with a pair of chopsticks until large, fat flakes form. Add the oil and knead in the bowl for about 5 minutes, until the dough is elastic, smooth, and just slightly tacky.

Cover with a tea towel and let rest for about 1 hour at room temperature, or until doubled in size.

(recipe and ingredients continue)

THE DOUGH

2 teaspoons sugar

133 grams (½ cup plus 1 tablespoon) warm water

½ teaspoon active dry yeast

180 grams (1¼ cups) all-purpose flour

70 grams (½ cup) pastry flour or cake flour

½ teaspoon baking powder

½ teaspoon kosher salt

1 tablespoon vegetable oil, plus more for greasing

MAKE THE OIL PASTE: Combine the flour and the oils in a small saucepan and heat over medium-low heat, stirring continuously, to toast the flour until it is lightly golden, about 2 minutes. Add the Sichuan peppercorns and salt, stirring with a spatula until the paste is the color of peanut butter and very fragrant. Immediately remove from the heat and scrape the paste into a small bowl. Cover and place in the refrigerator—it will thicken as it chills.

When the dough has risen, gently knead the dough in the bowl to eliminate any air bubbles.

On a lightly greased surface, use a rolling pin to roll the dough into a rectangle about 24 inches long × 12 inches wide, making the dough as thin as possible without breaking. Using a spatula, spread the cooled oil paste evenly on the surface. Roll it tightly from the long side, jelly-roll-style, to form a log, then cut it into 6 equal-size sections.

Taking one piece, pinch the ends tightly to seal in the oil paste, then fold the two ends toward the middle, like folding a letter, and press with your palm to adhere. Flip it over, and flatten into a ¾-inch-thick disk. Some of the oil paste will leak out; pat the excess into the dough to coat both sides—this will lock in the dough's moisture and create a crumbly, flaky exterior. Repeat with the remaining sections to make 6 shaobing total.

Place the sesame seeds on a plate and dip both sides of each disk into them, lightly pressing to coat, then roll out the dough into a ½-inch-thick oval or round disk, adhering the sesame seeds to the surface. Place on a greased surface, cover the shaobing with a damp tea towel, and allow them to rest and rise for 30 minutes.

In the meantime, place a pizza stone or flat baking sheet on a rack in the bottom third of the oven and preheat it to 400°F.

When the oven is ready, lay the shaobing on the hot pizza stone and bake for 10 to 12 minutes, flipping halfway through, until the dough has puffed up and the bottom is a nice golden brown. Let cool slightly before eating.

THE OIL PASTE

40 grams (5 tablespoons) all-purpose flour

2 tablespoons vegetable oil

1 tablespoon toasted sesame oil

½ teaspoon ground Sichuan peppercorns

¾ teaspoon kosher salt

⅓ cup raw white sesame seeds

CONGEES & SWEET SOUPS

Porridges and soups embody a dual role in the Chinese diet: they're "health maintaining" foods (養生 yǎngshēng) that regulate the body and ensure balance in the wisdom of traditional Chinese medicine, but also tasty and satisfying in their own right. Congees, called 稀飯 xīfàn, "thinned rice," or 粥 zhōu, porridge, can be as simple as a plain rice congee with savory pickled toppings (page 285), or a sweetened treasure-trove of a porridge studded with whole grains, seeds, nuts, and dried fruits (Eight Treasure Congee, page 287).

At the end of a meal, apart from the usual offering of cut fresh fruit, Chinese people love a good dessert soup, typically lightly sweetened. After indulging on richly flavored, salty dishes, there's nothing better than settling back and nursing a bowl of velvety pumpkin soup (page 297), a chilled clear soup with gelatinous waves of silver ear fungus (page 298), or a fragrant black sesame blended porridge (page 294). Many of the sweet soups in this chapter can be eaten as breakfast, dessert, or as a snack any time in between and are delicious both hot or chilled, like Red Bean Soup (page 292). Compared to cloyingly sugary, rich desserts, these are light dishes that satisfy your sweet tooth and double as wholesome nourishment.

PLAIN CONGEE

Dàmǐ zhōu

大米粥

SERVES 4

Simmer a handful of rice in a big pot of water, and the individual rice grains will eventually burst open and melt, transforming the liquid into a smooth, gentle mass with a milky-white color. In China, congee is generally regarded as the ultimate comfort food. It's easy to digest and kind on the stomach if you're feeling under the weather, and if you're feeling fancy, you can jazz it up with plenty of garnishes.

Traditionally, you make congee by cooking the rice on the stove for over an hour, but for faster results, you can freeze the uncooked rice first. Freezing changes its structure and makes it easier to break down, drastically cutting the cooking time to about 15 minutes. You don't even need to defrost it—add the frozen rice directly to the water in the pot. To prep frozen rice, rinse and drain the rice, divide it into ¾-cup portions, and freeze it. For maybe the easiest and quickest results, my mom has always made congee in her electric pressure cooker, which doesn't require any monitoring or stirring.

To reheat congee, heat it over low heat on the stove with extra water (it will thicken when left in the refrigerator) and stir until it bubbles.

Place the rice in a sieve and rinse it thoroughly under running water until the water runs clear, then drain well. If using frozen rice (see headnote), skip this step.

STOVETOP: Place the drained rice and 6 cups (1.4L) water in a large, heavy-bottomed pot. Bring it to a full boil over high heat, then reduce the heat to maintain a simmer. Partially cover the pot and cook on low heat, stirring to the bottom occasionally with a wooden spatula or spoon. After a while, the rice will blossom and break apart.

Cook, stirring occasionally, until the congee is thickened to your liking and satiny in consistency. This will take 60 to 70 minutes if you're using uncooked rice, or about 15 minutes for frozen rice. At any point, pour in more water if you want a thinner congee. Remove from the heat, ladle into bowls, and serve.

PRESSURE COOKER: Transfer the rinsed and drained rice to the pressure cooker pot and add 6 cups (1.4 L) water. Program to cook on the manual setting on high pressure for 15 minutes and set the pressure valve to seal. After the timer beeps, allow the pressure to release naturally for about 15 minutes. (Do not quick release the pressure—the starchy liquid will clog the valve.) Open the lid and give everything a stir to incorporate. Add more water if you want a thinner congee. Ladle into bowls and serve hot.

¾ cup (150 grams) uncooked short-grain or Thai fragrant rice

(recipe continues)

MUSHROOM CONGEE WITH TOFU SKIN & GREENS

Fǔzhú xiānggū zhōu

腐竹香菇粥

Serves 4

½ cup (20 grams) broken pieces of dried tofu skin sticks

1 tablespoon vegetable oil

2 cups thinly julienned assorted fresh mushrooms

Kosher salt

1 cup finely chopped choy sum, spinach, gai lan, bok choy, yu choy, or other greens

1 teaspoon mushroom bouillon powder (optional)

Ground white pepper

Toasted sesame oil, for serving

This savory, green-flecked congee is my favorite way to use up the broken bits and jagged pieces of dried tofu skin sticks that inevitably get left in the bottom of the bag. You can substitute fresh or frozen tofu skin.

Follow the instructions for basic congee above, but before cooking, add the dried tofu skin to the rice and water. While the porridge is cooking, heat the oil in a small skillet. Add the mushrooms and a pinch of salt and stir-fry until they have softened and released their liquid. Season with salt to taste.

When the congee is thickened to your liking (if cooking on the stovetop) or after the pressure releases, give it a stir and add the greens and sautéed mushrooms. Season with mushroom bouillon (if using) and salt to taste. Cover and allow the residual heat to wilt the greens. Ladle into bowls, sprinkle on some white pepper, and drizzle some sesame oil on top before serving.

CONGEE ADDITIONS

Some people find comfort in a bowl of plain congee, but many love it as a canvas for toppings and seasonings. Here are some of my favorites.

⊙ Chili oil or toasted sesame oil

⊙ White pepper

⊙ Crispy Fried Shallots (page 302)

⊙ Fried or Salt-Roasted Peanuts (page 304 or 305)

⊙ Scallions, thinly sliced

⊙ Cilantro, finely chopped

⊙ Preserved mustard tuber

⊙ A spoonful of Pickled Mustard Greens (page 306)

⊙ A scant spoonful of olive preserved mustard greens

⊙ Shredded roasted salted nori sheets

⊙ Fermented tofu

EIGHT TREASURE CONGEE

Bābǎo zhōu

八寶粥

SERVES 6 TO 8

One of my favorite memories from Guangzhou was waking up early on Laba Festival to make laba congee. Laba Festival falls on the eighth day of the last lunar month (臘月 *Làyuè*), and every year, people will cook a big pot of this winter porridge for their ancestors and then enjoy it with friends and family, since its bountiful ingredients symbolize a celebration of the harvest.

In my culinary school kitchen, a team of chefs simmered the soaked sticky rice, beans, dried fruits, and other grains in 5-liter stockpots, while the rest of us helped set up a table near the street by the ferry station. We ladled out the congee into lidded paper cups and then wove in and out of the crowd, offering them with our blessings. Later I took a cup myself and spooned up the hot congee gratefully, chewing on the treasures suspended in the thickened rice porridge—starchy lotus seeds, rich peanuts, plump golden raisins, and swelled jujube dates and sweet longan.

Since making the porridge is a tradition over a thousand years old, the ingredients can vary widely. Typically, people include different types of grains (white sticky rice, black rice or black sticky rice, cornmeal, millet, Job's tears, and oats), beans (mung beans, red adzuki beans, kidney beans), nuts (walnuts, chestnuts, almonds, peanuts), seeds (pumpkin seeds, lotus seeds, pine nuts), and dried fruits (raisins, dates, goji berries), which naturally sweeten the porridge. It's a very flexible and forgiving recipe, and if you don't have some of these ingredients, simply substitute more of the others. At home, my mom always makes it in her pressure cooker, which cuts down the active cooking time to almost nothing. Just soak everything the night before, then drain and add to the pot in the morning, and you can enjoy a hot bowl of it for breakfast.

In a large bowl, combine the black rice, red beans, mung beans, Job's tears, lotus seeds, and walnuts, cover with cold water, and soak for at least 4 hours or up to overnight. Transfer the soaked grains to a colander, add the sticky rice, and rinse under the tap, then drain. Discard the soaking water.

STOVETOP: Place the drained ingredients and 8 cups (1.9L) water in a large, heavy-bottomed pot. Bring to a full boil over high heat, then add the raisins, jujube dates, and dried longan. Lower the heat to maintain a gentle simmer. Cook for 60 to 70 minutes, stirring occasionally, until the porridge is thick and creamy and the fruits are soft.

(recipe and ingredients continue)

¼ cup (53 grams) black rice or forbidden rice, or replace with more sticky rice

¼ cup (55 grams) red adzuki beans

¼ cup (55 grams) mung beans

¼ cup (50 grams) Job's tears or Chinese pearl barley

Finally, stir in the salt, goji berries, and brown sugar and cook until the berries plump and the sugar dissolves. Taste and adjust the sugar if needed. Ladle into bowls and serve hot.

PRESSURE COOKER: Place the drained ingredients in the inner pot and add the raisins, jujube dates, and dried longan. Pour in 8 cups (1.9L) water, program to cook on the manual setting on high pressure for 30 minutes, and set the pressure valve to seal. After the timer beeps, allow the pressure to release naturally for about 20 minutes, then quick release. Open the lid, give the porridge a stir, add the salt, goji berries, and sugar, and stir to dissolve. Adjust the sugar to taste. If you want a thicker consistency, select the sauté mode, bring the congee back to a boil, and stir until it reaches your desired consistency. Ladle into bowls and serve hot.

Store any remaining congee in an airtight container in the refrigerator for up to 5 days—the leftovers are also delicious chilled.

¼ cup (30 grams) dried lotus seeds (substitute walnuts or slivered blanched almonds)

¼ cup (40 grams) walnut halves or shelled raw peanuts

½ cup (105 grams) round white sticky rice

¼ cup (38 grams) raisins

8 dried jujube dates

8 dried longan fruits

¼ teaspoon kosher salt

¼ cup (40 grams) dried goji berries

¼ cup (40 grams) rock sugar or Chinese brown sugar, plus more to taste

DESSERT

The category of dessert doesn't really exist in Chinese food, but sweets still play an important role in the Chinese culinary canon, though they're eaten mostly outside of the home. Chinese bakeries are warm, magical places that serve as hubs for the community, perfumed with the scent of baking dough and sugar. This is where you'll find treats like red bean pastries, baked pineapple buns, and egg tarts, purchased for a daytime meal or snack. In teahouses, sweet confections like sesame-encrusted puffy spheres, steamed sponge cakes, quivering nine-layer gelées, bouncy water chestnut *gao*, mochi-stuffed red dates, and flaky taro pastries are enjoyed with tea as part of dim sum. Sugar is used in moderation—the biggest compliment a Chinese person can give a dessert is *bu tai tian*— "not too sweet"!

At the end of a Chinese meal, you serve fruit. It is the healthiest dessert and takes little to no preparation. For guests at home, my mom will usually set out a plate of oranges; in fancy restaurants in China, you'll be served watermelon carved into the shape of arching swans or a basket and filled with sliced honeydew, mango, pineapple, dragonfruit, and other exotic offerings. Apart from fresh fruit, sweet soups made of soft, simmered fruit like pears and papaya, coconut milk–based soups, puddings with sago pearls, and red bean and mung bean soups are beloved in Cantonese cuisine—these are usually served hot or chilled at the end of banquets.

MILLET CONGEE

Xiǎomǐ zhōu

小米粥

SERVES 4 TO 6

Since millet is coarse and dry, it's most often cooked into congee in northern China: the hard yellow grains break down into soft and creamy flecks, and the satiny skin-like layer that develops on the surface of the bowl of congee is considered the most nutritious part. In traditional Chinese medicine, millet is said to support digestion, improve appetite, nourish qi, and prevent blood deficiencies. My mom likes to use northeast-style millet, a variety of millet that's larger and stickier; it can be found in the dried goods section of the Asian supermarket. This can be a plain congee to accompany savory dishes or steamed buns, or you can add some diced sweet potato, kabocha squash, and jujube dates or goji berries for natural sweetness.

STOVETOP: Place the millet in a sieve and rinse it thoroughly under running water until the water runs clear. In a heavy-bottomed saucepan, bring 4 cups (960 mL) water to a boil over high heat, then add the drained millet and sweet potato (if using).

Reduce the heat to maintain a slow simmer, partially cover, and cook for about 30 minutes, stirring occasionally. The porridge is done when the millet is tender and the grains have "bloomed." At this point you can either serve it or cook for 10 minutes more for a thicker, creamier consistency.

PRESSURE COOKER: Place the millet in a sieve and rinse thoroughly under running water until the water runs clear. Place the drained millet and 4 cups (960 mL) water in the inner pot. Program to cook on the manual setting on high pressure for 15 minutes and set the pressure valve to seal. After the timer beeps, allow the pressure to release naturally for about 15 minutes. (Do not quick release the pressure—the starchy liquid will clog the valve.)

Open the lid and give everything a stir to incorporate. If you want the consistency to be thicker, select the sauté mode and bring the congee back to a boil. Cook for a few more minutes, stirring occasionally, until the congee reaches your desired consistency. Ladle into bowls, top with jujube dates, if desired, and serve hot.

½ cup (100 grams) millet

1 cup diced peeled sweet potato, kabocha squash, or pumpkin (optional)

Handful of jujube dates or goji berries (optional)

RED BEAN SOUP

Hóngdòu tāng

紅豆湯

SERVES 4

Simmer red adzuki beans long enough and they'll release their starches and break down into a thick, rich porridge. Lightly sweetened with rock sugar, this wholesome treat is always anticipated at the end of a meal. For the Cantonese version, called "red bean sand," the beans are blended so the soup is not watery but thickened, with a hint of sandiness and a whisper of citrus aroma from dried tangerine peel. You can also add a tablespoon of sago or small tapioca pearls during the last 20 minutes for translucent, chewy little pearls suspended in the soup.

Rinse and drain the beans. Place them in a large bowl, cover with cool water, and soak in the refrigerator for at least 6 hours or up to overnight. Drain before using.

STOVETOP: Combine the beans, tangerine peel (if using), and 4 cups (960 mL) water in a heavy-bottomed saucepan. Bring to a boil over high heat and cook for 15 minutes, skimming off any foam or white residue that appears on the surface.

Turn the heat down to medium-low, cover, and cook, stirring occasionally, for 60 to 80 minutes more, until the beans are splitting apart and very soft. Over the course of cooking, add an additional 1 to 2 cups water as needed. If you want a slightly richer, creamier texture, use an immersion blender to partially break up the beans (or transfer half the beans to a blender and blend briefly, then return them to the pot).

Add sugar to taste and stir over medium heat to dissolve it. Cook for 10 to 15 minutes more, until the soup reaches your desired consistency. Remove from the heat and serve hot, warm, or chilled.

PRESSURE COOKER: Add the beans, tangerine peel (if using), and 4 cups (960 mL) water to the inner pot. Program the pressure cooker to cook on the manual setting on high pressure for 15 minutes and set the pressure valve to seal. After the timer beeps, allow the pressure to release naturally for 15 minutes, then quick release. If you want a slightly richer, creamier texture, use an immersion blender to partially break up the beans (or transfer half the beans to a blender and blend briefly, then return them to the pot).

Select the sauté function and bring the soup to a boil again. Add sugar to taste and stir over medium heat to dissolve it. Cook, stirring occasionally, for 10 to 15 minutes more, adding an additional 1 to 2 cups water as needed, until the soup reaches your desired consistency. Serve hot, warm, or chilled.

1 cup (200 grams) dried red adzuki beans

1 small piece (3 grams) tangerine peel, soaked in cool water for 30 minutes, white pith scraped off (optional)

¼ cup (40 grams) rock sugar, plus more to taste

Variation
MUNG BEAN SOUP

Lǜdòu tāng

綠豆湯

Eating mung bean soup is the best thing for your body in hot weather, my mom reminds me every summer. Unlike adzuki beans, which are warming in nature, mung beans are cooling, said to dispel an excess of inner heat, drain toxins, and relieve heatstroke and thirst.

This soup is best when thoroughly chilled—chew the cold beans and then sip the pale green liquid for an instant pick-me-up on a lethargic hot day. You can also add ¼ cup dried lotus seeds, dried lily bulbs, or a small head of snow ear fungus, for delightful starchy and slippery textures. To make mung bean ice pops, sweeten the soup and then freeze it in ice pop molds.

Follow the recipe for red bean soup (opposite) but replace the adzuki beans with 1 cup (200 grams) dried mung beans. Sweeten to taste, allow the soup to cool, then serve with a few added ice cubes.

THE VEGAN CHINESE KITCHEN

BLENDED BLACK SESAME PORRIDGE

Hēizhīmá hú

黑芝麻糊

SERVES 3

Often enjoyed for breakfast or dessert, *hu* or blended porridge can be rich and paste-like and eaten with a spoon, or thinned to a silky-smooth consistency and sipped like a drink, depending on your preference. Nutritionally, this stuff is liquid gold—black sesame seeds are a rich source of copper, magnesium, iron, and calcium, said to detoxify the body and nourish the hair. Many Asian supermarkets sell instant black sesame soup in powdered form to mix with boiling water, but they often contain added sugars and are rather skimpy on the black sesame. It's easy to make this at home, and you can customize it—add toasted pine nuts, peanuts, or walnuts for extra-rich nutty flavor. If you prefer a thicker consistency, decrease the amount of water.

Soak the black rice and sticky rice together in cool water for at least an hour.

Toast the black sesame seeds in a heavy-bottomed pan over medium heat, stirring continuously, until they begin to pop, about 1 minute. Lower the heat and continue to toast until they smell delicious, about 4 minutes. Wet a fingertip and taste the seeds—when fully toasted, they will be dry and crackly on the tongue and richly nutty, with no raw taste, and easy to crush between your fingers. Immediately transfer to a plate to prevent them from burning.

Rinse and drain the soaked rice and place it in a high-speed blender with the toasted sesame seeds and 1 cup (240 mL) water. Blend for 30 seconds on high speed to break up the grains, then add 2½ cups (600 mL) more water and blend on high until smooth and silky, about 1 minute more.

Strain the mixture through a fine-mesh sieve into a small, heavy-bottomed saucepan. Press the contents of the sieve to extract as much liquid as possible, then discard the solids. Bring the liquid to a simmer over medium-high heat, then turn the heat to low and cook for 10 minutes, stirring occasionally to prevent the rice from sticking to the bottom of the pot. The porridge will thicken, becoming dark and glossy. Add the salt and sugar and stir until dissolved. Adjust the seasoning to taste. Ladle into bowls and serve hot.

You can store any leftovers in the fridge for up to 3 days. To reheat, thin it with water and bring to a boil. Simmer for 1 minute before serving.

2 tablespoons (26 grams) black rice or Forbidden Rice or short-grain white rice

2 tablespoons (26 grams) round glutinous (sticky) rice

½ cup (70 grams) black sesame seeds

¼ teaspoon kosher salt, plus more to taste

2 tablespoons rock sugar or coconut sugar, plus more to taste

SIMPLE SWEET PUMPKIN SOUP

Nánguā gēng

南瓜羹

SERVES 4

Almost every vegetarian restaurant I visited in China offered *nan-gua geng*, a soothing sweet soup of blended squash. Straining the pureed squash makes it buttery and velvety in the mouth, with no hint of graininess. The perfect consistency is best described as gentle, *wen rou*. When I asked Chef Li Hongzhi to clarify, he responded, "A gentle soup doesn't move around in your mouth when you shake your head from side to side."

You can keep this simple, or add toasted flour dissolved with vegan butter or coconut oil, which slightly thickens the soup and lends a subtle fragrance. Although the name of this recipe translates to "pumpkin soup," I don't recommend pumpkin, as it can be watery or stringy—use a dense-fleshed, sweet winter squash like kabocha, butternut, red kuri, or Hubbard.

MAKE THE TOASTED PASTE (IF USING): Heat a clean, dry skillet over medium-low heat. Add the flour and toast, stirring continuously. You won't see any difference in the color for a while, but be patient and gradually it will start to darken to pale golden brown and smell faintly aromatic, about 4 minutes. At this point, stir in the coconut oil until smooth. Scrape the paste into a small bowl.

Peel the squash and cut it in half, then remove the seeds and core. Cut the squash into ¼-inch-thick slices until you have 20 ounces (570 grams) of squash flesh. Reserve the remaining squash for another use. Set up a steamer basket in a wok and bring the water to a boil over high heat. Place the squash slices in the steamer basket and steam until tender and almost falling apart, 5 to 6 minutes.

In a blender, combine the cooked squash and 2½ cups (600 mL) water. Puree just until smooth, about 20 seconds. The puree should be thin and pourable, but not too watery. Strain the puree through a fine-mesh strainer into a heavy-bottomed saucepan.

Slowly bring the soup to a boil over medium-low heat. Reduce the heat so that only a few small bubbles break the surface of the soup. Stir in the toasted paste, if using. The soup will thicken visibly. Add the sugar and salt and stir until dissolved.

Taste and add more sugar until the soup is as sweet as you like. Remove from the heat, ladle it into bowls, and top with a few toasted almond flakes before serving.

TOASTED PASTE (OPTIONAL)

1 tablespoon all-purpose flour or cake flour

1 teaspoon coconut oil or vegan butter

1 winter squash (24 to 28 ounces / 680 to 790 grams)

2 tablespoons (20 grams) rock sugar, plus more to taste

¼ teaspoon kosher salt

Toasted almond flakes, goji berries, or pine nuts, for garnish

SWEET PEAR & SILVER EAR SOUP

Bīngtáng yíněr

冰糖銀耳

SERVES 6 TO 8

My mom says her family served this dessert soup whenever guests came over—she always looked forward to it since it was a treat. Snow fungus, also called silver ear fungus (銀耳 yíněr), is said to be anti-inflammatory, good for healing a dry cough, and also beautifying, as it contains collagen that's good for the skin. Add the mildly sweet and cooling pear, and this is a soup that's perfect for the summertime, good either warm or chilled.

Look for the fungus in the dried goods section, and pick heads that are yellowish (avoid overtly white ones, as they may have been bleached). You have to be patient and cook the frilly snow ears for several hours until they take on a translucence, becoming syrupy and gelatinous. Using a pressure cooker makes this practically effortless.

Soak the dried fungus in a bowl of cold water until fully rehydrated, at least 1 hour or up to overnight. Wash thoroughly to rinse off any dirt and trim off any dark yellow-orange spots and tough root portions. Tear it into bite-size clusters. Combine 8 cups (1.9L) water, the fungus, and the lotus seeds (if using) in the inner pot of a pressure cooker or a large heavy-bottomed saucepan.

PRESSURE COOKER: Program the pressure cooker to cook on the manual setting on high pressure for 30 minutes and set the pressure valve to seal. When the timer beeps, allow the pressure to release naturally for 15 minutes, then quick release. Open the lid carefully and select the sauté function. Add the pear, jujube dates, rock sugar, and goji berries. Cook until the pear is soft, the dried fruits are plump, and the sugar has completely dissolved, about 10 minutes more. Taste and add more sugar, if needed.

STOVETOP: Bring the mixture to a boil, then reduce the heat to maintain a gentle simmer. Skim off any foam that rises to the surface. Simmer, covered, for 2 hours, until the fungus is completely translucent and silky soft. Add the pear, jujube dates, rock sugar, and goji berries. Cook until the pear softens and the sugar dissolves, about 5 minutes more. Taste and add more sugar, if needed.

Serve immediately while hot, or allow to cool, then refrigerate in an airtight container overnight and serve chilled.

1 large or 2 small heads dried silver ear fungus (¾ ounce / 20 grams)

¼ cup (1 ounce / 30 grams) dried lotus seeds (optional)

1 large Asian pear (13 ounces / 380 grams), peeled, cored, and cut into 1-inch pieces

6 to 7 dried jujube dates (1 ounce / 30 grams), pitted and halved

¼ cup (2 ounces / 60 grams) rock sugar or agave syrup, plus more to taste

2 tablespoons dried goji berries, rinsed

APPENDIX

STOCKS, CONDIMENTS & PICKLES

Red Chili Oil

Làjiāoyóu

辣椒油

MAKES ABOUT 1½ CUPS

Chili oil or "red oil" is a basic flavoring oil that's drizzled on dishes as a finishing touch or used in dressings for cold dishes and sauces—it adds a gorgeous ruby color and deep aroma, with a roasted back note of scorched chiles and nutty sesame seeds. Most Asian supermarkets will have Sichuan chiles, but if you can't find them, use Korean ground chile (gochugaru). Feel free to tweak this oil according to your preference: you can leave out the star anise or Chinese cinnamon and use just peppercorns and chiles, or add any of the following during the infusion: a 1-inch piece of fresh ginger (peeled and thinly sliced), 1 scallion or ¼ yellow onion (coarsely chopped), 2 peeled garlic cloves, 1 or 2 black cardamom pods, fennel seeds, a dried tangerine peel (*chenpi*), or extra sesame seeds.

- 1½ cups (360 mL) vegetable oil or other neutral-flavored oil

- 2 tablespoons whole Sichuan peppercorns

- 2 star anise pods

- 1 small Chinese cinnamon stick

- 2 bay leaves

- ½ cup (40 grams) coarsely ground dried Sichuan chiles, with seeds

- 1 tablespoon sesame seeds

Combine the oil, Sichuan peppercorns, star anise, cinnamon, and bay leaves in a small saucepan. Place the dried chiles and sesame seeds in a separate heatproof bowl and set aside.

Heat the oil over medium heat to 230°F (110°C), or until tiny bubbles rise slowly from the spices, and keep it at that temperature for about 10 minutes to infuse it with flavor. Reduce the heat if the spices appear to be darkening too quickly. When the oil has a gentle fragrance, remove it from the heat and strain out and discard all the spices.

Return the saucepan to medium heat and heat the oil to 320°F (160°C), or until a piece of ginger dropped in the hot oil bubbles up to the surface slowly. Pour a few tablespoons of the oil into the bowl of ground chiles and sesame seeds—the chiles will fizz and release a rich aroma. If the chiles bubble up too energetically, the oil may be too hot and could burn the chiles. Let it cool for 30 seconds, then pour again. Continue adding all the oil, stirring to the bottom, until the oil is rich red and has a toasty aroma. If the flavor is not as fragrant as you like, return the oil to the saucepan and heat over low heat for a few more minutes to continue to infuse it. Let cool, then transfer the oil and sediment to an airtight glass jar. Store in a cool, dark place for up to 4 months, or in the refrigerator indefinitely.

Scallion Oil

Cōngyóu

蔥油

MAKES 1 CUP

Scallions are one of the holy trinity flavors of Chinese cooking, but unlike garlic and ginger (the other members of the trinity), which seemingly last forever in the pantry, fresh scallions are harder to keep on hand. I'm also lazy and don't feel like washing and cutting fresh scallions every time I cook, and at times, I don't want the look of chopped scallion bits in a dish. This is where scallion oil comes in. Use this oniony, enticing golden oil to stir-fry vegetables in place of regular cooking oil, to dress noodles and fried rice, or to drizzle on steamed dishes and soups.

(recipe and ingredients continue)

12 scallions, cleaned and trimmed

1 cup (240 mL) vegetable oil or other neutral-flavored oil

Pat the scallions as dry as possible. Thinly slice them into circles or ovals.

Heat the oil in a wok over medium-high heat until shimmering. Add the scallions and stir them gently—the oil should be just hot enough that the scallions bubble gently along their edges. Cook the scallions over a steady low flame as they release their water and infuse the oil.

When the scallions are starting to darken and have a toasted aroma, 15 to 20 minutes, begin to stir continuously to help them develop an even golden color. Once they start turning brown and looking crispy, immediately remove the wok from the heat—overcooking will result in a burnt flavor.

Pour everything through a fine-mesh sieve set over a heatproof bowl and press the scallions with a spoon to squeeze out any remaining oil. The oil should be clear, with a slight greenish tinge. Discard the fried scallions—they should look pretty hammered if they've done their job properly—or reserve for one final use as a garnish for noodles.

Pour the strained oil into a lidded glass jar and store on the top shelf of your refrigerator for up to 2 weeks.

Crispy Fried Shallots & Shallot Oil

Yóucōng sū and Hóngcōng yóu

油蔥酥 · 紅蔥油

MAKES 1 CUP FRIED SHALLOTS and 1 CUP SHALLOT OIL

Fried shallots are a common ingredient in southern Chinese and Taiwanese cooking. As a garnish, the crisp, delicate morsels add a sweet, oniony crunch on cooked leafy greens, soups, cold dishes, and appetizers. Use the oil to add flavor to virtually any dish that needs a boost of umami.

1 cup (240 mL) vegetable oil or other neutral-flavored oil

4 large shallots, thinly sliced crosswise into ⅛-inch-thick slices and blotted as dry as possible

Heat the oil in a medium saucepan over medium heat to around 240°F (115°C). The oil should be just hot enough that a shallot ring dropped in bubbles gently along its edges.

Add the shallot rings, reduce the heat to low, and let the shallots fry steadily. Stir occasionally, more so at the end than at the beginning, until the rings have taken on a beautiful light bronze color. This will take 15 to 18 minutes.

Pour everything into a fine-mesh sieve set over a heatproof bowl. Shake off any extra oil, then spread the drained shallots on a paper towel–lined plate. They will still be soggy but will take on crispness as they cool.

Pour the strained shallot oil into a glass jar and store on the top shelf of your refrigerator for up to 2 weeks.

Use the fried shallots immediately or store them in an airtight container in a cool, dry place for up to 2 weeks or in the freezer for up to 3 months.

Fried Peanuts

Zhà huāshēng

炸花生

MAKES 1½ CUPS

Many Chinese cooks keep a jar of fried peanuts in their pantry, as they play a role in stir-fries and add a fragrant crunch to salads and cold dishes. The crisp, glossy peanuts are also irresistible as a snack or appetizer. Don't be intimidated by deep-frying or the technique of starting them in cold oil: the peanuts don't absorb any oil but rather expel their internal water in a continuous fizz of bubbles, becoming snappy and crisp. To accomplish that effect, you want the oil hot enough to evaporate water and force out the peanuts' moisture, but not so hot that they darken too quickly before fully crisped. To evaluate our batches in culinary school,

the teacher would roll a peanut between his fingers: no greasiness and papery skins meant it was fried perfectly.

> **1½ cups (235 grams) shelled raw peanuts, preferably with skins**
>
> **2 cups (480 mL) vegetable oil or other neutral-flavored oil, at room temperature**
>
> **Kosher salt**

Place the peanuts and oil in a medium pot. Over medium-low heat, bring the oil up to 240°F (115°C). You should see tiny, vigorous bubbles surrounding the peanuts as their water molecules are driven out. Stir the peanuts continuously, keeping the oil temperature at 240°F (115°C).

After about 15 minutes, the peanuts will be fragrant and start to make a cracking sound. When they are lightly golden under their skins, 3 to 5 minutes more, increase the heat to raise the oil temperature to 280°F (137°C). Cook for another

HANNAH CHE

15 seconds to expel any absorbed oil—this step will make them crispier—then immediately lift the peanuts out with a skimmer or slotted spoon.

Transfer the peanuts to a paper towel–lined plate—the peanuts will continue to darken as they cool. Sprinkle generously with salt while they're hot. The peanuts will crisp up gradually, so wait until they cool completely before enjoying them. Store in an airtight container or a lidded jar in a cool, dry place for up to 3 months.

Salt-Roasted Peanuts

Yánchǎo huāshēng

鹽炒花生

MAKES 1½ CUPS

My friend's dad from Foshan uses a bag of table salt to toast raw peanuts in his wok instead of frying them. It's an ingenious method: the salt reaches a high temperature but doesn't burn or melt, and the peanuts can tumble around in the slippery, hot salt grains, roasting evenly on all sides until fragrant and golden brown. Don't discard the salt—you can reuse it for future batches. These can be substituted in any recipe that calls for fried peanuts.

> 1½ cups (235 grams) shelled raw peanuts
>
> 2 cups (360 grams) fine-grained table salt or kosher salt

In a clean, dry wok, combine the peanuts and salt. Heat over medium-low heat, turning the peanuts continuously with a spatula to heat them evenly. Keep roasting and stirring until you hear faint crackling sounds, 8 to 10 minutes. When the peanuts are fragrant and turn a light golden color under their skins, lift them out with a slotted spoon and shake off the salt. Spread the hot peanuts on a plate to cool and crisp up, then serve.

Let the salt cool completely before storing in an airtight container or lidded jar for future salt-roasting.

Chinese Sesame Paste

Zhīmájiàng

芝麻醬

MAKES ABOUT 1½ CUPS

Chinese sesame paste is not the same as tahini, which is lighter in color, runnier in texture, and ground from lightly toasted sesame seeds. Using roasted sesame seeds results in a richly nutty flavor and deep peanut butter–like color.

> 1½ cups (210 grams) raw white sesame seeds
>
> 2 tablespoons toasted sesame oil

Pour the sesame seeds into a dry wok or skillet and set it over medium heat. Cook, stirring continuously, for 2 minutes, until the seeds are fragrant and starting to pop. Continue to stir for 5 to 6 minutes more, until the popping sounds decrease and the sesame seeds have darkened to a golden color and crumble easily between your fingers. Pour the seeds onto a plate and let cool slightly.

Place the warm sesame seeds in a food processor or high-speed blender. Pulse continuously for 5 to 6 minutes (if using a blender, start on low speed and then increase to high, and stir continuously with the tamper), until a crumbly paste forms. Stream in the sesame oil and process until the paste is smooth. Store in a covered jar in the refrigerator for up to 2 months.

PICKLED & PRESERVED FOODS

Pickled Mustard Greens

Xuěcài

雪菜

MAKES 1 QUART (500 GRAMS)

Also called snow vegetable, pickled mustard greens got me hooked on Chinese-style preserving. All you do is chop the leafy greens, knead them with salt until they give up their juices, then leave them to cure for a week. The fermentation mellows the mustard greens' bitterness and tames their volatile pungency. You can eat this as a relish, cook it into soups, and add it to fried rice, stews, and stir-fries to balance their richness and give them an edge of savory funk.

I'll have to admit—I eat this pickle most frequently as a topping on avocado toast (forgive me, my ancestors). Just thinking of its mustardy, salty, and juicy sour crunch with buttery avocado makes my mouth water. Trust me when I say you'll go through a jar of this quickly.

> **About 2 pounds (950 grams) fresh mustard greens, any variety**
>
> **2 tablespoons (24 grams) kosher salt (roughly 2.5 percent of the greens' weight)**

Wash the greens thoroughly, first soaking them in a large bowl of water to rinse away the gritty silt and dirt, especially between the leaves and at the base of the stalks. Dry the greens thoroughly:

either spin in batches in a salad spinner, or string them up on a clean clothes hanger (this is easier if the stems are still attached) and hang them in a cool, dark place to dry overnight. Traditionally, you'd sun-dry them—if you have a spot with direct, strong sunlight, place the wet greens on a baking sheet or a clean tea towel and lay them out in the sun for a few hours until the leaves look wilted and slightly shriveled.

Coarsely chop the stems and greens into ½-inch pieces and transfer to a large bowl or baking sheet. With clean hands, sprinkle on the salt and scrunch it thoroughly into the greens, as if you were kneading dough, until the volume has reduced by at least half. The greens will give off pungent fumes and start to release their juices. Let them sit for 5 minutes, then massage them one last time—the leaves should now be wet and dark.

Transfer the greens to a sterilized quart-size mason jar or fermentation crock. Pack in the greens, an inch at a time, using the end of a sterilized spoon or wooden rolling pin to press each layer down.

Place a weight on top to fully submerge the greens in their own liquid. If you don't have a weight, my trick is to take one of those little rice cooker measuring cups and place it on top of the greens, then screw the lid on—the base of the cup will press down and submerge the top layer under the liquid. You can remove the cup after a few hours, when the greens have exuded enough of their own juices to completely cover the greens.

Seal the jar and leave to ferment at room temperature away from direct sunlight. Open once a day to allow any gases to escape, press the greens down so that they're still covered in the liquid, and then reseal. The greens will usually take 4 to 7 days to ferment, depending on the room temperature. When the pickle is sour to your liking, transfer to the fridge. It will keep for up to 3 months.

HANNAH CHE

THE VERSATILE MUSTARD CABBAGE

Mustard greens (芥菜 *jiècài* in Mandarin or *gai choy* in Cantonese) are used for a whole range of Chinese preserves and prized for their hardy, crunchy texture, mild bitterness, and nose-tickling pungency. The entire cabbage is chopped and simply fermented for pickled snow vegetable (雪菜 *xuěcài*), preserved whole as sour mustard cabbage (酸菜 *suāncài*), or salted, steamed, and dried until reddish brown and floppy for Hakka mustard greens (梅乾菜 *méigān cài*). The dark leaves are finely chopped and salted in Sichuanese preserved mustard greens (芽菜 *yácài*), an important ingredient in dandan noodles, and preserved in oil with Chinese olives as the oily and unctuous Cantonese condiment olive vegetable (橄欖菜 *gǎnlǎn cài*). Finally, the bulbous heads are brined in spices into Sichuan pickled tuber (榨菜 *zhàcài*), which is more commonly found slivered in little condiment packs.

In Asian supermarkets, you'll see many green vegetables named "mustard," which can be confusing. "Big mustard cabbage" (大芥菜 *dà jiècài*) is the largest variety, with thick, wide, and twisty stalks, and it's often used for pickling because of its uniquely crunchy stems. "Mustard cabbage" (包心芥菜 *bāoxīn jiècài*) is the stubbier, rounder head, and is also called "heart mustard." The lengthy, leafier greens with spiky fronds are called "bright vegetable in snow" (雪裡紅 *xuělǐhóng*), also known as potherb, mizuna, or Japanese mustard; since their stems are more tender, they're great for stir-frying.

Pickled Sour Chinese Cabbage

Dōngběi suāncài

東北酸菜

MAKES 2 QUARTS (1 KILOGRAM)

One of the oldest traditions in northeastern China is preserving napa cabbage through fermentation. My mom says that during the harvest, when beautiful heads of napa cabbage were brought into town, every family in their neighborhood would be salting them in crocks to store in their dirt cellars for winter. It's the Chinese equivalent of sauerkraut or a mild cabbage kimchi (though far simpler), and you can find it now at any large Asian supermarket, sold in packs in the refrigerated section. When you make it yourself, you have the freedom to ferment it as long as you like for the best flavor. In our family, we either eat it straight, stew it in soups, or chop it up thinly to add to stir-fries and bun and dumpling fillings (see page 261).

> 2 medium heads Chinese napa cabbage (about 6½ pounds / 3 kilograms)
>
> 60 grams (¼ cup plus 1 tablespoon) kosher salt (2 percent of the cabbage's weight)

Remove the outer leaves of the cabbage. Using a sharp knife, cut the white stem portion lengthwise in half, then slowly pull apart the cabbage into 2 pieces. Don't cut the leafy parts with the knife; they will separate as you tear the stem apart. Cut each in half to divide the cabbage into quarters, then repeat to cut it into eighths.

In a large bowl, sprinkle the salt evenly onto the cut sides of each cabbage wedge, between the leaves, and all over the stem. Pile the pieces in a bowl, cover loosely with a clean tea towel to shield it from dust, and set it aside at room temperature for at least 8 hours, or overnight, until the leaves are slightly reduced in size and the stems are pliable and able to bend without snapping.

The next day, sterilize a 3.6-liter glass jar or 2 quart-size glass jars with boiling water. Clean and sterilize a large rock or glass fermentation weight that will fit in the mouth of the jar. Pack the cabbage wedges tightly into the jar and set the weight on top. If they're packed down, there should be enough liquid released to cover the cabbage completely, but if not, make a 2% brine by dissolving 1 tablespoon kosher salt in 2 cups (480 mL) water and add what you need. If you've made previous batches, you can speed up the fermenting process by adding some old pickling brine.

Seal the jar and leave it at room temperature away from direct sunlight to ferment. The leaves will gradually turn yellow in color and develop a bright sourness. After 2 weeks, the cabbage will be ready to eat, but the flavor will be best after 30 days. When the cabbage is sour enough for your liking, store the jar in the refrigerator for up to 2 months—the taste and texture will continue to change over time.

Kombu Stock

Kūnbù gāotāng

昆布高湯

MAKES 1 QUART (1 LITER)

This is my go-to stock when I'm short on time, as it doesn't require cooking—all you need to do is soak a piece of kombu in a jar of water overnight in the refrigerator. Kombu, or kelp seaweed, comes in dried brownish-black sheets rich in glutamic salts, the naturally sweet flavor enhancer that creates umami. This clear, pure stock fills the mouth with a light, smooth taste and adds a hidden undertone of savoriness to dishes, deepening the flavors without overwhelming them.

(recipe and ingredients continue)

If you see white crystals on the kombu, don't rinse or wipe them off—they contain mannitol sugar, which occurs naturally in the drying process and provides much of the umami taste.

½ ounce (14 grams) kombu, about 4 × 6 inches

In a medium bowl or glass jar, soak the kombu in 1 quart (1 liter) cool water for 4 to 6 hours at room temperature or overnight in the refrigerator. After soaking, remove the kombu and store the liquid in the fridge in an airtight container, where it will keep for up to 1 week.

If you want a stronger dashi, transfer the liquid and the soaked kombu to a medium saucepan and simmer for 8 to 10 minutes.

You can reuse the kombu by simmering it in another 4 cups (960 mL) water for a secondary stock. I like to cook the leftover kombu in a pot of rice to give the rice a savory flavor.

Light Vegetable Stock

Shūcài gāotāng

蔬菜高湯

MAKES ABOUT 3 QUARTS (3 LITERS)

For a mild-flavored broth, Chinese vegetarian chefs rely on fresh vegetables, which always vary according to the season. Traditionally, the base of many stocks in Buddhist temple cooking is fresh soybean sprouts, which add depth; I often use dried soybeans instead, since they're more convenient to keep on hand and add the same umami flavor as they simmer. This stock is a milky golden color and slightly sweet because of the carrot and daikon radish, which balance the grassiness of the soybeans. It freezes well and can be used for dishes that require a delicate, light-colored base for a braise or stew, like Pea Shoots in Silky Soup (page 57) and Coconut Clay Pot Taro and Edamame (page 127).

¼ cup (45 grams) dried soybeans, or 2 heaping cups (110 grams) fresh soybean sprouts

2 tablespoons vegetable oil

1 pound (450 grams) carrots, thinly sliced

8 ounces (225 grams) green cabbage, cut into 1-inch pieces

14 ounces (400 grams) daikon radish, thinly sliced

2 celery stalks, thinly sliced (1 cup)

4 scallions, white and green parts, cut into 2-inch segments

1 teaspoon kosher salt

Rinse the dried soybeans in a large bowl, then drain and cover with cool water. Soak for at least 2 hours and up to overnight, until plump. Drain well.

Heat the oil in a 6-quart pot over high heat until shimmering. Add the carrots, cabbage, radish, celery, scallions, and salt and cook for 8 to 10 minutes, stirring occasionally, until they are softened and starting to brown in some places. You may skip this step, but it adds extra flavor to the stock.

Add the drained soybeans (or fresh soybean sprouts, if using instead) and 4 quarts (4 liters) water to the pot and bring to a boil over high heat. Reduce the heat to low and gently simmer, uncovered, for 60 to 75 minutes, until the stock is golden in color and slightly reduced.

Remove the solids with tongs or a skimmer, and then strain the stock, working in batches if necessary, through a fine-mesh sieve set over another large pot or bowl. Gently press the vegetables and beans to extract as much liquid as possible and repeat with the remaining stock and vegetables. (You can discard the solids, lightly dress them to eat, or add them to another stew or soup.) Let the stock cool before storing it in an airtight container in the refrigerator for up to a week. It can also be frozen in airtight containers or zip-top bags for up to 3 months.

FOR CABBAGE

napa cabbage, savoy cabbage, bok choy

FOR CARROT

corn on the cob (cut into 1-inch slices), dried jujube dates

FOR DAIKON

bamboo shoots, turnip, kohlrabi, rutabaga

FOR CELERY

zucchini, celeriac, Chinese celery, jicama, broccoli or cauliflower stalks

FOR SCALLIONS

onions, shallots, leeks, cilantro stems

Rich Vegetable & Mushroom Stock

Sù xiāntāng

素鮮湯

MAKES ABOUT 3 QUARTS (3 LITERS)

Flavorful and full-bodied with a dark amber color, this stock utilizes dried and fresh mushrooms for deep aroma, as well as chestnuts for body. It's delicious heated up and drunk straight as a broth or used in any braised dish or stew that calls for a flavorful stock. You can also use it for a quick noodle soup like Tomato Noodle Soup (page 252).

2 tablespoons vegetable oil

2 medium onions, thinly sliced

1 pound (450 grams) carrots, thinly sliced

3 or 4 celery stalks, thinly sliced (2 cups)

4 garlic cloves, smashed with the blade of a knife

1 teaspoon kosher salt

1 ounce (28 grams) dried shiitake mushrooms, rinsed

4 ounces (112 grams) fresh mushrooms of any variety, cleaned and trimmed, caps and stems thinly sliced

3 ounces (84 grams) whole peeled chestnuts (6 or 7; optional)

1 tablespoon whole white peppercorns, lightly cracked with the blade of a knife (optional)

⅓ cup (80 mL) Shaoxing wine

Heat the oil in a 6-quart pot over high heat until shimmering. Add the onions, carrots, celery, garlic, and salt and cook, stirring occasionally, for 8 to 10 minutes, until the vegetables are softened and starting to brown in some places. You may skip this step, but it adds extra flavor to the stock.

Add the dried and fresh mushrooms, chestnuts (if using), and white peppercorns (if using) and cook for another 2 minutes. Pour in 4 quarts (4 liters) water and the wine and bring to a boil over high heat. Reduce to low heat and simmer, uncovered, for 60 to 75 minutes, until the stock is amber in color and slightly reduced.

Remove the solids with tongs or a skimmer, then strain the stock, working in batches if necessary, through a fine-mesh sieve set over another large pot or bowl. Gently press the vegetables to extract as much liquid as possible. Discard the solids in the sieve and repeat with the remaining pot contents. Let the stock cool before storing it in an airtight container in the refrigerator for up to a week. It can also be frozen in airtight containers or zip-top bags for up to 3 months.

Variations

FOR ONIONS

scallions, shallots, leeks, cilantro stems

FOR DRIED SHIITAKE MUSHROOMS

replace half with dried tea tree or porcini mushrooms for varied flavor

FOR FRESH MUSHROOMS

more dried shiitake mushrooms, eggplant (cut into thick slices)

ACKNOWLEDGMENTS

THREE YEARS AGO, I was sitting in a practice room at music school, sorting through two degrees' worth of frayed concerto scores and books I'd accumulated in my locker, when I found a cookbook that I'd been meaning to return to a friend. I remember flipping through the glossy pages and wondering if I could ever write a cookbook myself. At that moment, it was a vague, unattainable pipe dream, completely unrelated to what I thought I should be doing. But life is wild, and one heck of a journey later, we've somehow gotten to the acknowledgments; although it'd be impossible to name everyone who has played a part in this book, I want to thank a few people in particular:

Francis Lam, for being the greatest editor I could've wished for—I shrieked when I got off our first phone conversation, I felt so lucky knowing this book would be in the best hands. Thank you for believing in my vision and for trusting me, for your eternal patience across the thousands of miles and various time zones (I'll never forget that 4:00 a.m. Zoom meeting from the internet cafe), for the humor and insight you imparted along the way, and for asking all the wise questions that helped shape this book into something so much better than that massive AF manuscript I first turned in. Big thanks to the talented team at Clarkson Potter: **Jen Wang**, for designing these pages into a thing of beauty; **Paige Resnick**, **Darian Keels**, **Kelli Tokos**, **Kathy Brock**, and **Patricia Shaw**, for the hard work you put into every line and paragraph, every printing spec, and all the unseen and untold effort that goes into making a book. You all made my dreams come true, literally.

Joanne Lee Molinaro, book and soul sister: I will never forget our conversation at the Houston marathon that fateful January. Thank you for giving me advice and for cheering me on—in some ways, you started this whole thing. **Charlie Brotherstone**, agent extraordinaire; thank you for believing in me and in this book from day one and working the behind-the-scenes magic to make it all happen. Also, I'm thrilled that I have an excuse now to visit London.

To my mentors and colleagues in China: **Wen Wenhui**, for being not just an intimidatingly skilled vegetarian chef but an extraordinarily kind and generous teacher; **Liu Yuguo**, tofu *shifu*, for sharing your lifetime of knowledge with me; **Liu Yupei**, **Cai Haojie**, **Wang Kai**, and other colleagues, for the misery we endured, cheung fun breakfast runs, harrowing adventures on the Guangzhou metro, and endless laughter; **Coleman Yee** and **Jeh Ling Wang**, for the birthday dinner and for making me feel at home in a new city; **Na Mucuo**, **Chang Ru**, **Wang Laoshi**, **Li Laoshi**, **Liu Yuanyuan**, and the rest of the staff at the Guangzhou Vegetarian School, for welcoming me with open arms and teaching me so much. Thank you to **Chef Li Hongzhi**, my vegan hero in Harbin, for answering all my questions with so much patience; **Feng Suping**, for taking me around Chengdu and feeding me delicacies; **Uncle Yin Jingzhe**, for all the wonderful food you introduced me to in Suzhou.

I couldn't have done this without my family. **Mom**: Thank you for telling me to trust my intuition, even if it meant getting on next-day flights, for teaching me Chinese, for washing endless dishes when I made a mess of your kitchen during weeks of shooting, and for always providing brutally honest feedback on my food. **Dad**, your unconditional support means the world to me; thank you for driving me around for Chinese ingredients and tolerating me at my hangriest, and for your insight and edits on the manuscript. **Ben**, **Isaac**, and **Rebekah**: I'm so lucky to have you as siblings—thanks for the laughs and for ensuring there were no leftovers. Special thanks to **Elizabeth Che**, my sister and talented photo assistant, hand model, sounding board, creative consultant, and so much more—you are a true artist and I couldn't have done this book without you.

Jiayi Zheng: Thank you for always answering my panicked texts and calls, for letting me send you every image and design from this book, for your wise, grounding life advice and creative insight, and for being the first person to cook from this book. At this point we're going to be in each other's lives forever and I am very okay with that. **Shirley Xu, Grace Lim, Chandler Yu, Rūta Kuzmickas, Anna Chi, Gloria Quintanilla,** and **Yoseph Maguire,** my people from day one (!): Thank you for always checking in, for patiently listening to me vent during this entire process, and for providing support from afar. **Jon and Grace Scalet, Cathy Cao, Liana DeMaris, Katie Bryant, Nathan Chan,** and the rest of my family at Roots: You formed my support system in Taipei; thank you for helping me in immeasurable ways when the writing was rough. **Peggy and Bruce,** I will never forget your generous hospitality and our glorious vegan dim sum outings.

My recipe testers: **Jen Han, Jessica Babine, Hanna Donato, Jackie Cordero, Emily Lavieri-Scull, Echo Jiang, Candice Cadena, Connie Park, Flora Zhu, Robert Syvarth, Emily Shea, Lokyi Choy, Maryann Shangkuan, Silvia Soh, Kevin Hsu, Ngo Yoke Kwang, Ngo Ke Ni, Ngo Jun Wen, How Jin Yip, Christine Hsieh, Afia Amoako, Erika Kwee, Daphne Wang, Pat Donahue, Melissa Ramos, Justyna Czyszczoń, Olivia Hu, David Li, Ariel Lin, Mathison and Alyssa Ingham, Ally and Austin Smither-Lewellen, Delaney Eng, Sarah Obermaier,** and **Megan and Daniel Tavani**—you saw these recipes in their roughest form and provided invaluable feedback; thank you for your time and your much-needed encouragement.

Grandma, Uncle Chengjun, and **Aunt Xiaoming:** I had the best time in Harbin quarantining and cooking with you.

To **God**—there's nothing I can write here that could fully describe what you mean to me. You are faithful and you've brought me through.

Finally, to all the readers of my blog, who've supported me since I was Hannah Chia making avocado toast and smoothie bowls on the weekends: We've come a long way, and you're the reason this book exists. Thank you.

INDEX

Note: Page references in *italics* indicate recipe photographs.